THE
FAMILY HEALTH
COOKBOOK

THE
FAMILY HEALTH
COOKBOOK

Alice White
and
The Society for Nutrition Education

Foreword by Dr. Jean Mayer

David McKay Company, Inc.
NEW YORK

Library of Congress Cataloging in Publication Data

White, Alice, 1943-
The family health cookbook.

Includes index.
1. Cookery. 2. Nutrition. I. Society for
Nutrition Education. II. Title.
TX715.W578   641.5'63   80-14965
ISBN 0-679-51053-2

Illustrations by Durell Godfrey

Book Design by Tere LoPrete

1 2 3 4 5 6 7 8 9 10

MANUFACTURED IN THE UNITED STATES OF AMERICA

Acknowledgments

We would like to thank those members of the Society for Nutrition Education who generously contributed nearly half the recipes for this cookbook. They represent the entire United States and parts of Canada—included are graduate and undergraduate nutrition students and professional nutrition educators who work in health care programs, hospitals, government agencies, professional nutrition organizations, colleges and universities, the food industry, and as independent nutrition consultants.

Many thanks to all who helped!

Mary Ann Abeyta-Behnke
Martena Ainsworth
Jane Armstrong
Deborah Bolecz
Suzanne S. Cheung
Childrens Centers Nutrition Staff, San
    Francisco
Juno-Ann K. Clarke
Doris Cosgrove
Donald R. Davis
Annette Dickenson
Lisa Ferriero
Food and Diet Appraisal Research
    Group, USDA
Reva Frankle
Ruth A. Franklin
Linda Garcia
Joyce Gee
Karen Gordon
Ethel Graham
Christine Groppe
Joan Gussow
Helen Guthrie
Patricia Harper

Rae Hartfield
Cynthia Hazeltine
Cheryl Holtcamp
Linda Houtkeeper
Joanne P. Ikeda
A. Kazaks
Ann Kendall
Pat Kendall
Harriet Kuhnlein
Marjorie Marks
Yvonne Martin
Rena Mendelson
Margaret Mikkola
Jean Nebel
Kathryn Nicholl
Betsy Nobmann
Anita Owen
Leo Pearlstein
Susan Pisias
Vivian D. Prince
D. M. Rathman
Cynthia Reeser
Arnold Reisman
Marcia Rhodes

Gloria Runyan
Barbara Sheehan
Janice L. Sinclair
Alice Slingerland
Karen Smith
Sharon L. Tansley
Carolyn Templeton
Bob Ullrich
Helen Ullrich

United Fresh Fruit and Vegetable Association
Helen Urban
Levon G. Urbonas
Sue Van Dam
Avis R. Wals
Brenda Wetters
Norma Wightman
Mary Zmitrovich

We would also like to express our deep appreciation to the colleagues and friends who so generously offered editorial advice: Dr. Roslyn B. Alfin-Slater, Jane Armstrong, Dorothy Campbell, Dr. Joan Gussow, Dr. Helen Guthrie, Martha Mapes, Dr. Jean Mayer, Dr. Kristen McNutt, Margaret Phillips, Arnold Reisman, Dr. Judith Turnlund, and Helen Ullrich. Also, to those who tested the recipes: Margaret Mikkola, Dr. Rena Mendelson and her Simmons College nutrition students. And to Mary White, for her long hours typing the manuscript, and our publisher's editor, Cynthia Nelson, for her patience and support.

Alice White
and
the
Society for Nutrition Education

Contents

Foreword

Cooking well was never more popular than today. On TV and radio, in dozens of best-selling cookbooks, and in lavishly equipped home kitchens, fascinated Americans labor to produce gastronomic delights. Too often these culinary triumphs are achieved with an inordinate amount of time and money and a conscious neglect of good nutrition in the interest of "fine"cooking. Very often, too, weekends devoted to such cooking sprees are balanced by weekday meals consisting mainly of fast foods snatched on the run or convenience foods moved hastily from freezer to oven to table. Again, nutrition suffers, and in this case so does the palate.

One of the questions I am asked most frequently by readers of my books, articles, and newspaper column is how to produce tasty, easily prepared, reasonably priced, well-balanced meals that follow the dictates of good nutrition. Back in the '20s and '30s, when the vitamins were just being identified and the great nutritional deficiency diseases—pellagra, goiter, rickets, for example—were the enemy, the answer appeared to be simple: "Eat more!" More meat, eggs, milk, bread, vegetables. Eat heartily of good foods and you would eat well. Today we know it's more complex than that. There are about forty identified essential nutrients that must be obtained—some of them, like the trace minerals, in minute quantities— from our daily bread, and there may even be more still to be discovered. At the same time, the doctrine of "More!" coupled with the increasingly sedentary life of most Americans, has contributed to our national epidemic of obesity. Thus, we must still eat a wide variety of good foods to ensure getting all the essential nutrients and yet eat less. Less total food, and also less total fat, saturated fat, cholesterol, sugar, salt, if we would practice nutritional preventive medicine against the new diseases of dietary excess—heart disease, hypertension, diabetes, and the like.

The Family Health Cookbook, prepared by Alice White and the Society for Nutrition Education, of which I was once president, addresses this problem. With the clarity of the '30s it focuses on the dietary needs of the '80s. I believe it will help you to cook well and eat healthfully, to plan and prepare a good diet that is also a daily treat.

Jean Mayer

Introduction

The idea that how we eat has something to do with how we look at the world and how the world looks at us has been popping in and out of the public consciousness ever since Adam first bit that apple. It wasn't until the end of the eighteenth century, however, that the evolution of science allowed for an experimenal approach to nutrition, and over the next hundred years scientific nutrition began to attract more and more attention. In the early 1900s, when researchers discovered the relationships between individual nutrients and states of physical deficiency, nutrition finally took its place as a recognized science. Since then, our awareness of the importance of nutrition has continued to grow. Just within the past decade, we have witnessed a proliferation of nutrition information in the popular press; an abundance of new nutrition books; regular nutrition columns in many newspapers and magazines; an annual National Nutrition Week in March (soon to become an entire month)*; the initiation of nutrition education programs in most schools; increasing visibility for nutritionists working in industry, hospitals, public health, and world organizations; and an expressed federal government commitment to develop a workable policy on food and nutrition.

Unfortunately, awareness itself does not necessarily lead to understanding. In an attempt to satisfy the urge for fitness, some people kid themselves with half measures; putting alfalfa sprouts on everything or eating soyburgers with "the works." Others consume a breakfast composed of fifteen vitamin and mineral tablets, or "all-natural" cereals that are more than 50% sugar.

Without question, the smoke from contemporary cooking has sent up an SOS signal. The widespread desire for "a proper diet," combined with the nutrition information glut, has created a need for expert help in relating sound nutrition to food. *The Family Health Cookbook* has been developed to fill this need. This is not a nutrition textbook, nor is it "just another cookbook." It resolves much of the confusion and many of the concerns that people have about nutrition and translates the most up-to-date scientific information into good-tasting dishes with improved nutri-

---

* As of this printing, a National Nutrition Month has been instituted.

tion. The recipes have been planned with due consideration for the spiraling cost of food, the need to conserve food in view of world shortages, and national health problems related to nutrition, such as heart disease, obesity, hypertension, and diabetes.

The recipes in this book have come from the files of the author as well as those of nutrition educators from all parts of the U.S. and Canada who are members of the Society for Nutrition Education. All recipes were carefully selected and tested to meet the highest standards for nutritional quality and sensory appeal. Whether you are contemplating a family feast or a brown-bag special, we hope that you will enjoy using our cookbook and discovering the benefits of sound nutrition through good eating.

Table of Equivalents

GOING FROM CUSTOMARY UNITS TO METRIC UNITS

When You Know	Multiply By	To Find
teaspoons	5	milliliters
tablespoons	15	milliliters
fluid ounces	30	milliliters
cups	0.24	liters
pints	0.47	liters
quarts	0.95	liters
gallons	3.8	liters
ounces	28	grams
pounds	0.45	kilograms
inches	2.5	centimeters
feet	30	centimeters
square inches	6.5	square centimeters
degrees Fahrenheit	5/9 (after subtracting 32)	degrees Celsius

GOING FROM METRIC UNITS TO CUSTOMARY UNITS

When You Know	Multiply By	To Find
milliliters	0.03	fluid ounces
liters	2.1	pints
liters	1.06	quarts
liters	0.26	gallons
grams	0.035	ounces
kilograms	2.2	pounds
millimeters	0.04	inches
centimeters	0.4	inches
square centimeters	0.16	square inches
degrees Celsius	9/5 (then add 32)	degrees Fahrenheit

TEMPERATURES

Degrees Fahrenheit	Degrees Celsius	
0°	−18°	highest temperature to store frozen foods safely
32	0	water freezes
40	4	correct temperature for refrigerator
98.6	37	body temperature
140	60	hot tap water
212	100	boiling point of water at sea level
225	107	to warm foods in the oven
250–275	121–135	very slow oven
300–325	149–163	slow oven
350–375	177–191	moderate oven
400–425	214–218	hot oven
450–475	232–246	very hot oven

We have used the following abbreviations in this book:

gram = g
milligram = mg (one thousandth of a gram)
microgram = μg (one millionth of a gram)
teaspoons = tsp
tablespoons = tbsp

PART I

The Facts about Food and Health

Answers to Some Basic Questions

The following questions and answers are designed to highlight a few general nutrition principles for you.

What are nutrients?

Nutrients are the chemical substances in foods which must be consumed in adequate amounts to supply the body with the materials and energy necessary to allow it to grow and move and make repairs. Water is another essential component of nutrition because it carries some of the nutrients into the body and removes waste materials from it. There are five major categories of nutrients: protein, carbohydrate, fat, vitamins, and minerals. Only three of these—protein, carbohydrate, and fat—supply energy (measured in calories) to the body. Vitamins and minerals do not supply calories but help us effectively *utilize* the calorie-producing nutrients. In addition, vitamins and minerals have specific functions in the body that cannot be carried out by any other material. Foods supply us with packages of all of these nutrients—one or more of the calorie-producing nutrients (carbohydrate, protein, and fat)—along with vitamins and minerals.

Vitamins are essential in our diets since we cannot manufacture sufficient amounts of them in our bodies. Although we require only small amounts of vitamins, a shortage will cause deficiency diseases which, if severe enough, can be fatal. Two large classes of vitamins are identified, based on their solubility. *Water-soluble* vitamins (the B vitamins and vitamin C) can be excreted by the body, so they need to be supplied frequently; *fat-soluble* vitamins (vitamins A, D, E, K) are stored in the fatty areas of the body, which means that they can be toxic if eaten in excess. For this reason, it is not a good idea to greatly exceed the Recommended Dietary Allowances (pages 6–7) for fat-soluble vitamins.

Minerals are essential components of our teeth, bones, and every cell in the body, including soft tissue, muscle, blood, and nerves. In addition to being part of the structure of the body, minerals also help to maintain its internal environment by their involvement in such functions as blood clotting, respiration of the cells, fluid balance, and activation of enzymes. Minerals must be supplied in food (some are supplied in water). Some of the minerals (calcium, phosphorus, magnesium, sodium, potassium, and others) are called *macrominerals* because the body requires relatively large amounts of them—approximately 1 gram—or the weight of a paper clip. Other minerals (iron, iodine, manganese, copper, zinc, fluoride, chrominum, molybdenum, cobalt, and selenium), required in much smaller amounts (1/100 to 1/10,000 as much), are called *microminerals* or *trace minerals,* but they are just as necessary to adequate nutrition. Both macrominerals and trace minerals are required in the diet but, like the fat-soluble vitamins, they can be toxic at excessively high levels of intake.

How can I be sure to have a balanced diet?

Most nutritionists would agree that the two most important principles to apply are:

· Eat a wide *variety* of foods
· Eat foods that provide a *high nutrient density*

Why is variety so important?

Variety assures you that the elusive nutrients for which there is no single food source of particularly high value (iron and some of the B vitamins, for example) or nutrients which vary greatly in amount from one food to another (such as some of the trace minerals) probably will be included in your diet. You can eat the same menu every day, but you risk missing the elusive nutrients or those that have not yet been identified.

What does "high nutrient density" mean?

Foods that offer high nutrient density are those that *provide the most nutrients from the least amount of calories.* Since many of us are too sedentary and too many of us are overweight, we cannot afford to rely primarily on foods that are richly composed of sugars and fats, and ones that have had nutrients *permanently* removed during processing. Alcohol also adds a lot of extra calories (7 calories for each gram of alcohol) with hardly any nutritional value. Refined and processed sugars not only contribute to dental caries but "dilute" the value of many diets by satisfying the appetite with plenty of calories, but essentially no nutrients. The nutrient density of milled or "refined" cereal products is also nowhere near as high as that of their whole-grain counterparts. If we continually substitute products made from white or what's often labeled "wheat" flour (which is still white flour), such as English muffins or hamburger buns, for whole wheat or rye products, with their content of nutrients and fiber, we are bound to shortchange ourselves nutritionally. But—more on all this later.

Which foods have the highest nutrient density?
Foods with the highest nutrient density seem to fall into about six major categories. To be sure that you are getting all the nutrients you need—the known as well as the unknown—think in terms of getting a *variety* of foods every day from each of the following groups, with emphasis on the first four groups:

1. *Whole grain cereal products*—breads, crackers, cereals, pasta, and other dishes made from whole grains, such as: whole-grain barley; brown rice; buckwheat; cornmeal; millet; oats; rye; whole wheat and whole wheat products, such as bulgur, cracked wheat, wheat germ, and whole wheat berries.
2. *Dark green and deep orange vegetables*—dark leafy greens, such as spinach, kale, beet greens, and turnip greens; broccoli; carrots; winter squash; rutabagas; sweet potatoes; and sweet red pepper.
3. *Other vegetables*—potatoes; zucchini; summer squash; and bush beans.
4. *High vitamin C vegetables and fruits*—dark green and deep orange vegetables (as above); cabbage; Brussels sprouts; tomatoes; tomato juice; green or red pepper; cauliflower; turnips, asparagus; citrus fruits and their juices; melon; berries; and papaya.
5. *Lowfat milk, yogurt, and cheeses.*
6. *High-protein sources*—dried beans and peas; lentils; poultry; fish; shellfish; lean meats; eggs; nuts; and nut "butters."

In addition, if you need to add fat—for preparing salad dressings, stir-frying or sautéing—use small amounts of polyunsaturated oils (such as safflower, corn, or sunflower) or margarines made from them.

I know generally what I should be eating but how can I be certain that I'm getting all the nutrients I require for my individual bodily needs —based on my height, weight, sex, and age?
Most nutritionists agree that if you meet your *Recommended Dietary Allowances** (RDA), the chances of your suffering from nutrient deficiency are slim (even if *you* may not be). People have often heard of the RDA's but don't really understand what they represent. The RDA's are estimates of the levels of intake of essential nutrients which will meet

* The 9th edition of the RDA's (revised 1980) is available from:
   Printing and Publishing Office
   National Academy of Sciences
   2101 Constitution Avenue
   Washington, D.C. 20418

	Age (years)	Weight (kg)	Weight (lbs)	Height (cm)	Height (in)	Protein (g)	Vitamin A (µg R.E.)[b]	Vitamin D (µg)[c]	Vitamin E (mg α T.E.)[d]	Vitamin C (mg)	Thiamin (mg)
Infants	0.0-0.5	6	13	60	24	kg X 2.2	420	10	3	35	0.3
	0.5-1.0	9	20	71	28	kg X 2.0	400	10	4	35	0.5
Children	1-3	13	29	90	35	23	400	10	5	45	0.7
	4-6	20	44	112	44	30	500	10	6	45	0.9
	7-10	28	62	132	52	34	700	10	7	45	1.2
Males	11-14	45	99	157	62	45	1000	10	8	50	1.4
	15-18	66	145	176	69	56	1000	10	10	60	1.4
	19-22	70	154	177	70	56	1000	7.5	10	60	1.5
	23-50	70	154	178	70	56	1000	5	10	60	1.4
	51+	70	154	178	70	56	1000	5	10	60	1.2
Females	11-14	46	101	157	62	46	800	10	8	50	1.1
	15-18	55	120	163	64	46	800	10	8	60	1.1
	19-22	55	120	163	64	44	800	7.5	8	60	1.1
	23-50	55	120	163	64	44	800	5	8	60	1.0
	51+	55	120	163	64	44	800	5	8	60	1.0
Pregnant						+30	+200	+5	+2	+20	+0.4
Lactating						+20	+400	+5	+3	+40	+0.5

a The Allowances are intended to provide for individual variations among most normal persons as they live in the United States under usual environmental stresses. Diets should be based on a variety of common foods in order to provide other nutrients for which human requirements have been less well defined.

b Retinol equivalents. 1 Retinol equivalent $= 1$ µg retinol or 6 µg carotene.

c As cholecalciferol. 10 µg cholecalciferol $= 400$ I.U. vitamin D.

d α tocopherol equivalents. 1 mg d-α-tocopherol $= 1$ α T.E.

e 1 NE (niacin equivalent) is equal to 1 mg of niacin of 60 mg of dietary tryptophan.

f The folacin allowances refer to dietary sources as determined by *Lactobacillus casei* assay after treatment with enzymes ("conjugases") to make polyglutamyl forms of the vitamin available to the test organism.

Water-Soluble Vitamins					Minerals					
Riboflavin	Niacin	Vitamin B6	Folacin [f]	Vitamin B12	Calcium	Phosphorus	Magnesium	Iron	Zinc	Iodine
(mg)	(mg N.E.) [e]	(mg)	(µg)	(µg)	(mg)	(mg)	(mg)	(mg)	(mg)	(µg)
0.4	6	0.3	30	0.5 [g]	360	240	50	10	3	40
0.6	8	0.6	45	1.5	540	360	70	15	5	50
0.8	9	0.9	100	2.0	800	800	150	15	10	70
1.0	11	1.3	200	2.5	800	800	200	10	10	90
1.4	16	1.6	300	3.0	800	800	250	10	10	120
1.6	18	1.8	400	3.0	1200	1200	350	18	15	150
1.7	18	2.0	400	3.0	1200	1200	400	18	15	150
1.7	19	2.2	400	3.0	800	800	350	10	15	150
1.6	18	2.2	400	3.0	800	800	350	10	15	150
1.4	16	2.2	400	3.0	800	800	350	10	15	150
1.3	15	1.8	400	3.0	1200	1200	300	18	15	150
1.3	14	2.0	400	3.0	1200	1200	300	18	15	150
1.3	14	2.0	400	3.0	800	800	300	18	15	150
1.2	13	2.0	400	3.0	800	800	300	18	15	150
1.2	13	2.0	400	3.0	800	800	300	10	15	150
+0.3	+2	+0.6	+400	+1.0	+400	+400	+150	h	+5	+25
+0.5	+5	+0.5	+100	+1.0	+400	+400	+150	h	+10	+50

g The RDA for vitamin B12 in infants is based on average concentration of the vitamin in human milk. The allowances after weaning are based on energy intake (as recommended by the American Academy of Pediatrics) and consideration of other factors such as intestinal absorption.

h The increased requirement during pregnancy cannot be met by the iron content of habitual American diets nor by the existing iron stores of many women; therefore the use of 30–60 mg of supplemental iron is recommended. Iron needs during lactation are not substantially different from those of non-pregnant women, but continued supplementation of the mother for 2–3 months after parturition is advisable in order to replenish stores depleted by pregnancy.

Reproduced from: Recommended Dietary Allowances, Ninth Edition (1979, in press), with the permission of the National Academy of Sciences, Washington, D.C.

the needs of the majority of healthy persons in the United States, as established by the Food and Nutrition Board of the National Academy of Sciences' National Research Council, a group of well-respected nutrition scientists (the membership changes periodically so that a variety of opinions are represented). About every five years RDA's are updated, based on the latest research information. It's important to understand that the RDA's are *recommendations*—people often confuse them with *minimum requirements* when, in fact, they include an additional allowance for all the nutrients to meet the needs of most people. An exception is the calorie RDA. An extra allowance here would not be in the best interest of all the overweight people in our population. Since the requirements of each individual are difficult to determine, and the RDA's are generous in order to meet the needs of entire populations, failure to meet the RDA does not automatically indicate a deficiency state. However, it is important to keep in mind that if your consumption of a nutrient regularly falls below the RDA, the risk of not fulfilling your needs increases.

The term "U.S. RDA" is used frequently these days—what does this mean?

The U.S. Recommended Daily Allowances are found on food labels. They are a regulatory standard derived by the Food and Drug Administration (FDA) from the Recommended Dietary Allowances. In general, the U.S. RDA's represent the *highest* nutrient levels for any group (according to age and sex) on the RDA table. Foods required to conform with the U.S. RDA labeling regulations include those for which the manufacturer has made a nutritional claim or products to which the manufacturer had added nutrients; many other foods are voluntarily labeled. For all these items the manufacturer is required to list calories per serving; protein, carbohydrate, and fat content in grams per serving; and the percentage U.S. RDA for protein, vitamin A, vitamin C, thiamin, riboflavin, niacin, calcium, and iron. There are twelve other nutrients which the manufacturer may elect to show. Cholesterol, saturated and polyunsaturated fats, and sodium are also often listed, since many consumers find the information useful. Special U.S. RDA's have also been established for infants, children under 4 years, and pregnant women and nursing mothers. These U.S. RDA's are listed on the labels of vitamin and mineral supplements and on infant and toddler foods.

The U.S. RDA's are a big help to consumers in comparing and evaluating individual servings of food products both for their nutrient density and caloric value.

Are the nutrients for which there are RDA's and U.S. RDA's the only ones we need to think about?

No. There are known nutrients which have yet to be assigned RDA's because research is still "in progress." Although the RDA's provide estimates of appropriate levels of calories and seventeen well-known nutrients for seventeen categories of persons according to age and sex, there are at least fifty nutrients overall to be considered. And for some of these nutrients, particularly the trace elements, the human nutritional need has not been definitely established.

Fifty or more nutrients is mind-boggling for most people. Is there any simple way to check the nutrient status of our diets?
Yes, one way is to keep an eye on what nutritionists call the *indicator nutrients*—protein, calcium, iron, vitamin A, thiamin (vitamin B-1), riboflavin (vitamin B-2), niacin, and vitamin C (note that these are the same nutrients that must be listed when a food product has nutrition labeling). They are called indicator nutrients because they can be used as a rule-of-thumb guide to assess our diets. If you are getting these nutrients from their best natural food sources, you are probably getting adequate amounts of the other nutrients as well. In order to use the indicator nutrients as a guide, however, *your foods must be from natural or lightly processed sources.* Highly processed or synthetic foods that have been fortified with a few nutrients just don't count because the presence of added nutrients does not necessarily indicate that other nutrients are also present. For example, a synthetic, powdered, orange-flavored fruit drink may be fortified with vitamin C—but that's about its *only* selling point nutritionally. By comparison, real orange juice supplies folacin, potassium, vitamin A, some calcium, and niacin, as well as vitamin C.

The recipes in this cookbook have been calculated to determine if they qualify as excellent sources of any of the indicator nutrients. In order for a recipe to be called an "excellent" source of any of these nutrients, it must contain the nutrient at the following percentage of U.S. RDA:

Indicator Nutrients:	% of U.S. RDA:	Or at Least:
Protein	25% of 65 g	16 g
Calcium	10% of 1 g	100 mg
Iron	10% of 18 mg	1.8 mg
Vitamin A	25% of 1000 µg R.E. or 5000 I.U.	250 µg R.E. or 1250 I.U.
Thiamin	10% of 1.5 mg	0.15 mg
Riboflavin	10% of 1.7 mg	0.17 mg
Niacin	25% of 20 mg	5 mg
Vitamin C	25% of 60 mg	15 mg

Which foods are the best sources of the indicator nutrients?
Best Protein Sources (see pages 14–16 for more information)
Poultry, Fish, Shellfish, Meat; Milk, Yogurt, Cheese, Eggs; Lentils, Dried Beans, Dried Peas, Tofu (soybean curd); Nuts and nut butters.

Best Calcium Sources (see page 43 for more information)

Milk (all types), Yogurt, Cheese, Cottage cheese, Ice cream, Ice milk; Artichokes, Broccoli, Dark leafy green vegetables*; Tofu (soybean curd), Dried beans and lentils; Oysters, Small fish eaten with bones; Almonds.

Best Iron Sources

Liver and other organ meats; Cooked dried beans, peas, and lentils; Dark leafy green vegetables; Whole-grain breads and cereals, Enriched breads and cereals, Fortified cereals; Meats; Oysters, Clams, Shrimp, Sardines; Blackstrap molasses; Prune juice, Tomato juice; Dried fruits; Nuts and nut butters.

Best Vitamin A Sources

Liver; Egg yolk; Fortified margarine; Whole milk, Whole milk products, such as cheese and yogurt, Fortified nonfat or lowfat milk; Chili powder; Dark leafy green vegetables, such as beet greens, broccoli, collard greens, kale, mustard greens, spinach, Swiss chard, turnip greens; Deep orange vegetables and fruits, such as carrot, hot pepper, sweet potato, winter squash, yam, apricot, cantaloupe, mango, papaya, persimmon, pumpkin, tomato, watermelon.

Best Thiamin Sources

Whole-grain and enriched breads and cereals; Wheat germ; Legumes, such as dried, cooked beans and peas; Pork, Organ meats, such as liver, kidney, and heart; Leafy green vegetables; Nuts, such as peanuts, Seeds, such as sesame and sunflower.

Best Riboflavin (Vitamin B-2) Sources

Milk, Cheese, Yogurt, Eggs; Liver, Kidney; Legumes; Whole-grain or enriched breads and cereals; Dark leafy green vegetables (as above).

Best Niacin Sources

Liver and other organ meats, Lean meats, Poultry, Fish; Legumes, such as dried, cooked beans, peas, and lentils; Whole-grain or enriched breads and cereals; Wheat germ; Nuts and nut butters; Seeds.

Best Vitamin C (Ascorbic Acid) Sources

Vetgetables, such as asparagus, broccoli, Brussels sprouts, cabbage, cauliflower, dark leafy greens (as above), green peas, green pepper, kohlrabi, potato (white or sweet), turnip, vegetable juices made from vegetables on this list; Fruits, such as avocado, cantaloupe, cranberry juice, grapefruit and its juice, guava, honeydew melon, mango, orange and its juice, papaya, strawberries, tangerine and its juice, tomato and its juice, watermelon.

---

* Except for spinach and Swiss chard, which contain high concentrations of oxalic acid that combines with the calcium, making it insoluble and unavailable for use by the body.

Do the indicator nutrients represent all of the six major food categories mentioned previously?

Yes, they do. By doing a cross-reference, you will find that all of the best food sources of the indicator nutrients fall into the major food categories described on page 5. So if you select a variety of these foods each day to fit all the major food categories, you really can't miss out on achieving a well-balanced diet.

We read a lot today about the U.S. Dietary Goals. What are they?

Concern by some nutritionists over the effects of excess fats, sugars, cholesterol, salt, and alcohol prompted the Senate Select Committee on Nutrition and Human Needs to issue a set of dietary guidelines based upon available scientific information. Released in 1977, the Senate staff report* noted that our eating habits have changed radically during the last fifty years and warned that they are as much a threat to our health as smoking because of the role they play in such conditions as obesity, diabetes, cardiovascular disease, hypertension, cirrhosis, certain types of cancer (of the breast and colon), and dental caries. The Goals, which were revised by the Senate staff in late 1977, recommend that we:

1. Decrease consumption of animal protein foods and increase emphasis on vegetable protein sources; protein should represent about 12% of our total caloric intake.
2. Increase consumption of complex carbohydrates and "naturally occurring" sugars to a level of about 48% of caloric intake.
3. Reduce the use of refined and processed sugars by about 45% so that they represent no more than 10% of our total caloric intake.
4. Reduce overall fat consumption from 40% to approximately 30% of caloric intake.
5. Reduce consumption of saturated fat to a level of about 10% of total caloric intake; substitute polyunsaturated and monounsaturated fats, each to a level of about 10% of caloric intake.
6. Reduce cholesterol consumption to about 300 milligrams daily.
7. Limit sodium intake by reducing consumption of salt (including foods high in salt) to about 5 grams or less a day.
8. Decrease alcohol intake.
9. Consume only as many calories as needed for energy to avoid overweight; and, if overweight, decrease caloric intake and increase exercise.

* U.S. Senate Select Committee on Nutrition and Human Needs, *Dietary Goals for the United States*, Second edition, Government Printing Office, Washington, D.C., 1977.

If we follow the U.S. Dietary Goals, our calories will be consumed in the following proportions:

Complex carbohydrates and "naturally occurring" sugars			48%
Refined and processed sugars			10%
Total fat			
saturated fat	10%	⎫	
polyunsaturated fat	10%	⎬	30%
monounsaturated fat	10%	⎭	
Protein			12%
			100%

Has the government taken any official steps regarding the Dietary Goals?
   Yes, as a result of the Dietary Goals and recent scientific studies, the following seven recommendations have been developed by a joint committee of the USDA and HEW:

1. Eat a variety of foods.
2. Maintain ideal weight.
3. Avoid too much fat, saturated fat, and cholesterol.
4. Eat foods with adequate starch and fiber.
5. Avoid too much sugar.
6. Avoid too much sodium.
7. If you drink alcohol, do so in moderation.

For more information about these guidelines, send for:

   Nutrition and Your Health—Dietary Guidelines for Americans
   Superintendent of Documents
   U.S. Government Printing Office
   Washington, D.C.   20402

   On the following pages we'll take a closer look at protein, carbohydrate, and fat, and how each fits in with the nutrition principles outlined so far. Specific guidelines are provided for getting these important nutrients from the best sources, and in the proper amounts. We have also included a few words on the role of sodium in the diet.

PROTEIN

   Protein is by far the most well-known and well-respected nutrient in America. It has earned its reputation rightfully when we consider the vital function it serves in the body. Proteins are not only the major building blocks of muscles, tendons, skin, and other tissues, but they are also the main constituents of hemoglobin (which carries oxygen to body cells and removes carbon dioxide from them), of enzymes and some hormones (which assist in body processes), of antibodies (which help to fight infections), and of nucleic acids (which determine who we are via our genes). Proteins can also provide energy—on the order of 4 calories per gram.

How do we get the right kinds of protein to meet all of these sophisticated needs?

Since every cell requires specific proteins, our bodies must have a pool of building materials from which to work. When we eat animal and vegetable protein foods, they are broken down in the digestive tract and absorbed as single amino acids. The body then manufactures its own variety of proteins from these amino acids by combining them in an infinite number of configurations to produce highly specialized protein structures. Our bodies are able to produce most of the amino acids, but eight or nine of them must be provided by our foods. Indispensable for humans, these are called the *essential amino acids*. To make new protein in the body, we need to supplement our body's protein pool with a good daily supply of these amino acids from a mixed diet that contains adequate protein—and calories, so that the protein will be used to build and repair our bodies, rather than for energy.

How much protein do we need?

This varies only slightly for adults. Infants and growing children, however, need relatively more protein when compared on a body weight basis. Pregnant women and breast-feeding mothers need much more than other women. And persons who are recovering from serious illnesses or burns usually need increased protein as well. Since protein is not stored in the body and is constantly being turned over, we need a fresh supply from protein sources in our diets every day; but unless we are building a large amount of new tissue, we need to replace only the amount we lose each day.

The recommendation for adults, based on a diet consisting of mixed protein sources—animal and vegetable—is a little less than 1 gram per kilogram (about 2 pounds) of body weight per day. This means that the "average" man needs about 56 grams of protein daily, while the "average" woman needs about 44 grams of protein each day. (For other categories, check the RDA chart on pages 6–7.)

Since protein has such an important role in the body, and since we need to replace our supply daily, why do the U.S. Dietary Goals recommend that we keep our protein intake at only about 12% of total calories?

Because most Americans tend to think that "more is better" when it comes to protein—some people even spend extra money unnecessarily for protein supplements to satisfy this misconceived notion. On the average, most adults in this country consume 80–90 grams or more of protein daily! But as you can see from the accompanying Protein Chart, it doesn't take a great quantity of food to meet our daily protein needs. For example, a breakfast which includes two slices of whole wheat bread with one egg and one cup of nonfat milk provides about 20 grams of protein. That is more than half of the recommended protein intake for a 7–10-year-old child, nearly half of the 44 grams of protein recommended for women, and more than one-third of the 56 grams recommended for men.

PROTEIN CHART

Food	Amount	Protein (grams)	Calories
MILK:			
whole	1 cup	9	160
lowfat (with 2% non-fat milk solids added)	1 cup	10	145
skim	1 cup	9	90
buttermilk (skim)	1 cup	9	90
nonfat, instant dry	¼ cup	6	60
CHEESE:			
cheddar	1 ounce	7	115
cottage, creamed	½ cup	15	130
uncreamed	½ cup	12	85
YOGURT, PLAIN:			
from whole milk	1 cup	8	150
from partially skimmed milk	1 cup	8	120
ICE MILK:			
hardened	1 cup	6	200
soft-serve	1 cup	8	265
ICE CREAM:			
(10% fat)	1 cup	6	260
EGG:	1 large	7	80
FISH:			
light and dark, cooked	3 ounces	20–25	125–175
SHELLFISH:			
clams, raw/mussels, cooked	4–5	8	55
oysters, raw	½ cup	10	80
crab/lobster, cooked	½ cup	12	70
scallops, cooked	3 ounces	20	95

PROTEIN CHART *(continued)*

Food	Amount	Protein (grams)	Calories
POULTRY (WITHOUT SKIN):			
light and dark, cooked	3 ounces	25	145–175
MEAT, COOKED:			
ground beef, 10% fat	3 ounces	23	185
21% fat	3 ounces	20	235
lamb	3 ounces	22	240
organ meats (heart, kidney, liver)	3 ounces	23–28	160–215
pork	3 ounces	21	310
veal	3 ounces	24	200
LEGUMES:			
dried, cooked	½ cup	7–8	90–115
mung sprouts, raw	½ cup	2	20
tofu (soybean curd)	4 ounces	9	85
CEREAL GRAIN PRODUCTS:			
barley, whole-grain, cooked	½ cup	4	135
bran cereal (100% bran), uncooked	½ cup	5	90
cornmeal, unrefined ground, uncooked	½ cup	5	215
macaroni, enriched, cooked	1 cup	5	155
millet, whole-grain, cooked	½ cup	3	95
oatmeal, cooked	1 cup	5	130
rice, cooked brown	1 cup	5	230
white, enriched	1 cup	4	225
spaghetti/noodles, enriched, cooked	1 cup	7	200
wheat berries, cooked	½ cup	5	110
wheat, bulgur, cooked	½ cup	7	225
wheat, cracked, cooked	½ cup	4	110
wheat germ	2 tablespoons	4	45
unprocessed bran	½ cup	4	55

PROTEIN CHART *(continued)*

Food	Amount	Protein (grams)	Calories
BREADS:			
pumpernickel/ whole wheat/rye	1 slice	3	60–80
white, enriched	1 slice	2	65
NUTS:	2 tablespoons	2–5	80–115
NUT BUTTERS:	1 tablespoon	4	95
SEEDS:	2 tablespoons	3–5	95–100
YEAST:			
brewer's debittered; torula	2 tablespoons	6	40–45
VEGETABLES, COOKED:			
artichoke	1 medium	3	60
broccoli	1 medium stalk	6	45
Brussels sprouts	1 cup	7	55
corn	1 medium ear or ½ cup	3	70
greens:			
collards (leaves)	1 cup	7	65
kale (leaves)	1 cup	5	45
spinach (leaves)	1 cup	5	40
Swiss chard (leaves)	1 cup	3	30
peas, fresh	1 cup	9	115
potato, baked	1 large	4	145
winter squash, baked	1 cup	4	130

What happens to the excess protein that most of us consume?

When we eat more protein than our bodies need, the excess is first used as energy or, if not needed for energy, is stored as fat in the body. Since we can get all the energy we need from carbohydrates and fats, this represents an enormous waste of a nutrient that is costly, both in terms of the resources required to produce it and in terms of our food budgets.

What is meant by the "quality" of protein foods?

Proteins that supply a good balance of all of the essential amino acids are classified as "high-quality" proteins. Animal protein foods—meat, fish, poultry, eggs, milk, cheese—are of high quality. This means that they are of an amino acid composition close to the one we require and are easily utilized by the body. Consequently, we need a relatively small amount of these foods to meet our daily protein needs. Protein foods low in one or more of the essential amino acids are of lower quality. Vegetables, grains, legumes, and nuts are considered to be of poorer quality because, even though they contain all of the essential amino acids, they are relatively low in one or more of them (usually lysine, tryptophan, and/or methionine).

What is meant by "complementary proteins"?

When we know the limiting amino acid(s) in vegetable proteins, we can combine foods in what is known as complementary fashion and end up with a higher-quality protein. For example, most grains are low in lysine and high in methionine; legumes have just the opposite pattern—high in lysine and low in methionine. So these two groups complement each other very nicely. Also, by adding small amounts of animal protein to vegetable protein sources, you can markedly improve the amino acid balance. For example, a glass of milk, an egg, an ounce of cheese, or small amounts of meat, fish, or poultry will improve the usefulness to the body of such vegetable protein foods as dried beans, peas, cereal grains, nuts, and even fresh vegetables, some of which are surprisingly high in protein. (See the following Complementary Vegetable Protein Chart for suggestions on how to get high-quality protein.)

COMPLEMENTARY VEGETABLE PROTEIN CHART

The following combinations make it possible for the strengths of one vegetable protein food to balance the weaknesses of another, thus increasing their overall protein value. There are a number of vegetable protein foods that fit together this way and seem to be made for each other.

Combine	With	Examples

CEREAL GRAINS   +
 barley
 bulgur
 cornmeal
 cracked wheat
 kasha (buckwheat)
 millet
 oats
 rice
 whole wheat berries
 whole-grain breads,
    crackers, muffins,
    biscuits, pasta
	LEGUMES
	 dried beans
	 dried lentils
	 dried peas
	
	 or
	
	 BREWER'S
	 YEAST
	 (add 1–2 tbsp to hot
	 cereals, soups, pilaf,
	 and other grain
	 dishes)
		• rice with black bean sauce
		
		 • split pea soup and corn bread
		
		 • lentil barley soup
		
		 • baked beans with brown bread
		
		 • cracked wheat and bean salad
		
		 • tofu (soybean curd) with rice

COMPLEMENTARY VEGETABLE PROTEIN CHART *(continued)*

Combine		*With*	*Examples*
LEGUMES (as above)	+	SEEDS AND NUTS cashews peanuts* sesame seeds sunflower seeds walnuts nut butters	· garbanzo bean/ tahini (sesame seed paste) dip · roasted soybean/ sunflower/peanut snack mix
PEANUTS or PEANUT BUTTER	+	SUNFLOWER SEEDS	· peanut butter and sunflower seed sandwich or cookies
RICE	+	SEEDS sesame seeds sunflower seeds	· sesame seed/rice pilaf or pudding

The quality of vegetable protein foods can also be improved substantially by adding *small* amounts of animal protein foods to them.

| MILK AND MILK
PRODUCTS
POULTRY
FISH
SHELLFISH
EGGS
LEAN MEAT | + | VEGETABLE
PROTEIN
FOODS
legumes
nuts
nut butters
seeds
vegetables
whole grains | · macaroni and cheese
· broccoli with cheese
sauce
· bean soup with small
pieces of meat
· chili beans with
grated cheese
· sesame seed/whole
wheat crackers with
cheese
· bulgur salad with
yogurt dressing
· stir-fried vegetables
with small pieces of
poultry, fish, or lean
meat
· whole wheat/cheese
pizza |

* Peanuts are botanically similar to legumes and are classified as such; however, their amino acid profile resembles nuts and seeds, so they are listed with this group.

Is it true that most animal protein foods are low in calories?

No, this is probably the most common misunderstanding about animal protein foods. Many people believe that foods such as steak, fish, or eggs are low in calories and are good "diet" foods. The fact is that such foods not only supply us with 4 calories per gram of protein but they often contain a good many calories from fat as well; and each gram of fat supplies 9 calories. For example, whole milk brings into your diet a total of 20 calories for each gram of protein, whereas skim milk gives us only 10 calories for the same quantity of protein. The Protein Chart shown earlier, outlines the protein and calories found in some common animal and vegetable protein sources.

CARBOHYDRATES

Carbohydrates are probably more misunderstood than any other nutrient. A widespread myth (second only to our overemphasis on protein) is the notion that foods high in carbohydrates are fattening extras which should be avoided if possible. The truth of the matter is, carbohydrates are an essential component of our diets and provide the major source of body energy for most of the world.

All carbohydrates are made of carbon, hydrogen, and oxygen combined in chains of varying lengths to make "complex" carbohydrate (starches) and "simple" carbohydrate (sugars)—both of which provide energy—and cellulose (also a complex carbohydrate), which is not digested and therefore does not supply energy but does provide us with fiber (roughage). In the gastrointestinal tract digestible carbohydrates (both the complex starches found in grains and starchy vegetables and the simpler sugars found in milk and fruits) are eventually broken down to glucose. When glucose is released into the bloodstream, it is carried to all cells, including the brain cells, where it is the major fuel source. Excess glucose is stored in the liver as glycogen, to be released as needed, or it is converted to body fat.

Why do the Dietary Goals advise us to increase our consumption of complex carbohydrates and "naturally occurring" sugars?

There is considerable evidence that our diet and our health might improve if a major portion (about 48%) of our caloric intake were derived from these carbohydrates. The preferred ones are those that contain relatively large amounts of vitamins, minerals, fiber, and some protein—as well as carbohydrate. Starchy foods, such as whole grains, legumes, and vegetables all have these characteristics. Some of our carbohydrates can also be supplied by naturally occurring sugars, such as those found—along with vitamins, minerals, and fiber—in fresh fruits and some vegetables.

Why are "whole-grain" breads being emphasized—isn't enriched white flour as nutritious as the whole-grain flours, such as whole wheat, rye, cracked wheat, oat, and bran?

No. Unfortunately, flours that have been "refined" by milling processes that remove the bran, or outer coat of the kernel, and the inner germ have a considerable number of nutrients removed from them as well. The law only requires that iron, niacin, thiamin, and riboflavin be put back into the flour during "enrichment." Some of the nutrients that are not returned to the refined flour are the very ones that many Americans are short of—vitamin B-6, folacin, and zinc, for example. We also lose the valuable fiber from the outer coat which is so important to the health of the digestive tract.

Why is fiber so important?

Fiber is the structural part of plants that provides the bulk and stimulation necessary to move waste materials through the intestines. Since most fiber is not digested, it provides no energy to the body. However, because of the function it serves, it is an essential component of an adequate diet. The bulk provided by fiber holds water in the feces—thus softening them and aiding in elimination—distends the colon, and stimulates normal intestinal function by helping to initiate the contractions necessary for normal bowel movement. Low fiber intake contributes to the incidence of diverticular disease and has been suggested (though *not* proven) to be the cause of colon cancer. While Americans have become more aware of the merits of fiber in recent years, many people still have diets that are relatively low in fiber.

What are the best food sources of fiber?

We get plenty of fiber from 1) whole-grain breads and cereal products, particularly bran and whole-meal varieties, 2) legumes, especially dried beans, 3) leafy vegetables, such as broccoli, Brussels sprouts, cabbage, and romaine lettuce, 4) root vegetables, such as carrots, parsnips, rutabagas, and turnips, 5) vegetables with skins and seeds, such as unpeeled potatoes, tomatoes, and corn, 6) fruits with skins and seeds, such as unpeeled apples, pears, peaches, plums, cherries, and strawberries, 7) and nuts. Another simple way to add fiber to your diet is to sprinkle a tablespoon or so of unprocessed bran into cereals and recipes where it won't be noticed, such as meat loaf, chili, stuffings, breads, and soups.

Does fiber perform any other function in our diets?

Yes, fiber is bulky and helps to fill us up without the extra calories normally found in other foods. Only the *digestible* carbohydrate found in high-fiber foods is calorie-producing. True fiber is undigestible and therefore supplies no calories. This makes most whole grains and legumes important in weight-reducing or weight-maintenance diets, contrary to popular belief that they are "fattening."

But, if we increase our consumption of carbohydrates this way, won't we be getting too many calories?

Carbohydrates provide us with the same number of calories as protein—4 calories per gram (as compared with the 9 calories per gram yielded by fats). And, ounce-for-ounce, carbohydrate foods are actually lower in calories than most protein foods which carry with them a substantial amount of fat.

The following chart compares the caloric values for representative foods from the major food categories:

	Carbohydrate (4 cal/g)	Protein (4 cal/g)	Fat (9 cal/g)	Approx. Total Calories
Whole milk, 1 cup	12	9	9	165
Skim milk, 1 cup	13	9	Trace	90
Vegetable, ½ cup	5	2	—	30
Fruit, 1 small piece	10	—	—	40
Bread, 1 slice	15	2	—	70
Meat, 1 ounce	—	7	5	75
Margarine, oil (or butter) 1 teaspoon	—	—	4-5	35-45

As you can see, only an ounce of raw hamburger has about the same number of calories as a slice of bread, so a "quarter pounder" at about 235 calories (cooked) would have almost twice as many calories as the 140-calorie bun it's served on.

However, what we eat with carbohydrate foods as well as what we add to them increases their caloric value. One-half cup of plain cooked carrots, for example, gives us only about 30 calories, but when we glaze them with butter and brown sugar, we can easily add another 150 calories (as well as masking their natural flavor). A slice of bread goes into—and comes out of—the toaster at about 70 calories; after we add butter and jelly it may end up with at least triple that calorie level.

Why, then, are carbohydrates so often equated with bad eating habits?

The bad reputation that attached itself to carbohydrates as a group really applies to the refined and processed sugars that we add to foods. Sugars provide us with virtually nothing but calories and therefore tend to crowd out more important nutrients. Because sugars make things so tasty, leading to overconsumption, they are also associated with obesity. Obesity, in turn produces an increased risk of diabetes and heart disease. Tooth decay is another major concern because when any sticky sugar or carbohydrate adheres to the tooth surface, it provides food for the bacteria in our mouths which are responsible for dental caries.

*If the refined and processed sugars added to our foods are harmful to
our health, why do the Dietary Goals recommend that we only "reduce"
our consumption of them by half? Why not cut them out altogether?*

This would be difficult to do because more and more of the added sugar
in our foods is added not at the table but in the factory, where manufacturers do it for us—often quite liberally. And it's not just the ubiquitous
table sugar (sucrose) that we need to be concerned about. Sugar is found
in such obvious sources as soft drinks, candy, cookies, pastries, cakes,
ice cream, sherbet, fruit-flavored yogurt, fruits packed in syrup, and
sugar-coated cereals, but it also lurks less conspicuously in such items
as "fruit-flavored" drinks and many non-sugar-coated cereals.

Check your food labels carefully for the many types of added sugar:
dextrose, maltose, lactose, fructose, glucose, maple syrup, corn syrup,
honey, molasses, dextrins, and brown sugar. And don't be misled by the
health food store varieties—raw sugar and turbinado sugar—they're
all sugar! Consumption of refined and processed sugars in the United
States averages well over 100 pounds per person each year. The most
current USDA statistics (1978) show that the "average" American consumed about 138 pounds of refined and processed sugar that year—or
about 14 tablespoons (nearly 1 cup) of sugar each day. This represents about 645 extra calories per day from added sugar alone! This also
equals about 1¼ pounds of extra body weight per week if these calories
are not being used for energy. Keep in mind that 1 pound of body weight
represents about 3500 calories. So just 100 extra calories each day—
more than the calories you need for energy—will amount to about 36,500
extra calories annually, or that 10-pound weight gain that may mysteriously
appear *on you* each year.

*But aren't some sugars, such as those found in honey, brown sugar, and
molasses, more nutritious than regular table sugar?*

Slightly, but not enough to cause a significant improvement in our diets
since their calories are accompanied by only insignificant amounts of
vitamins and minerals. The exception to this is molasses, which supplies
1.2 milligrams of iron per tablespoon, plus some calcium and B vitamins.
Blackstrap molasses supplies 3.2 milligrams of iron per tablespoon, but,
unfortunately, its characteristic strong flavor limits its use.

*How can we reduce our consumption of sugar if we don't control most
of the sugar added to our foods?*

Begin by cutting down on the sugar that you do control. Try to wean
your sweet tooth from these sugars by adding less and less at the table,
until you can enjoy foods for their own natural flavors. In the kitchen,
cut down on the amount of sugar added to recipes (as we have done in
this cookbook)—many foods taste just as good with less than half the
sugar called for in most recipes. When you shop, look for foods without

added sugars and avoid buying foods in which these sweeteners are among the first three to four ingredients listed.

FATS

Fatty substances are part of a large chemical family known as *lipids*. They are called *fats* if solid at room temerature, and *oils* if liquid at room temperature. Lipids are further classified as *visible* or *invisible*; visible if easily identified (as in butter, cream, cream cheese, margarine, oil, shortening, mayonnaise, salad dressing, and the fat around the edges of meat), and invisible if they are hidden in foods (as in whole milk and its products, egg yolks, the fat flecks buried in meat, dark-fleshed fish and poultry, poultry skin, pastries, nuts, and avocados).

Fats are essential in the diet in a number of ways. They carry the valuable fat-soluble vitamins A, D, E, and K; they add flavor to foods; they provide a major source of calories for energy; and they remain in the stomach longer than protein or carbohydrates, thereby helping to delay the onset of hunger. In the body, fat stores provide insulation, thus aiding in the maintenance of body temperature; they also form a protective layer around vital organs, acting somewhat like the cushion and springs in a bicycle seat.

If fats are so important, why do the Dietary Goals advise us to reduce our overall consumption of fat to 30% of caloric intake?

Because high fat intake has been associated with heart disease and (although not yet proven) cancer of the breast and colon. Also, too much fat in the diet may lead to obesity. Some of us consume as much as 40% or more of our calories in the form of fats, and fats are the *most concentrated* source of calories we can possibly get, supplying 9 calories per gram as compared with the 4 calories per gram from carbohydrates and protein.

How can we cut down on fat?

There are a number of ways to substantially reduce the fat content of our diets:

1. Reduce consumption and portion size of animal protein foods, particularly meats; and especially avoid fatty and processed meats, such as frankfurters, cold cuts, bacon, and sausage.
2. Select the leanest cuts of meat and remove all visible fat from meats *before* cooking.
3. Cook meats on a rack to allow invisible fat to drain off.
4. Substitute small portions of light-fleshed poultry and fish in place of meat; remove the skin from poultry *before* cooking.

5. Eat more vegetable protein sources, such as dried peas, beans and lentils, in place of meat, fish, and poultry.
6. Bake, broil, or cook in liquid instead of frying; if you do fry, use a small amount of fat, as in stir-frying.
7. Defat broths, soups, stews, and gravies as described in the Soup section (see Index).
8. Use lowfat milk, yogurt, and cheese in place of whole milk products, skim Neufchatel cheese in place of cream cheese, and lowfat yogurt instead of sour cream.
9. Apply margarine, oil, mayonnaise, salad dressings, peanut and other nut butters, with a light hand.
10. Cut down on desserts high in fat, such as ice cream, pastries, pies, cheesecake, and other cakes (particularly ones with butter or cream frosting).

Why do we need to reduce our saturated fat intake to 10% of total calories and substitute polyunsaturated and monounsaturated fats, each at levels of about 10% of caloric intake?

Because many nutrition scientists feel that the *type* of fat we eat may be important too. There are numerous studies showing that a high intake of saturated fat is associated with high blood cholesterol level, which is thought to be one of the risk factors involved with heart disease. Polyunsaturated and monounsaturated fats, while they have the same caloric value as saturated fats, seem to affect the blood cholesterol differently; polyunsaturated fats tend to *lower* blood cholesterol levels in some people, whereas monounsaurated fats appear to *have little effect* on blood cholesterol one way or the other.

How do we know which foods contain these different types of fats?

Most fat-containing foods have some of each type of fat—saturated, polyunsaturated, and monounsaturated—but in varying proportions. *Saturated fats* are usually solid at room temperature and are found largely in such animal products as meat, dark oily fish, poultry skin, egg yolk, butter, lard, whole milk, and products made from it, such as cheese and yogurt. Exceptions to this are *saturated vegetable fats*, such as *coconut oil*—found in most synthetic coffee creamers and whiteners, or sprayed on some crackers and snack foods (and who knows what else, since the food labels are not presently required to say)—*palm oil, cocoa butter* (found in chocolate), and *some hydrogenated vegetable margarines and shortenings*, depending on how they are made (see next question). *Polyunsaturated fats* are found in relatively large proportions in plant foods, such as safflower, corn, sunflower, sesame, soybean, and cottonseed oils and in margarines made from these oils. *Monounsaturated fats* are found in relatively large proportions in avocados, olive and peanut oils, and in most nuts.

What does it mean to "hydrogenate" fats?

This is a process whereby hydrogen is added to liquid fats, changing them to solid or semi-solid fats. Generally, the harder the product becomes, the higher the degree of saturation. This means that vegetable oils, which are normally unsaturated, become saturated during hydrogenation; some margarines and all hydrogenated vegetable fats are good examples of this. So be sure to buy margarines that list "liquid oil" as the first ingredient—this is often more true of the tub margarines than those in sticks, but not always, so it's a good idea to read the labels.

We often hear that polyunsaturated fats are high in "essential fatty acids" —what does this mean?

Fatty acids are the basic building blocks of all fats. They have carbon chains of varying lengths which are identified according to how saturated or unsaturated they are with hydrogen. *Essential fatty acid* refers to two polyunsaturated fatty acids, linoleic acid and arachidonic acid, which are absolutely necessary for our nutritional well-being. However, linoleic acid is the only fatty acid that *must* be available in our diets since we cannot manufacture it ourselves. As long as linoleic acid is available, our bodies are able to use it to synthesize arachidonic acid and other important fatty acids. Linoleic acid is necessary for keeping skin healthy, strengthening of cell membranes, maintaining proper transportation of other fats in our bodies, and prolonging blood clotting time. Good sources of linoleic acid are safflower, corn, cottonseed, sesame, soybean, and sunflower oils. We need only a very small amount of linoleic acid—about 1 or 2% of our total caloric intake. One tablespoon of one of the polyunsaturated oils mentioned above used daily in cooking is enough to prevent deficiency—and this does not include the linoleic acid present in other foods as well. Diets which contain a mixture of animal and vegetable fats to provide 20–30% of the calories will almost certainly meet the body's needs for linoleic acid.

What is cholesterol?

Cholesterol is a waxy lipid which is involved in a number of important bodily functions. For example, it serves as a structural material for cell membranes; it is used to make bile salts which are necessary for digestion; it helps in the formation of sex hormones and hormones of the adrenal glands, such as cortisone; and, in the skin, it helps to produce vitamin D in the presence of sunlight.

Why then, do the Dietary Goals recommend that we limit the cholesterol in our diets to 300 milligrams daily?

The cholesterol issue is still quite controversial. As mentioned earlier, studies have shown that too much cholesterol in the blood of some people may create a greater risk for the development of atherosclerotic heart disease. This suggests that people who have high blood cholesterol levels probably should watch out for excess cholesterol in their diets. The "average" American consumes 400–500 milligrams of cholesterol each day—a level far above the average in countries where there is little heart disease. While further research is needed on this issue, it seems that it would do no harm for us to cut down on foods that are high in cholesterol. Furthermore, since we can manufacture our own cholesterol (mainly in the liver), it appears that adequate levels can be maintained in the body even if its dietary intake of cholesterol is reduced.

How can we reduce the cholesterol level of our diets by 25–35%, as suggested in the Dietary Goals?

It's simple—just keep in mind that cholesterol is only found in foods of animal origin; *vegetable food sources contain no cholesterol.* So begin by emphasizing more vegetable protein sources in your diet, such as legumes (dried beans and peas and lentils), whole grains, nuts, and nut butters in place of animal protein sources. Use small amounts of light-fleshed fish and poultry and relatively little or no meat or other foods high in saturated fats. Use lowfat dairy products (lowfat milk, cheese, and yogurt); vegetable oils and margarine in place of butter, salt pork, lard, and other animal fats; and eat plenty of fresh fruits and vegetables. Reduce both the saturated and total fat content of your diet *substantially,* as outlined earlier. And reduce animal products that are particulary rich sources of cholesterol, such as egg yolk, shrimp, and organ meats. The following chart compares many of these foods for cholesterol, as well as caloric content.

CHOLESTEROL CONTENT OF SOME COMMON FOODS

Food	Amount	Cholesterol (milligrams)	Calories
Whole milk	1 cup	35	160
Skim milk	1 cup	5	90
Cheese:			
American, pasteurized processed	1 ounce	25	105
cheddar	1 ounce	30	115
cottage			
creamed	½ cup	25	130
uncreamed	½ cup	7	85
cream cheese	1 tablespoon	15	60
Cream:			
half and half	1 tablespoon	7	20
heavy	1 tablespoon	20	55
light	1 tablespoon	10	30
sour	1 tablespoon	8	25

CHOLESTEROL CONTENT OF SOME COMMON FOODS
(continued)

Food	Amount	Cholesterol (milligrams)	Calories
Ice milk	1 cup	25	200
Ice cream (10% fat)	1 cup	55	255
Yogurt (made from partially skimmed milk), plain	1 cup	17	125
Egg	1 large	250 (yolk only; white has no cholesterol)	80
Lean meats, cooked	1 ounce	25	75
Liver, cooked	1 ounce	125	60
Kidney, cooked	1 ounce	225	70
Frankfurter	1	35	155
Poultry, cooked	1 ounce	25	50
Fish, cooked:			
dark oily flesh	1 ounce	40	55
light flesh	1 ounce	20	40
Shrimp	5 large	45	35
Other shellfish, cooked or raw	1 ounce	15–25	20–35
Vegetable protein sources:			
legumes, grains, vegetables	½ cup	0	15–115
nuts	1 ounce	0	120
nut butters	1 tablespoon	0	95
Fruits, all types, unsweetened	½ cup	0	40
Margarine, made from vegetable oil	1 tablespoon	0	100
Butter	1 tablespoon	35	100
Vegetable oil	1 tablespoon	0	120
Mayonnaise	1 tablespoon	10	85
Vegetable shortening	1 tablespoon	0	110
Lard	1 tablespoon	13	115
Bacon, lean	2 strips	14	90

ABOUT SALT

Why do the U.S. Dietary Goals advise us to reduce consumption of salt to 5 grams or less daily?

Mainly because excess salt consumption is known to be associated with the high incidence of hypertension (high blood pressure) found in the United States—and hypertension is a *major* risk factor in the development of cardiovascular disease. Actually, it's the *sodium* contained in salt that is associated with hypertension; and salt—or sodium chloride (NaCl)— is about 40% sodium. (This means that the Dietary Goal of *5 grams of salt translates to about 2 grams of sodium daily.*) Most dinner tables nowadays are seen as incomplete without a salt shaker. In fact, to many Americans it's nearly as essential as a fork. Nutritionists have become concerned in recent years about the increased use of salt—not only the salt we use in cooking or liberally apply to foods at the table (often without tasting them first), but also the salt consumption that is becoming more and more controlled by food manufacturers who add large amounts of salt and other sodium-containing compounds to many commercial food products. As a result the average figure for salt consumption in the U.S. ranges from about 6 to 18 grams per person daily. If you consume 12 grams of salt per day, you use about 10 pounds per year, which is equivalent to about six of the large-sized (26-ounce) containers of salt sold in food markets! Fortunately, many people are able to excrete any extra sodium, and it causes no apparent health hazard; but for many other people, too much sodium may be harmful.

But, isn't sodium necessary to keep our body fluids properly balanced?

Yes, we do need some sodium—but under normal conditions, most of us only need about 200 to 300 milligrams of sodium daily (or about ½ gram of salt) to maintain sodium balance. This is very easy to obtain without salting foods *at all* because sodium occurs naturally in most foods. For example, 2 cups of milk alone supply 250 milligrams of sodium, which would meet the average person's daily requirement. (See Sodium Content chart on pages 29–31.)

What about this naturally occurring sodium; is it included in the Dietary Goal of 2 grams per day?

No, the Dietary Goal does not include the sodium we get naturally from foods, which is estimated on average to be about 1 gram daily. The *sodium limit* actually being advised, then (including both the naturally occurring sodium and the sodium in salt added to foods), is about *3 grams per day* (the equivalent of 8 grams of salt). This may sound like a lot, but when you reach for the salt shaker, be aware that just 1 teaspoonful contains about 5 grams of salt (2 grams of sodium), or about two-thirds of the Dietary Goal.

How can we decrease our sodium consumption to stay within this limit?
There are a number of ways to reduce sodium intake effectively:

1. Cut down on salt added at the table—in fact, avoid having the salt shaker on the table at all—and only add salt, if desirable, *after* tasting the food.
2. Reduce the salt and seasoned salt used in cooking; use half, or less, the amount called for in recipes (as we have done in this cookbook.)
3. In place of salt, season foods with onion and garlic (fresh or powdered), herbs, spices, vinegar, lemon, or lime juice. (See Index for Herb and Spice Chart.)
4. Decrease use of foods processed with large amounts of salt—whether visible (as on crackers, chips, and pretzels) or hidden (as in many condiments, canned foods, processed meats and fish, and frozen dinners). Read the ingredient labels on cans and packages carefully and look for the words *sodium* or *Na, salt,* and *soda.*

    The following chart comparing the sodium content of some common foods will probably surprise you.

SODIUM CONTENT OF SOME COMMON FOODS

Food	*Amount*	*Sodium (mg)*	*Calories*
Lowfat milk or yogurt	1 cup	125	90–120
Cheese:			
American, pasteurized			
processed	1 slice	240	80
American, pasteurized			
processed cheese			
spread	1 ounce (2 tbsp.)	460	40
cheddar	1 ounce	200	115
cottage, uncreamed	½ cup	210	85
Parmesan	2 tablespoons	80	40
Egg	1 large	60	80
Lean meats, cooked	1 ounce	25	75
Cured meat (such as ham)	1 ounce	255–350	75
Dried chipped beef	1 ounce	1290	60
Cold cuts (bologna,			
salami)	1 ounce	390	90
Frankfurter	1	550	155
Poultry, cooked	1 ounce	20	50
Fish, fresh, cooked	1 ounce	30–60	40–50
Shellfish:			
fresh, raw or cooked	1 ounce	20–60	25
canned	1 ounce	280	25
Sardines	1 ounce	235	60

SODIUM CONTENT OF SOME COMMON FOODS *(continued)*

Food	Amount	Sodium (mg)	Calories
TV dinner	1	715–1320	250–550
Frozen pot pie	1	875–1025	425–510
Lean bacon	2 medium strips	150	85
Legumes:			
dried beans and			
peas, cooked	½ cup	1–13	95–115
lentils, cooked	½ cup	negligible	105
Fresh leafy green vegetables:			
collards, kale, beet			
greens, cooked	½ cup	25	20
spinach or dandelion			
raw	½ cup	20	7
cooked	½ cup	45	20
Swiss chard, cooked	½ cup	60	15
Other fresh vegetables	½ cup	2–5	15–70
Canned vegetables	½ cup	250–300	15–70
Pickled vegetables			
(such as sauerkraut)	½ cup	880	20
Tomato juice or V-8	½ cup	245	25
Fresh tomato	1 medium	5	25
Fruit, unsweetened	½ cup	negligible	40
Whole cereal grains,			
cooked	½ cup	negligible	70–90
Bread (all types			
containing salt)	1 slice	130	70
Cold cereal, unsalted			
(shredded wheat)	1 ounce	10	110
Cold cereal, containing			
salt	1 ounce	230–300	70–95
Soup, canned (diluted			
with an equal volume			
of water)	1 cup	720–1050	50–170
Bouillon	1 cube	780	30
Snack foods:			
crackers			
saltines or soda	5	155	60
oyster crackers	½ cup	100	250
olives			
black (Greek)	5 large	435	45
green	3 large	280	15
peanuts			
salted	1 ounce	120	165
unsalted	1 ounce	trace	165

SODIUM CONTENT OF SOME COMMON FOODS *(continued)*

Food	Amount	Sodium (mg)	Calories
peanut butter			
salted	1 tablespoon	100	95
unsalted	1 tablespoon	trace	95
pickles, dill	1 medium		
	(2 ounces)	930	5
pizza, commercial	⅛ of 14-inch		
	pie	455	155
potato chips	1 ounce	100	170
pretzels	5 twisted thins	505	115
	1 large rod type	235	55
Condiments:			
prepared mustard	1 tablespoon	195	15
sweet relish	1 tablespoon	105	20
tomato catsup	1 tablespoon	155	15
soy sauce	1 tablespoon	1320	10
Worcestershire sauce	1 tablespoon	250	10
Salted butter or			
margarine	1 teaspoon	45	35
Unsalted butter or			
margarine	1 teaspoon	trace	35
Vegetable oil	1 teaspoon	trace	40
Mayonnaise	1 teaspoon	35	30
Commercial salad dressing:			
blue cheese	1 tablespoon	165	75
French	1 tablespoon	220	65
Italian	1 tablespoon	315	85
Russian	1 tablespoon	130	75
Thousand Island	1 tablespoon	80	115
Seasonings:			
salt, seasoned salt, sea salt	1 teaspoon	2130	0
chili powder	1 teaspoon	25	negligible
herbs and other spices	1 teaspoon	negligible	negligible
Baking powder	1 teaspoon	315	5
Low sodium baking powder	1 teaspoon	trace	5
Baking soda	1 teaspoon	1360	0

SPECIAL NEEDS

Pregnant women and breast-feeding mothers, babies, children of various ages, and adolescents all have special nutritional needs. In this chapter we have provided information and specific guidelines to help you recognize and meet the nutritional requirements in these special areas.

PREGNANT WOMEN AND BREAST-FEEDING MOTHERS

Do calorie requirements increase during pregnancy?

Most definitely. During pregnancy, an increase of approximately 300 calories (or 15%) is needed above normal daily requirements. This need varies with maternal age, activity, height and pre-pregnancy weight: adolescents, active women, exceptionally large-framed women, and underweight women generally have even greater caloric needs during pregnancy.

What are the calorie needs of mothers during breast-feeding?

The energy involved just to produce breast milk requires an additional 200–400 calories each day. This, plus the caloric content of the milk itself, means that a mother requires an extra 700–1000 calories per day (over normal caloric needs) when breast-feeding. The fat deposits that a mother stores during pregnancy provide 200–300 of these calories per day, leaving a minimum of 500 calories daily that need to be provided by food sources. And, since the fat deposits are usually exhausted after three months, the entire 700–1000 calories needed daily must come from a mother's diet if she continues to breast-feed beyond that time.

Do nutrient needs also increase during pregnancy and breast-feeding?

Yes, all of the Recommended Dietary Allowances increase during pregnancy and breast-feeding (except for iron during breast-feeding—which is at the same level, 18 milligrams daily, as for nonpregnant women of child-bearing age). These increases are highlighted in the RDA chart (see page 6). This means that the extra calories needed during pregnancy and breast-feeding should come from foods that have a high nutrient density, as discussed earlier.

What is the average recommended weight gain during pregnancy?

A number of studies show that a normal infant birth weight of 7.5 pounds requires an average prenatal maternal weight gain of about 24 to 30 pounds. It is important, therefore, for women to gain *at least* 24 pounds during a normal pregnancy to be certain that all needs are met—the mother's as well as the baby's.

At what rate should this weight be gained?

Normally, 2 to 4 pounds (1 to 2 kilograms) are gained during the first trimester (12 weeks), followed by an average of about 1 pound (0.5 kilograms) per week during the last two trimesters (28 weeks).

Does this weight gain apply to women who are overweight before pregnancy?

Yes, it does. Women who are overweight at the onset of pregnancy should be encouraged to increase their physical activities (such as walking) rather than severely restricting their diets. Of course, these women should be especially careful not to dilute their diets with extra calories from foods high in sugars and fats. Overweight can be dangerous to both mothers and their babies, so the weight should be lost *before* becoming pregnant again.

Doctors have traditionally advised women to restrict their use of salt during pregnancy to prevent edema (swelling resulting from fluid retention). Is this still recommended?

No, since maternal and fetal tissues require salt during pregnancy, it should not be excluded from the diet. Also, *iodized* salt should be used because of the increased iodine needs during pregnancy. In cases of edema, most physicians advise against excessive sodium intake by restricting the use of highly salted foods, such as those mentioned in the discussion on salt.

Are nutrition supplements normally needed during pregnancy and lactation?

Except for supplements of iron, folacin, and possibly vitamin B-6, routine multivitamin and mineral supplementation is not necessary during pregnancy and lactation if the diet is adequate. And no supplements, not even iron and folacin, should be taken without your doctor's advice.

Iron is essential to the formation of hemoglobin, the protein in red blood cells which carries oxygen throughout the body. During pregnancy, the mother's blood volume increases by nearly 50%, and in order to maintain her hemoglobin level, she requires a daily intake of more than 18 milligrams of iron.

When folacin, a B vitamin essential to the reproduction and growth of red blood cells, is low in the diet, large, immature red blood cells (called megaloblasts) are formed, resulting in megaloblastic anemia. During pregnancy the folacin recommendations double (from 400 micrograms to 800 micrograms per day) and during lactation the recommendation increases by 25% (from 400 to 500 micrograms per day). Since it is difficult to get the recommended amounts of iron and folacin from food sources alone during pregnancy and lactation, a daily supplement (of 30–60 milligrams of iron and 400–800 micrograms of folacin) is usually prescribed by the doctor.

THE FIRST YEAR OF LIFE

We hear a lot of controversy today about breast-feeding versus commercial infant formulas. Which milk is better for babies?

There are advantages to both breast milk and commercial formula, but there is no question that breast milk is the preferred infant food for a number of reasons. Breast milk is already sterile and at the right temperature for your baby; there is no danger of error, as there is in mixing a formula; breast milk is always available and convenient so you have more time to relax and enjoy being close to your baby. Also, during the first few days after delivery, a mother's breasts produce a yellowish fluid called *colostrum* which carries antibodies that provide newborn babies protection against infections that is not available from any other source.

Are vitamin/mineral supplements needed for the breast-fed baby?

Breast milk supplies all of the required nutrients in adequate amounts except for iron, fluoride, and possibly vitamin D. Babies are usually born with enough iron stored in their livers to last for the first few months. But since many young mothers (especially teenagers whose own bodies are still growing) are either very low in iron or actually anemic during pregnancy when the baby is gathering an iron supply, most pediatricians prescribe for the breast-fed baby an iron supplement (of 7 milligrams per day) by at least four months of age—and some pediatricians prescribe iron from birth—just to be on the safe side. A fluoride supplement (0.25 milligram per day) is usually prescribed from birth to increase resistance of developing teeth to caries. And many pediatricians recommend a vitamin D supplement (of 400 International Units per day) from birth as an extra margin of safety against rickets, since the vitamin D content of human milk is variable.

If it is necessary to bottle-feed, what type of formula should be used?

If you decide not to breast-feed, or are unable to for any reason, there are a number of commercial formulas available and there is evaporated milk formula which you can make yourself. These substitutes for breast milk are modified to make them resemble human milk as closely as possible. Commercial formulas are more convenient to prepare than evaporated milk formula and their cost is generally directly related to the ease of preparation—the least expensive varieties are the powdered and concentrated liquid formulas that you must dilute with water; the ready-to-feed formulas requiring no dilution are usually the most expensive. Whatever kind you decide to use, choose one that is fortified with iron and vitamins. If you decide to prepare your own evaporated milk formula you should give the baby a vitamin C supplement in drop form of 20 milligrams per day from birth and an iron supplement of 7 milligrams by four months of age. If you live in an area where the fluoride content of the drinking water used to dilute the formula is less than 0.3 parts per million, a fluoride supplement of 0.25 milligrams per day will probably be recommended by your pediatrician.

When should babies be introduced to semi-solid foods?

Babies get all the essential nutrients needed from breast milk or iron-fortified formula (plus supplements as mentioned on page 35) until they have developed the muscular control to accept or refuse semi-solid food. When babies are able to sit with support, they have usually developed enough control of their head and neck muscles to begin eating from a spoon. Also, they will be able to indicate a desire to eat by opening their mouths and leaning forward, and to indicate that they have had enough food by leaning back or turning away. *This generally occurs around five to six months—and, nutritionally, babies do not need semi-solid foods before this age.* If babies are not developed enough to show that they are hungry or full, parents may inadvertently be forcing them to overeat. and eating habits that encourage overeating early in life may become established and lead to obesity later on.

What foods should be offered to the baby first?

Commercially prepared iron-fortified infant cereals should be the first food introduced to babies around five to six months of age (or when they are developed enough to eat and to refuse food) and continued at least until eighteen months. An iron supplement is usually no longer necessary for breast-fed babies (or babies receiving homemade evaporated milk formula) once they begin eating iron-fortified infant cereal. Baby cereals in jars (fortified with ferrous sulfate) and dry baby cereals (fortified with electrolytic iron) satisfy the baby's iron needs best because they provide an iron source that is highly absorbable in the body, and they are easy for babies to eat and digest. The jarred baby cereals, however, are usually much more expensive than the dry baby cereals.

In what order should other foods be introduced to babies?

After the baby has completely accepted cereal, check with your nutritionist or pediatrician about introducing strained vegetables, fruits, and meats. There is no absolute rule about which type of food to offer first, but it is a good idea to begin introducing foods that provide vitamin C (such as strained fruits and vegetables) so that your baby will be accustomed to them when he or she makes the transition from vitamin-containing breast milk or formula to whole milk, which has a much lower content of vitamin C.

Are there any foods to which young babies are particularly allergic?

Babies commonly have allergic reactions to foods but they generally outgrow them in time. By introducing foods individually and waiting several days before introducing another new food, the culprit foods can be identified more easily. For example, young babies can usually tolerate plain rice or barley cereal, rather than mixed cereals. Also, babies are frequently allergic to egg whites during the first year so it's best not to offer them until the baby is at least a year old. However, egg yolk, cooked and mashed into cereal or formula, can be introduced to babies whenever they are ready to begin eating semi-solid foods during the first year. (By the way, it is less expensive to buy fresh eggs than baby egg yolks sold in jars . . . just use the leftover egg whites in other cooking for the family.)

Are homemade baby foods recommended by nutritionists?

Homemade baby foods are an economical and easy way to feed your baby *providing* you use high-quality ingredients; do not add unnecessary extras, such as salt, monosodium glutamate, sugar, or other sweeteners to them; and prepare them with the utmost cleanliness—clean hands, clean kitchen, clean utensils, clean food, and clean storage containers. Homemade baby foods offer the advantage of using the same foods prepared for the family meals, which can be separated *before* salt and other seasonings are added and puréed for the baby to eat right away—or frozen for later use.

How should homemade baby foods be prepared?

By following these simple guidelines:

· Be sure that everything is absolutely clean.
· Use fresh foods, or if using frozen foods be certain that they do not have salt, sugar, or other unnecessary ingredients added to them. (Home-

made baby food, prepared from canned foods or those cooked in salted water, are considerably higher in sodium than are commercially prepared baby foods. Also, regular canned fruits and vegetables should not be used in preparing baby food because of the potentially high lead content of the cans.)

· Be sure to remove all skin, pits, and seeds from fruits and vegetables and excess fat and gristle—and the bones—from meat and poultry.
· Add a small amount of water to foods and cook them just until tender (it is best to steam or bake baby foods so that valuable vitamins will not be lost), and be sure to save unsalted cooking liquid for puréeing.
· Place the cooked food into a baby food grinder, blender, food processor, or simply mash with a fork through a strainer . . . add enough cooking liquid, broth, milk, or water to blend the food to baby food consistency (meats usually require much more liquid).
· Avoid overcooking, overblending or overmashing foods to minimize damage to vulnerable vitamins and polyunsaturated fats.
· Never put the same spoon back into the food if you taste the baby food . . . it can cause the food to spoil and can spread any germs from your mouth to the baby.

How should homemade baby foods be stored?

Homemade strained baby foods can be stored in ice cube trays or individual ice cube containers. After the food is frozen, the cubes can be popped out and stored in tightly sealed plastic bags in the freezer. *To thaw*, place frozen cube in a custard cup or other heatproof dish and set the dish in hot water. Be sure to date and label all frozen baby foods and try to use foods within one month so they will not lose their nutritional value.

Avoid freezing foods that have been stored in the refrigerator even for one day.

Avoid refreezing foods that have been previously frozen—even after making them into baby food.

Avoid storing home-prepared baby foods in the refrigerator for longer than two days.

Are commercially prepared baby foods reasonable alternatives to the homemade ones?

Baby food manufacturers have made major strides in improving the quality of baby foods by removing much of the salt and sugar once added to them. However, it is still advisable to read labels carefully and choose baby foods with the least number of unnecessary ingredients added . . . remember, contents are listed on ingredient labels in descending order of use. It is usually best to buy *plain, rather than mixed*, vegetables, fruits, meats, and poultry for the best values nutritionally and economically.

Are there any important things to know about using commercial baby foods?

Yes, sanitation is just as important when using commercial baby foods as it is when you prepare homemade baby foods. For example:

- Always wash the baby food jar *before* opening.
- When you open the jar, listen for a "pop" sound. This will tell you that the protective seal has not been previously broken (and that bacteria have not contaminated the food).
- Put the amount of food that you think the baby will eat in a clean dish, replace the jar lid, and refrigerate the remaining food in the jar immediately . . . the leftover food should be used within two days.
- *Do not* feed directly from the jar unless you know that the baby will eat the entire contents of the jar . . . there are digestive enzymes in the baby's saliva (and in yours) that will break down food and cause it to liquify.
- Throw away any food remaining in the dish after the baby is finished eating.

When should "junior" foods be introduced to babies?

When the baby is eating a variety of strained foods, it's a good time to begin to offer foods with more texture. You really do not need to buy "junior" foods—they are usually an unnecessary expense. Instead, try chopping and mashing foods that are prepared for family meals, such as:

- well-cooked and ground, chopped, or mashed meats (with all bones, gristle, and fat removed), such as meat loaf or minced chicken livers
- omelets
- enriched or whole wheat noodles or macaroni
- soft, ripe fruits
- tuna or soft, flaked fish with all bones removed
- coarsely chopped or mashed vegetables without skins or stringy texture
- very soft, well-mashed rice and beans
- tofu (soybean curd)

What about "finger foods"? When should they be made available to babies?

When the baby is able to chew and pick up foods, begin to offer foods that are easy to handle, such as:

- peeled ripe fruits without seeds, such as banana, apple, pear, peach, nectarine, or papaya slices
- *cooked* vegetables, such as tender green beans, peeled white or sweet potatoes, or carrots
- small pieces of cooked meat, poultry, or fish
- cheese cubes or strips
- pieces of hard-cooked egg or omelet

· dried-out and toasted whole wheat, oatmeal, or rye bread or crackers, such as melba toast, zwieback, teething biscuits, or graham
crackers.

Avoid offering foods that may cause the baby to choke, such as:

- · popcorn
- · potato chips
- · nuts
- · dry cereals

- · corn
- · peas
- · berries
- · raw vegetables

- · meat, fish, or
 poultry with bones
- · raisins

***Babies are often seen sleeping with a bottle of milk or juice. Is this
practice recommended by pediatricians and nutritionists?***
Many pediatric experts are concerned that the natural sugar in milk
and juices can linger in the baby's mouth and damage teeth if the baby
sleeps with a bottle. Some pediatricians and nutritionists feel so strongly
about this that they do not recommend introducing fruit juice until the
baby is able to drink it from a cup. Babies have no real nutritional need
for fruit juices before this time *providing* they are receiving vitamin C
from breast milk, iron-fortified formula, vitamin drops, or strained fruits
and vegetables. Be sure to check with your pediatrician and/or nutritionist
about this.

When do babies usually begin drinking from a cup?
As babies begin to eat a wide variety of foods, they are generally
switched (by the doctor) from breast milk or iron-fortified formula to
whole milk. This is also a good time for babies to be introduced to the
cup. Water and unsweetened fruit juices can be offered from the cup as
well. It is not necessary to buy expensive, commercially prepared baby
fruit juices—and particularly avoid buying fruit "drinks" because they
contain large amounts of added sugar and do not compare favorably in
nutritional value to real fruit juices.

TODDLERS (1–3 YEARS) AND PRESCHOOLERS (3–6 YEARS)

***Why is it that young children frequently have poor appetites and finicky
eating behavior?***
After babies triple their weight and add about 50% to their length
during the first year of life, their growth rates obviously have to slow
down—causing appetites also to slow down during the next few years.
Appetites often vary from one meal to the next, depending on the child's
rate of growth, activity level, and state of health. Adults frequently over-
estimate the amount of food that young children are able to eat. It is much
better to offer small servings and let children ask for more than to over-
whelm them with adult-size portions. Toddlers should also be allowed
plenty of time to finish meals. Remember that their eating skills are being

perfected and they need time to practice. They are also learning more about the different types of foods and how they feel, smell, and taste. After a reasonable period of time, and if the child is obviously no longer interested in the food, parents should quietly remove it. Sometimes unfinished food from meals can be saved for a later snack when the child is hungrier.

Food jags are also common at this age, likes and dislikes change frequently, and children often ritualize the preparation of food. For example, foods have to be cut to a particular size or served on a particular dish. Children at this age are reaching for independence and need to be in control to some extent. Usually, if adults do not focus attention on these demands, they will soon be outgrown.

Young children are generally interested in frequent snacks. Should this practice be encouraged?

Most children this age need to eat an average of five to seven times during the day in order to fulfill their increased nutritional needs. Snacks between meals should be high in nutritional value and spaced so that they do not interfere with family meals. They should be easy for a hungry child to pick up with the fingers since most children this age are not yet skilled in eating with utensils. And it is also important to avoid giving children snacks high in sugar of any type. Sugars not only dilute the nutritional value of the food but are harmful to developing teeth. Keep in mind that it is not only the *type* of sweets that are eaten but also the *frequency* with which they are eaten that leads to dental problems. When sugary foods are continuously consumed throughout the day, the incidence of dental caries is greatly increased; and even more so if the snack has a sticky consistency.

The following are good snacks for children this age:

- small pieces of cheese with apple slices or a whole wheat cracker
- hard-cooked eggs (quartered)
- cooked green beans (whole)
- peanut butter or toasted cheese sandwiches on whole wheat bread (quartered)
- oranges cut in wedges (this shape is preferred by most children)
- plain yogurt with unsweetened fruit and wheat germ

When young children flatly refuse to eat nutritionally important foods such as vegetables, what can adults do?

Often when children this age refuse healthful foods it is simply because their taste buds are very sensitive to strong flavors. Children generally prefer soft or crisp textures; mild, delicate flavors; and single foods to combination dishes such as casseroles. They commonly dislike strongly flavored or highly spiced foods, so it's wise to cut down on the seasoning in family meals. If an entire group of foods, such as meat or fish, is refused, substitutes of equal nutritional value need to be offered. For example, eggs, cheese, or boneless tender pieces of poultry (without skin) that are easier to chew might solve the problem in this case. Fortified powdered milk added to meat loaf, soups, or hot cereals might be the answer for a child who is refusing to drink milk. However, if children show dislike for only one or two foods, remember that they are entitled to their likes and dislikes just like anyone else.

Toddlers and preschoolers are more likely to drink too much milk. Is this a serious problem?

Yes, it can be. When children fill up on milk (which is a poor source of iron) and refuse to eat important solid foods that supply iron, they may develop "milk anemia" from a lack of iron. Two to three cups of milk daily is enough for children this age.

OLDER CHILDREN (6–11 YEARS) AND ADOLESCENTS (11–18 YEARS)

School-age children and adolescents are notorious for snacking between meals—particularly while watching television and right after school. What can parents do to encourage nutritious snacks?

Try to keep a variety of nutritionally valuable snacks on hand, such as:

- unsweetened fruit juices
- a variety of fresh and dried fruits—it's best if some of these are pre-prepared, such as pineapple wedges or orange sections
- cherry tomatoes or precut raw vegetables, such as carrot, green pepper, celery, or cucumber sticks
- plain yogurt with unsweetened applesauce and cinnamon
- mixtures of whole-grain cereals (such as Granola, see Index) with dried fruits and nuts
- small strips of cold meat, chicken, turkey, or cheese
- peanut butter or other nut butters
- homemade sandwich spreads, such as bean, cottage cheese, egg or tuna (see Index for sandwiches and snacks)
- whole-grain crackers or Whole Wheat Pretzels (see Index)

Do nutrient needs change during adolescence?

Very much so. For example, the RDA for protein is higher at this age because adolescents are building new lean body mass and (particularly true of males) muscle mass. Adolescents need about 45 (males 11–14 years) to 46 (females 11–18 years) grams of protein each day as compared with the 34 grams per day used when they were 7–10 years old. Older adolescent males (15–18 years) need even more protein—about 56 grams daily. In addition to higher protein allowances, almost all of the RDA's for vitamins and minerals increase as well. (See RDA chart pages 6–7.)

Which nutrients are adolescents typically lacking most of all?

Studies have shown that adolescent diets are often low in calcium, iron, ascorbic acid (vitamin C), and vitamin A. In the case of vitamins A and C (and many of the other vitamins also) deficiencies occur mainly because adolescents frequently miss meals—particularly breakfast and lunch, make poor food choices, and lack variety in their diets (particularly fruits and vegetables). Adolescents are often deficient in calcium and iron for these same reasons but mainly because of important physiologic changes:

Iron needs increase by 75% during adolescence due to increased blood volume and muscle mass, a rise in hemoglobin (in males), and menstrual losses for females. Consequently, both males and females require 18 milligrams of iron daily instead of the 10 milligrams per day needed during preadolescence.

Calcium is absorbed in large amounts as bone growth accelerates during adolescence. To accommodate these increased needs and as an extra margin of safety, the RDA for adolescent males and females is 1200 milligrams of calcium per day—or 400 milligrams more than during preadolescence.

How can adolescents be sure to get enough calcium?

The easiest way for adolescents to meet their calcium needs is by consuming adequate amounts of milk and milk products:

	Mg of Calcium	Calories
Whole milk, 1 cup	290	160
Buttermilk (skim), 1 cup	295	90
Skim milk, 1 cup	295	90
Yogurt (made from whole milk), plain	270	150
Yogurt (made from partially skimmed milk), plain	295	125
Cheddar cheese, 1 ounce	215	115
Creamed cottage cheese, 1 cup	230	260
Uncreamed (lowfat) cottage cheese, 1 cup	180	170
Ice cream, 1 cup	200	260
Custard, 1 cup	300	305

Even with erratic eating habits, a teenager can easily meet his or her RDA for calcium by drinking 4 cups of milk or equivalent each day—preferably skim or lowfat milk if excess weight is a problem.

PART II

The Recipes

Introduction to the Recipe Section

These recipes have been selected to help you put the nutrition principles we've just discussed to practical use. We have chosen tasty recipes with a high nutrient density and ones that will help to minimize your intake of calories, salt, sugar, cholesterol, and fat—particularly saturated fat. Also included are several recipes to help switch the emphasis in your diet from animal to vegetable protein sources. With each recipe we have given a breakdown of the calorie, protein, fat, and sodium content per serving, along with a listing of any indicator nutrients (see page 9) for which the recipe is an excellent source. The example that follows illustrates how you can use this information. We hope you will refer to this cookbook often to be nutritionally well read—and well fed.

HOW TO USE THE RECIPE NUTRITION INFORMATION

Example:

A 20-year-old woman wants to maintain her weight on 1800 calories a day. She decides to prepare Lentil Surprise Stew (see Index), and when she looks at the bottom of the recipe page she has the following information at her fingertips:

Calories: She knows right away that one serving of the recipe provides *300 calories*—about one-sixth of her caloric goal for the day.

Protein: The RDA chart (see pages 6–7) lists the protein RDA for someone her age and sex at 44 grams per day; one serving of this recipe supplies *18 grams*, or more than one-third of her RDA.

Fat: To stay within the Dietary Goal for a total fat intake that does not exceed 30% of total calories (see Index), she is aiming for no more than about 540 of her total calories for the day to be supplied as fat calories. There are *12 grams* of fat per serving in this recipe. She knows from the chart on page

21 that there are 9 calories per gram of fat, so this recipe supplies *108 calories* per serving from fat alone, or about one-fifth of her fat calorie intake for the day.

Sodium: The recipe has *300 milligrams* of sodium per serving—about 15% of the 2 grams (2000 milligrams) per day recommended in the Dietary Goals.

Iron,   From the discussion about indicator nutrients, she knows
Vitamin A,   that, in one serving, she'll be getting at least 10% of the
Thiamin,   U.S. RDA for *iron* (1.8 milligrams), 25% for *vitamin A*
and   (250 micrograms R.E., or 1250 I.U.s), 10% for *thiamin* (0.15
Riboflavin: milligrams), and 10% for *riboflavin* (0.17 milligrams).

SOME SPECIFICS ABOUT THE NUTRIENT CALCULATIONS

1. *Optional ingredients* have not been included in the recipe calculations.
2. Recipes that call for *"salt to taste"* have been calculated *without any added salt.* It is important to keep in mind that each ½ teaspoon of salt added to a recipe supplies about 1070 milligrams of sodium, or about one-third the maximum daily amount that is recommended for the "average" person. (See Index for more information about sodium and salt intake.)
3. Recipes calling for *"sugar or honey to taste"* have been calculated *without any added sugar or honey.* If the recipe calls for "1 tablespoon honey (or to taste)" only 1 tablespoon of honey has been included in the calculation. For each extra tablespoon of honey, add 65 calories; and for each extra tablespoon of sugar, add 45 calories.
4. Some recipes call for *"defatted stock—or use canned."* These recipes have been calculated using the figures for *homemade* stock (see Index), which has about 55 milligrams of sodium per cupful. If defatted *canned* broth is substituted, the sodium content of the recipe will be much higher, since each cup of commercially prepared broth supplies approximately 750 milligrams of sodium. Bouillon has an even higher sodium content—about 960 milligrams per cube (or about 480 milligrams per teaspoon).
5. All calculations for meat recipes have been based on figures for *raw* meat *except* in recipes where the cooking method allows a substantial amount of the fat to be drained off, as with roasted meats; for these recipes, calculations have been based on figures for *cooked* meat since a large number of calories are lost in the discarded fat.
6. Nutrient breakdowns are not given for the recipe variations, unless otherwise indicated.

SOUPS

"Soup of the evening, beautiful soup!" Soups are certainly worthy of the emotion displayed by the Mock Turtle when he sang this for Alice. From low-calorie, delicate, iced soups to the hot and heartier varieties, soups can act as snacks or as accompaniments to turn the humblest of meals into elegant affairs—or serve as the meal itself. Soups are soothing restoratives and, in fact, this quality was responsible for the coining of the word "restaurant." An eighteenth-century French tavern keeper named Boulanger sold soups to weary travelers as restoratives, and the idea of restaurants quickly caught on in Paris. Try making some homemade soup to have on hand in place of the less nutritious restoratives we have become accustomed to.

Few other food categories offer cooks so much opportunity for individual creativity—and with the minimum of culinary expertise required. Just about any ingredient can be used in soups. They are a good way to use leftovers, particularly leftover meats, poultry, fish, pasta, rice, and vegetables. Some soups can be simmered on top of the stove for hours (while you do other things); others can be quickly prepared using the blender method with broth, skim milk, vegetables, and seasonings. Furthermore, with homemade soups, *you* are in control of how much salt goes into them. This is an important advantage since most canned soups are very highly salted. They contain an average of about 1000 milligrams of sodium per cupful (when prepared with an equal volume of water), or more than many people need in an entire day!

So, whatever your motives—greater taste and higher nutritional value for relatively few calories and a controlled salt content, or an opportunity to express your creativity and please your friends and family—get into the habit of preparing your own soups.

To make soups extra special, garnish them with any of the following:

· chopped fresh chives
· grated cheese
· pumpkin, sunflower, or sesame seeds
· chopped nuts
· whole-grain croutons
· chopped fresh herbs, such as parsley, chervil, or dill weed
· chopped fresh greens, such as watercress
· fresh sprouts
· finely diced fresh vegetables, such as tomato, scallion, celery, broccoli, cauliflower, or green pepper—or any other vegetable

BASIC SOUP STOCKS

Soups can be made with water or commercial broths, but the real key to delicious soups is using homemade stock. When preparing other foods, THINK STOCK. Save those bones, fresh vegetable scraps, stems, and potato peelings. Add herbs and water to cover and simmer for 2–3 hours (longer for meats with bones).

You may or may not wish to strain the stock, depending on the type of soup you plan to make. But be sure to defat any stock that is made from meat or poultry.

DEFATTING STOCK

If time allows:
Allow the stock to cool.
Strain if you wish.
Cover and store in refrigerator for several hours until the fat rises to the top and hardens. Remove the hardened fat and discard.
In a hurry:
Skim off fat carefully from the surface with a spoon, *or*
Apply an all-white paper towel (avoid dyes from colored paper towels) to surface and blot up fat. Replace towel as needed until all the visible fat is removed. A piece of ice can be wrapped inside the towel to speed up this process.

Stocks can be stored in jars in the freezer for later use (be sure to leave some space at the top of the jar since liquid expands when it freezes!). Some of the stock can be frozen in ice cube trays, then popped into plastic storage bags, tightly sealed, and stored for later use in recipes requiring small amounts of stock. These cubes are also convenient as a quick pick-up. Just heat one and drink it in place of commercial bouillon cubes, which are excessively high in salt.

Basic Vegetable Stock

1 cup well-scrubbed potato peelings*

2 onions (or 4 scallions or 4 leeks), chopped

2 carrots, sliced

2 stalks celery, sliced

6 cups water

1 Bouquet Garni (see Index)

* Or use any leftover vegetable scraps, stems, or peelings (except those in the cabbage family, which tend to give a strong flavor).

Place vegetables in a large pot. Add water (be sure it covers the vegetables) and the bouquet garni. Simmer for about 1 hour, or until vegetables are very soft; cool.

Strain and store in jars in freezer. (Be sure to leave 1½-inch space at top of jar to allow for expansion of liquid when it freezes.)

Yield: 1 quart
Per cup: Calories: Negligible; Protein: Negligible; Total Fat: Negligible; Sodium: Negligible

Basic Light Stock

2½ pounds chicken or fowl (uncooked, skinned), or pork bones or veal knuckle or shank or a combination of any of these*

2½ quarts water

2 medium carrots, sliced

1 large onion, chopped (or 2 leeks, sliced)

2 stalks celery, including the tops, chopped

1 small white turnip (optional)

1 Bouquet Garni (see Index)

2 peppercorns

1–2 cloves

* If whole chicken is used, remove from pot when meat is tender (after about 1 hour), allow to cool, remove meat from bones, and use in other recipes, for chicken salad, or added to the soup later. Return bones to the stock for remainder of cooking time.

Rinse bones and meat well with lukewarm water. Cover with water and bring to boil; if there is a lot of scum on the surface, discard the water,

(continued)

rinse bones again, cover with water again, and bring to a boil. If there is not much residue, just skim carefully.

Add remaining ingredients and simmer, covered, for 1–1½ hours, or until the meat has completely separated from the bones. Remove the meat and separate from the bones; there will be about 3 cups of cooked, chopped chicken (for salads, sandwiches, etc.). Return the bones to the broth and cook 1½ hours, or until they begin to soften. If the water level evaporates a great deal while the stock is simmering, add some boiling water.

Cool at room temperature. Strain (through a strainer lined with cheese-cloth if a clear stock is desired) and refrigerate for several hours. Defat the stock (as described on page 50).

Store in jars in the freezer. (Be sure to leave 1½ inches at the top of the jars to allow for expansion during freezing.)

Yield: 1½ quarts (plus 3 cups chopped, cooked chicken if whole chicken is used)
Per cup: Calories: 20, Protein: 3 g; Total Fat: Trace; Sodium: 55 mg

SPEEDY BLENDER SOUPS

Delicious homemade creamed vegetable soups can be prepared in 20–30 minutes by using a few shortcuts, such as frozen vegetables in place of fresh and an electric food processor or blender in place of a hand-operated food mill or strainer. Here is a simple technique for making low-calorie creamed vegetable soups in a hurry.

BASIC PROPORTIONS FOR CREAMED VEGETABLE SOUPS

1 Cup Servings	Water or Defatted Stock	Vegetables	Potato Starch*	Skim Milk
2	1½ cups	1 cup	1½ T	½ cup
4	2½ cups	2 cups	3 T	1 cup
6	6¼ cups	3 cups	4 T	1½ cups

* Rice starch or arrowroot starch may be substituted for the powdered or dehydrated potato starch.

Bring water or stock to a boil.

Chop vegetables in a food processor (or by hand). Add vegetables to water, season with pepper (and herbs if desired), and bring back to boil. Lower heat and simmer 10–15 minutes, or until vegetables are tender.

Purée three-quarters of the vegetables in a food processor or blender, return to pan, and continue to simmer with the non-puréed vegetables. (Some people prefer to purée all of the vegetables for a completely smooth soup, which is fine. However, when you leave a small amount of the vegetables whole, the soup has more texture.)

Dissolve the starch in the cold milk, mixing thoroughly, then stir mixture into the vegetable purée. Continue to cook until the soup thickens. Season to taste.

Per Cup (made with asparagus): Calories: 70; Protein: 5 g; Total Fat: Trace; Sodium: 55 mg
Excellent Source of: Riboflavin and Vitamin C

Spanish Bisque

4 large ripe tomatoes, coarsely chopped (about 3 cups)	¼ teaspoon garlic salt (or to taste)
1 cup plain lowfat yogurt	⅛–¼ teaspoon hot pepper sauce (or more to taste)
3–4 tablespoons chopped scallion	1 medium-size ripe avocado
½ teaspoon ground cumin (or to taste)	1–2 teaspoon lemon juice Croutons (optional)

Put tomatoes in blender and purée. Whip in yogurt until smooth. Stir in 2 tablespoons scallion, cumin, garlic salt, and hot pepper sauce.

Peel avocado and cut into thin slices; sprinkle with lemon juice and add to soup (do not purée the avocado). Cover and chill 1–2 hours.

Serve garnished with remaining chopped scallion and, if desired, croutons.

Size of Serving: 1 cup   *Number of Servings:* 4
Per Cup: Calories: 170; Protein: 6 g; Total Fat: 11 g; Sodium: 180 mg
Excellent Source of: Calcium, Vitamin A, Thiamin, and Vitamin C

Gazpacho by the Cupful

1 medium tomato, peeled and diced	1 tablespoon chopped onion
¼ cucumber, peeled and chopped	2 sprigs parsley, chopped
¼ green pepper, seeded and chopped	⅛ teaspoon garlic powder Dash hot pepper sauce

Combine all ingredients in blender and liquify.
Chill and serve.

Size of Serving: 1 cup   *Number of Servings:* 1
Per Cup: Calories: 50; Protein: 2 g; Total Fat: Trace; Sodium: 30 mg
Excellent Source of: Iron, Vitamin A, and Vitamin C

Cucumber Yogurt Soup

The *fresh* dill and mint are key ingredients here.

1 quart plain lowfat
  yogurt
1½ cups defatted chicken
  broth (see Index or use
  canned)
1 garlic clove, crushed
2 large cucumbers,
  peeled—one should be
  coarsely chopped, the
  other halved, seeded,
  and thinly sliced

Salt to taste
Dash pepper
1 tablespoon minced
  fresh dill
1 tablespoon minced
  fresh mint

Combine yogurt and chicken broth in a bowl; mix well. Place 1 cupful of yogurt/broth mixture in blender with garlic and the chopped cucumber with seeds. Turn on "chop" speed for 10 seconds; the cucumber should be finely chopped, not puréed.

Add blender mixture to mixture in bowl along with seeded, thinly sliced cucumber, seasonings, and fresh herbs. Cover and chill thoroughly; serve in chilled soup bowls.

VARIATION: Use 2 tablespoons chopped walnuts and 2 whole (including the tops) scallions, finely chopped, in place of the dill weed and mint.

Size of Serving: 1 cup   *Number of Servings:* 6
Per Cup: Calories: 100; Protein: 6 g; Total Fat: 3 g; Sodium: 100 mg
Excellent Source of: Calcium and Riboflavin

Lithuanian Cold Beet Soup

1 quart skim buttermilk
2 cups cooked julienne
  beets or 1 16-ounce can
  julienne beets including
  liquid (canned beets are
  higher in sodium, unless
  low-sodium canned beets
  are used)

5 whole scallions, finely
  chopped
1 medium cucumber,
  pared and diced
2 medium hard-cooked
  eggs, chopped
1–2 tablespoons fresh
  (or dried) dill weed

In a 2-quart bowl, mix together the buttermilk, beets (including liquid), chopped scallions, and diced cucumber. Chill thoroughly. A half hour before serving, place in freezer so that it becomes icy cold. Ladle into chilled soup bowls, and garnish with chopped egg and dill weed.

Size of Serving: 1 cup   *Number of Servings:* 8
Per Cup: Calories 85; Protein: 7 g; Total Fat: 2 g; Sodium: 195 mg
Excellent Source of: Calcium and Riboflavin

Borscht by the Bowlful

5 *tablespoons plain*	1 *thin slice onion,*
lowfat yogurt	*chopped*
1 *thin slice lemon, peeled*	¼ *cup cooked diced beets*
	¼ *cup crushed ice*

Combine 4 tablespoons yogurt, lemon, onion, and beets in blender; whirl for 20 seconds. Add ice; blend 10–15 seconds.
     Serve garnished with 1 tablespoon yogurt.

Yield: 1 cup
Per Cup: Calories: 60; Protein: 4 g; Total Fat: 2 g; Sodium: 60 mg
Excellent Source of: Calcium

Pumpkin Pumpkin Soup

Serve this delicate soup cold or hot.

1½ *tablespoons vegetable*	⅛ *teaspoon ground*
oil	*nutmeg (or to taste)*
1 *small onion, finely*	1½ *cups lowfat milk*
minced	⅛ *teaspoon garlic salt*
1 *tablespoon enriched*	*Freshly ground pepper*
all-purpose flour	*to taste*
2½ *cups defatted chicken*	1 *tablespoon potato*
stock	*starch (optional)*
1½ *cups puréed pumpkin*	¼ *cup cold water*
¼ *teaspoon ground*	*(optional)*
ginger (or to taste)	¼ *cup minced fresh*
	chives

Heat oil in a large heavy pan; add onion and sauté until tender. Gradually stir in the flour and cook 2–3 minutes over low heat, stirring constantly. Gradually stir in the chicken stock; stir over low heat with a wire whisk until mixture is smooth.
     Add pumpkin purée and spices; mix well. Gradually stir in the milk; season to taste with garlic salt and pepper. If a smoother soup is desired, cool slightly and purée in blender. Return to pot and thicken, if desired,
(continued)

by mixing the potato starch with cold water; mix in some of the hot soup, then add gradually to the soup, stirring constantly.

Cool to lukewarm, then chill in refrigerator before serving. (Or if soup is to be served hot, keep warm over low heat to prevent curdling.)

Mix well with whisk and serve garnished with fresh chives.

Size of Serving: 1 cup   *Number of Servings:* 6
Per Cup: Calories: 100; Protein: 5 g; Total Fat: 5 g; Sodium: 225 mg
Excellent Source of: Calcium, Vitamin A, and Riboflavin

Avgolemono (Greek Egg Lemon Soup)

4 cups defatted chicken
stock (see Index or use
canned)—this is best if
it contains tiny pieces
of chicken
⅓ cup uncooked brown
rice
½ teaspoon salt

¼ teaspoon pepper
2 large eggs, beaten (or
½ cup 'imitation'
cholesterol-free eggs)
3–4 tablespoons lemon
juice (or to taste)
1–2 tablespoons snipped
fresh dill weed

Combine stock and rice; cover and simmer 15–20 minutes; add salt, and pepper.

Beat eggs until light and frothy, then beat in 2 tablespoons lemon juice.

Spoon about ½ cup of the hot stock into the egg mixture, stirring constantly, then gradually add egg mixture to the stock in the pot, stirring continually. Heat 2–3 minutes, stirring all the time; avoid boiling because the soup will curdle.

Add remaining lemon juice to taste, if desired; adjust seasonings. Serve garnished with fresh dill.

Size of Serving: 1⅓ cups   *Number of Servings:* 4
Per Serving: Calories: 120; Protein: 8 g; Total Fat: 3 g; Sodium: 355 mg
Excellent Source of: Iron

Carrot Soup

2 tablespoons margarine
8 medium carrots, thinly
sliced
4 small tomatoes, peeled
and chopped
2 cups defatted chicken
stock
1 cup water

1 teaspoon nutritional
yeast
1 teaspoon sugar
Pinch salt
1 quart skim milk
2 teaspoons finely chopped
fresh parsley
4 teaspoons fresh alfalfa
sprouts

Melt margarine in a skillet and sauté the carrots over low heat until tender. Add tomatoes and sauté for 2 minutes.

In a 3-quart saucepan, heat the chicken stock with the water, yeast, sugar, and salt and add carrot mixture. Cover and simmer for 30 minutes. Stir in the milk and reheat (do not boil).

Serve garnished with parsley and sprouts.

Size of Serving: 1½ cups   *Number of Servings:* 6
Per Serving: Calories: 160; Protein: 8 g; Total Fat: 4 g; Sodium: 200 mg
Excellent Source of: Calcium, Iron, Vitamin A, Thiamin, Riboflavin, and Vitamin C

"Cream" of Broccoli Soup

1 *bunch fresh broccoli*
¼ *cup margarine*
1 *large onion, chopped*
1 *cup chopped celery*
1 *garlic clove, crushed*
½ *cup unsifted, enriched all-purpose flour*
4 *cups skim milk*
4 *cups defatted chicken stock (see Index)*
½ *teaspoon crushed thyme*
½ *teaspoon crushed marjoram*
¼ *teaspoon salt (or to taste)*
Pepper to taste
½ *cup finely chopped ripe tomato (optional)*
¼ *cup sliced toasted almonds (optional)*

Trim broccoli and cut into ½-inch-thick crosswise slices; cook in a small amount of boiling water until just barely tender; drain.

In a large saucepan, melt the margarine; add onions, celery, and garlic; sauté until onions are golden brown. Stir in flour; mix well and cook for 1–2 minutes. Gradually add milk, chicken stock, and herbs; stir over low heat until soup thickens slightly and bubbles. Keep soup at a simmer and add cooked broccoli, salt, and pepper; cook until heated through. Serve hot, sprinkled with chopped tomato and sliced almonds.

Size of Serving: 1½ cups   *Number of Servings:* 8
Per Serving: Calories: 180; Protein: 12 g; Total Fat: 6 g; Sodium: 270 mg
Excellent Source of: Calcium, Iron, Vitamin A, Thiamin, Riboflavin, and Vitamin C

The Heartier Ones

"Hayfoot, strawfoot, bellyful of bean soup," from a Civil War song, sums up the sustaining value of these rib-sticking soups. They were originally used by farmers, fishermen, pioneers, and other rugged individuals who had to depend on whatever they could forage for the soup pot. Served with some whole-grain bread, cheese, and fruit, these soups become a meal in themselves.

New England Clam Chowder

4 dozen softshell clams ("steamers") or 2 7½-ounce cans minced clams

2 tablespoons vegetable oil

1 large onion, finely chopped

4 medium potatoes, peeled and diced

2 cups skim milk

1 cup undiluted, skim evaporated milk

2–3 tablespoons margarine (optional)

¼ teaspoon salt (or to taste)

Freshly ground pepper to taste

Clean clams according to basic instructions outlined in recipe for steamed clams (see Index).

Place clams in a deep pot and cover with cold water. Bring to boil, reduce heat, and simmer, covered, just until the shells open. Remove from pot, cool; remove shells and chop clams into small pieces. Strain clam broth through a cheesecloth-lined strainer and save.

Heat oil in pot and sauté onion until translucent (do not brown). Add reserved clam broth and potatoes; simmer until potatoes are tender. Add chopped clams and milk (if a richer chowder is desired, add the margarine also); heat slowly over low heat (avoid boiling) for about 45 minutes. Season to taste with salt and pepper.

Size of Serving: 1½ cups   *Number of Servings:* 6
Per Serving: Calories: 270; Protein: 24 g; Total Fat: 7 g; Sodium: 220 mg
Excellent Source of: Protein, Calcium, Iron, Thiamin, Riboflavin, and Vitamin C

Soupe au Pistou

THE SOUP:

8 cups water
2 teaspoons kosher salt
1½ pounds zucchini and/
    or summer squash,
    sliced ½ inch thick
1 pound fresh green
    beans, cut in 1-inch
    pieces

2 cups cooked dried beans
    (see Index for
    directions) or canned
    cooked beans (if using
    canned beans, reduce
    the salt in the recipe to
    1¼ teaspoons) any
    type: fava, navy, pink,
    or black.
1 cup small elbow or shell
    macaroni
¼ cup Parmesan cheese

Bring water to a boil. Add salt, squash, green beans, and cooked dried beans; bring to boil, reduce heat, and simmer 10 minutes. Add macaroni; stir until it boils and cook for 12 minutes. Serve with Pistou and Parmesan cheese.

THE PISTOU:

1½ tablespoons minced
    fresh garlic
½ teaspoon kosher salt
½ cup finely chopped
    fresh basil leaves

2 tablespoons olive oil or
    other vegetable oil
4 ripe, peeled tomatoes,
    coarsely chopped

Crush garlic and salt together with the flat of a knife on a chopping board. Combine the garlic and salt in a bowl with the other ingredients. Serve cold or at room temperature; it is added to the hot soup at the table.

Size of Serving: about 2 cups   *Number of Servings:* 8
Per Serving: Calories: 150; Protein: 7 g; Total Fat: 4 g; Sodium: 700 mg
Excellent Source of: Iron, Vitamin A, Thiamin, Riboflavin, and Vitamin C

Hearty Portuguese Bean Soup

It's best to begin this soup the day before you plan to serve it so that it can be thoroughly defatted, thus lowering its contribution of saturated fats and cholesterol.

2 cups dried pinto beans
  (or use canned)
1 medium onion, chopped
1 pound fresh Portuguese
  sausage
1 large carrot, diced
1 turnip, peeled and diced
  (optional)

2 large potatoes, diced
1 small head cabbage,
  coarsely sliced
1 1-pound can tomatoes,
  crushed
¼ teaspoon pepper

If dried beans are used, cover them with boiling water and soak 1½ hours (or overnight in cold water). If canned beans are used, proceed directly as follows.

Add onions and meat and cook 1 hour; cool and refrigerate about 5–6 hours, or overnight, until there is a hard layer of fat on the top; skim off fat. Add carrot, turnip, potatoes, cabbage, tomatoes, and pepper; simmer 1½ hours.

Size of Serving: 2 cups   *Number of Servings:* 8
Per Serving: Calories: 390; Protein: 21 g; Total Fat: 16 g; Sodium: 90 mg
Excellent Source of: Protein, Iron, Vitamin A, Thiamin, Riboflavin, and Vitamin C

Fakisoupa (Greek Lentil Soup with Tomatoes)

1¼ cups dried lentils,
  thoroughly rinsed
1 medium onion,
  chopped
2 garlic cloves, crushed
2 teaspoons Italian
  seasoning
1 bay leaf

4–6 peppercorns
2 cups peeled tomatoes,
  fresh or canned
1 quart water
¼ cup olive oil or other
  vegetable oil
¼ teaspoon salt (or to
  taste)

Combine all ingredients except salt in a large soup pot. Bring to a boil, lower heat, and simmer for 1 hour. If desired, add salt to taste.
NOTE: 1 teaspoon basil, ¼ teaspoon oregano, ¼ teaspoon rosemary, ¼ teaspoon thyme, and ¼ teaspoon sage may be used in place of 2 teaspoons Italian seasoning.

Size of Serving: 2 cups   *Number of Servings:* 4
Per Serving: Calories: 355; Protein: 16 g; Total Fat: 14 g; Sodium: 160 mg
Excellent Source of: Protein, Iron, Thiamin, Riboflavin, and Vitamin C

Chinese Hot Sour Soup

4 large dried Chinese
mushrooms (available
in Oriental markets and
health food stores)

2 3 x 3 x 1-inch fresh tofu
(soybean curd), drained

½ cup fresh or drained,
canned bamboo shoots

1 quart defatted pork or
beef stock (see Index)

1 tablespoon soy sauce

1 teaspoon pepper (or to
taste)

¼ pound boneless pork
(tenderloin), cut into
narrow, 2-inch-long
strips

¼ cup white vinegar (or
to taste)

2 tablespoons cornstarch

3 tablespoons cold water

2 large egg whites,
lightly beaten

2 teaspoons sesame seed
oil

1 whole scallion, thinly
sliced

Cover mushrooms with 1 cup warm water and soak for 20–30 minutes, or until soft. Discard the water and slice mushrooms thinly, removing the stems. Shred the bamboo shoots and tofu as thinly as the mushrooms.

Combine the stock, soy sauce, pepper, mushrooms, bamboo shoots, and pork in a large pan; simmer 3–4 minutes. Add tofu and vinegar; bring to boil and then reduce to simmer.

Combine cornstarch with cold water and slowly pour it into the soup, stirring until soup thickens. Slowly pour in beaten egg; stir gently but constantly (soup will have a slightly curdled appearance).

Just before serving, remove from heat and stir in sesame seed oil. Serve sprinkled with scallions.

Size of Serving: 1½ cups   *Number of Servings:* 4
Per Serving: Calories: 140; Protein: 11 g; Total Fat: 6 g; Sodium: 410 mg
Excellent Source of: Iron

Mormon Split Pea Soup

2 cups dried green split
peas (1 pound)

8 cups water

1 cup chopped onion

½ cup chopped celery

½ teaspoon salt

½ teaspoon crushed dried
marjoram

¾ teaspoon pepper

1 pound ground lean pork

¾ teaspoon ground dried
sage

3 medium potatoes,
peeled and diced

Rinse peas and place in large Dutch oven or other heavy pot. Add water, onion, celery, ¼ teaspoon salt, marjoram, and ½ teaspoon pepper. Bring

(continued)

to a boil, then reduce heat and simmer, covered, about 1 hour, or until peas are tender.

Meanwhile, in a large mixing bowl, combine pork, ¼ teaspoon salt, ¼ teaspoon pepper, and sage; mix thoroughly and shape into meatballs using ½ tablespoon for each.

When peas are ready, drop in the meatballs and diced potatoes. Bring to a boil, then reduce heat and simmer, covered, about 15–20 minutes, or until meatballs and potatoes are done.

Size of Serving: 1½ cups   *Number of Servings:* 8
Per Serving: Calories: 375; Protein: 30 g; Total Fat: 9 g; Sodium: 205 mg
Excellent Source of: Protein, Iron, Thiamin, Riboflavin, and Niacin

VEGETABLES

Although vegetables are one of our greatest natural resources, they have spent generations sitting like wallflowers on side dishes. For years, vegetables have been the victims of bad press from a culture brought up on canned peas, string beans, and corn. Now, however, we can choose from an increasing variety of fresh and frozen vegetables found in modern supermarkets and in new farm-style stores specializing in locally grown produce. Be adventuresome and try a new vegetable each time you shop.

Vegetables offer us an abundance of unique flavors at low caloric values *providing* we avoid preparing them with high-calorie ingredients (such as butter, margarine, salt pork, sugar, and honey). Generally, it doesn't take much to enhance the natural flavors of vegetables. Try adding a little lemon or lime juice, vinegar, garlic, onion, tomato juice, meat or chicken broth, herbs, and spices (see the Herb and Spice Chart).

Vegetables also provide us with a good supply of fiber, vitamins (particularly vitamins A, C, and the B vitamins), and minerals (such as iron, potassium, and calcium). Generally, fresh, raw vegetables offer a better supply of nutrients than do cooked vegetables, because cooking often destroys the more vulnerable vitamins (vitamin C and the B vitamins). However, cooked vegetables have their place too. Some vegetables (carrots and spinach) actually have more nutrients (especially vitamin A) available after they have been cooked and slightly softened.

Although easy to prepare, vegetables need to be handled and cooked with care to prevent loss of valuable vitamins. This means protecting them from the damaging effects of heat, water, light, air, and alkalines (such as baking soda, which is sometimes added to preserve their green color and is very destructive to vitamin C). Here are some simple guidelines:

· *Keep vegetables as fresh as possible.* Store delicate vegetables in tightly closed containers in the refrigerator, and stronger root vegetables in a cool dry place. Avoid storing vegetables at room temperature or in uncovered containers.
· *Avoid peeling vegetables* unless they have a particularly tough or bitter skin. A large proportion of vitamins are stored just beneath the skin, so it's best to cook vegetables in their skin.
· *Wash vegetables quickly under a gentle stream of cool tap water;* drain in a colander or gently shake off excess water. Vegetables such as carrots or potatoes may be scrubbed lightly with a brush to remove difficult dirt spots.
· *Avoid cutting vegetables before washing them and do not soak them in water after cutting.*
· *Avoid cutting vegetables whenever possible.*

   Cook vegetables whole (green beans are particularly attractive this way), or cut them into large pieces to minimize the cut surface area exposed to harmful elements.

   Tear leafy greens rather than cutting them.

   Avoid dicing, shredding, or puréeing vegetables; if this is necessary, do it quickly and close to serving time.

· *Cook vegetables in as little liquid as possible—or none at all*—to prevent loss of water-soluble vitamins. For this reason, steaming is the preferred method of cooking vegetables because they are not required to stand in water. (Be sure to save any cooking liquid to use as vegetable stock.)
· *Keep vegetables tightly covered during cooking* to prevent steam from escaping; this will reduce the cooking time and nutrient losses.
· *Cook vegetables as quickly as possible.* Gradually shorten the cooking time and experience the pleasures of vegetables with far more flavor and texture than those that many of us left on our plates as children.

VEGETABLE COOKING METHODS

Steaming: For centuries the Chinese have known the benefits of cooking vegetables in bamboo steamers. This is such a simple, pleasurable way to cook vegetables that most people get hooked on it permanently once they have used a steamer. Steaming helps to retain the maximum amount of flavor, color, and, most importantly, nutrients.

Stackable bamboo steamers can be placed in 1–2 inches of boiling water (just enough to come up to the bottom of the steamer) in a wok, large skillet, or any other large pan. Place a single layer of vegetables in as many of the compartments as needed, cover tightly, and cook until tender. These steamers are a wonderful way to cook several different types of food at the same time.

Aluminum or stainless steel colanders or steaming baskets can also be used to steam vegetables—just be sure that the pot used to hold them has a tightly fitting cover. Some of these steaming baskets have the added advantage of adjusting to fit any size pot.

Because of their exceptionally high water content, some vegetables, such as spinach and other leafy greens, can be steamed perfectly well in a regular saucepan with just the moisture that clings to their leaves after they've been washed.

Boiling: If it is necessary to boil vegetables (steaming is preferred), add liquid sparingly to preserve the water-soluble vitamins. Use only enough liquid to prevent them from sticking to the pan. Most vegetables need only about ¼ to ½ cup of liquid for cooking; watery vegetables, such as zucchini and summer squash, require even less. Be sure to cook them tightly covered and *quickly.*

Pressure Cooking: Vegetables are generally cooked at 15 pounds pressure, but it's always best to check the manufacturer's directions; a slight deviation in pressure, time, or added liquid can make a great difference with pressure-cooked vegetables. And be sure to run cold water over the pan before opening it to reduce the pressure quickly and to prevent the vegetables from cooking further.

Braising: Braising vegetables is essentially steaming them in a very small amount of oil with a sprinkling of liquid. Heat the oil (about 1 tablespoon); add the vegetables and sauté lightly; add a small amount of liquid (2–3 tablespoons, or less if they have just been rinsed and are fairly moist or have a high natural water content—such as leafy greens, tomatoes, zucchini, or summer squash); cover tightly and cook over low heat until tender. *Note:* Vegetables cooked this way are higher in calories because of the added oil.

Baking: Many vegetables, such as potatoes, squash, eggplant, tomatoes, and pumpkin, can be baked in their own skin. Others, such as mushrooms, zucchini, summer squash, carrots, and parsnips, can be baked in a baking dish with a small amount of liquid to prevent sticking. Bake vegetables at 350°F. until tender when pierced with a fork.

Stir-Frying: This is another ancient Chinese method for cooking vegetables, as well as many other foods, singly or in combination. Stir-frying is basically sautéeing vegetables in a small amount of oil, quickly, over high heat. Vegetables are particularly tasty when stir-fried with sesame seeds or nuts, such as peanuts and cashews (these are also high in calories, so avoid them if you're watching your weight). Stir-frying is a good place to let your creativity take off because it's almost impossible to make a mistake—as long as you keep stirring and avoid overcooking.

Here's how: Heat a small amount of oil (about 1–2 tablespoons) in a wok or large skillet (for more flavor, add sliced garlic or ginger root, cook for a minute or two, and discard); add the sliced vegetables with your favorite herbs, spices, nuts, or seeds, plus a small amount of water or broth if the vegetables have a low water content (such as broccoli or cauliflower); cook quickly over high heat, stirring constantly, until the vegetables are slightly soft but still crunchy.

FRESH VEGETABLE CHART

Vegetable & (Peak Season)	Amount to Buy (4 Servings)	Buying, Storing, Preparing, and Serving Information	Cooking Timetable*
ARTICHOKE, GLOBE OR FRENCH (All year— peaks in March, April, May)	1 per serving	*Buy* plump, compact, green, heavy artichokes with tightly closed globes; avoid brown tips and discolored leaves. *Store* in plastic bag in refrigerator. *Prepare* by rinsing well and by slicing off the stem and the very top; snip off tips from outer leaves with scissors; from the top, reach inside with a spoon and remove the "choke," or fuzzy center, and discard. Stand upright in pot to cook. *Serve* hot or cold. Good with lemon sauce, vinaigrette dressing, or stuffed with fish, meat, or chicken.	*Steamed:* 35–45 minutes *Boiled* (in 1–2 inches water): 30–45 minutes *Pressure Cooker:*** 10–12 minutes
ARTICHOKE, JERUSALEM (Nov.– Jan.)	1 per serving	*Buy* firm tubers without wrinkles and free from blemishes. *Store* in a cool place, preferably outdoors. *Prepare* by scrubbing, scraping, and either leaving whole or slicing. *Serve* cooked with a lemon sauce or raw (peeled and sliced) in salads.	*Boiled* (in small amount water): Sliced—6–8 minutes Whole—12–15 minutes *Baked* (in jackets): 45 minutes

* These are approximate cooking times and will vary with the age of the vegetables, the temperature at which they were stored, how large and tough they are, the size of the cut pieces, and the thickness of the pan they are cooked in. Cook all vegetables until tender but still crisp, except for those that must be cooked soft enough to mash or purée. Cook all vegetables as quickly as possible to minimize vitamin losses due to heat and water exposure.
** 15 pounds pressure for vegetables.

FRESH VEGETABLE CHART *(continued)*

Vegetable & (Peak Season)	Amount to Buy (4 Servings)	Buying, Storing, Preparing, and Serving Information	Cooking Timetable*
ASPARAGUS (Mar.– June)	2 pounds (Approx. 5 stalks or 1 cup per serving, cooked)	*Buy* smooth stalks with tightly closed tips and green covering most of the stalk. *Store* 1–2 days in a tightly closed plastic bag or vegetable crisper in refrigerator. *Prepare* by washing thoroughly and bending the stalks until they snap easily. Tie the upper ends of the stalks together loosely and cook standing upright. *Serve* plain or with a lemon sauce; also delicious marinated and served cold.	*Steamed:* 12–15 minutes *Boiled* (in 1–2 inches water in bottom half of double boiler or coffee pot: 10–12 minutes *Pressure Cooker:* ½–1 minute *Braised:* 4–5 minutes *Stir-Fried:* 5–6 minutes
AVOCADO (May– June)	2 as a main course or ½ as part of a salad	*Buy* firm, unblemished pears for use in 2–3 days. For use within a day, buy ripe pears that are slightly soft when pressed. *Store* at room temperature to ripen; in refrigerator to retard further ripening. *Prepare* by cutting avocado in half vertically and removing pit and skin. Sprinkle with lemon or lime juice to prevent flesh from discoloring when in contact with the air. *Serve* whole halves stuffed, sliced for salads or garnishes, or mashed for dips.	Usually served raw.
BEANS, GREEN OR YELLOW (All year— peaks in June to Aug.)	1 pound (Approx. 1 cup per serving, cooked)	*Buy* small, firm, unblemished beans that snap crisply when bent. *Store* in a plastic bag or vegetable crisper in refrigerator. *Prepare* by rinsing well and by removing ends and strings from the side seams of the beans. Leave whole or cut in 1–2-inch lengths or French-style. Cook or blanch. *Serve* hot or cold with nuts, herbs, or vinaigrette dressing.	*Steamed:* 10–12 minutes *Boiled* (in 1 inch water): 8–10 minutes *Pressure Cooker:* 1½–3 minutes *Braised:* 5–6 minutes *Stir-Fried:* 6–8 minutes

(continued)

FRESH VEGETABLE CHART (continued)

Vegetable & (Peak Season)	Amount to Buy (4 Servings)	Buying, Storing, Preparing, and Serving Information	Cooking Timetable*
BEANS, LIMA (Peak July– Aug.)	2 pounds, fresh, unshelled (Approx. ½ cup per serving, shelled & cooked)	*Buy* crisp, full, unblemished pods. *Store* 1–2 days in a vegetable crisper or tightly closed plastic bag in refrigerator. *Prepare* by removing outer shell and cooking. *Serve* with a complementary herb, such as dill. Use hot as a side dish or cold in salads.	*Steamed:* 25–30 minutes *Boiled* (in 1 inch water): 20–25 minutes *Pressure Cooker:* 1–2 minutes *Braised* (blanched first): 8–10 minutes
BEETS (All year— peaks in June, July)	1 pound (Approx. ½ cup per serving, cooked)	*Buy* young, small, firm, round, unblemished beets with crisp, reddish-green leaves. *Store* up to 2 weeks (beets, not the greens) in a vegetable crisper or tightly closed plastic bag in refrigerator. (See directions for Greens.) *Prepare* by cutting off the tops about 1½ inches above the crown of the beets. Scrub well but avoid puncturing the skin so that beet juice will not escape during cooking. After cooking, cool and slip skins off using your fingers. *Serve* whole, sliced, diced, or shredded; hot or cold. Good plain, pickled in vinegar, or served with an orange or lemon sauce.	*Steamed:* 45–55 minutes *Boiled* (in 2 inches water): 35–45 minutes *Pressure Cooker:* 5–10 minutes *Baked* (425°F.): 1 hour
BROCCOLI (All year— peaks in Oct.– Apr.)	1 pound (Approx. 1 cup per serving, cooked)	*Buy* firm green stalks with compact, deep-green bud clusters. Avoid yellow flowering clusters (this is a sign of aging and woody texture). *Store* for 1–2 days in vegetable crisper or tightly closed plastic bag.	*Steamed:* 10–12 minutes *Boiled* (in small amount water): 8–10 minutes *Pressure Cooker:* 1½–3 minutes

FRESH VEGETABLE CHART *(continued)*

Vegetable & (Peak Season)	Amount to Buy (4 Servings)	Buying, Storing, Preparing, and Serving Information	Cooking Timetable*
BROCCOLI *(continued)*		*Prepare* by separating stalks, rinsing well, and trimming any woody ends and removing large leaves. Cut stalks in half lengthwise and cook whole or sliced in ½–1-inch pieces, or use raw. *Serve* plain or with sesame seeds or a sauce, such as lemon, fresh orange, or cheese. Also, delicious raw in salads or as an appetizer or snack with yogurt dip.	*Stir-Fried:* 5–6 minutes *Baked (350°F.):* 20 minutes
BRUSSELS SPROUTS (All year— peaks in Sept.– Jan.)	1 pound (Approx. ¾ cup per serving, cooked)	*Buy* small, firm, crisp heads with tight, dark-green leaves. Avoid yellowing, loose leaves. *Store* 1–2 days in a vegetable crisper or tightly closed plastic bag in refrigerator. *Prepare* by rinsing well, trimming the ends, and cooking. *Serve* plain or in a cheese, yogurt, or lemon sauce.	*Steamed:* 15–20 minutes *Boiled* (in ½–1 inch water): 10–12 minutes *Pressure Cooker:* 1–2 minutes *Braised:* 15–20 minutes
CABBAGE *Green Savoy Red Chinese or Bok Choy* (All year— peaks in Mar.–June)	1 pound (Approx. 1 cup raw or ½ cup cooked per serving)	*Buy* firm, hard heads that are heavy for their size and have dark green or red leaves. Avoid yellowing leaves. *Store* in a vegetable crisper or tightly closed plastic bag in refrigerator. *Prepare* by rinsing well and cutting into wedges. Remove the tough white core. Either cut into serving size wedges or shred. Cook or use raw. *Serve* plain, with vinegar; cooked with seeds, such as caraway, dill, mustard or celery; stuffed with rice and/or meat; or shredded raw for coleslaw and other salads.	*Steamed:* Wedges— 12–15 minutes Shredded— 8–10 minutes *Boiled* (in ½–1 inch water): Wedges— 8–10 minutes Shredded— 5–6 minutes *Pressure Cooker:* Wedges— 2–3 minutes Shredded— ½–1½ minutes *Braised:* 8–10 minutes

(continued)

FRESH VEGETABLE CHART *(continued)*

Vegetable & (Peak Season)	Amount to Buy (4 Servings)	Buying, Storing, Preparing, and Serving Information	Cooking Timetable*
CABBAGE *(continued)*			*Stir-Fried:* 2–3 minutes *Baked* (350°F.): Stuffed— 30–40 minutes
CARROTS (All year)	1 pound (Approx. ¾ cup raw, ⅜ cup shredded, or ½ cup diced, cooked per serving)	*Buy* thin, small, firm carrots. Avoid large, thick carrots with stringy offshoots (this usually indicates that they are woody and tough). *Store* for up to 2 weeks in a cool, dry dark area or in a tightly closed plastic bag or vegetable crisper in the refrigerator. *Prepare* by scrubbing carrots well (there is no need to peel them, thus losing valuable vitamins). Trim the ends and slice them crosswise into ¼-inch pieces, lengthwise into 2–3-inch x ¼-inch julienne sticks, or leave them whole. Cook or use raw. *Serve* plain; with spices, such as nutmeg or ginger; with sauces, such as orange, lemon or cheese; puréed; shredded raw for salads, coleslaw, or sandwiches; or cut into raw sticks for snacking.	*Steamed:* 8–10 minutes *Boiled* (in ½–1 inch water): 10–12 minutes *Pressure Cooker:* Whole— 3–5 minutes Sliced—1½–3 minutes *Braised:* 30–40 minutes *Baked* (400°F.): Whole— 35–45 minutes Sliced— 15–20 minutes
CAULIFLOWER (All year— peaks in Sept.– Nov.)	1 medium head, about 2 pounds (Approx. ¾ cup per serving, raw or cooked)	*Buy* firm, white, clean florets with green leaves. Avoid older ones with yellow leaves. *Store* up to 5 days in a vegetable crisper or tightly closed plastic bag in refrigerator. *Prepare* by removing outer leaves, any smaller leaves in the interior of the head and the core. Separate the florets	*Steamed:* Whole— 20–25 minutes Florets— 10–12 minutes *Boiled* (in 1 inch water): Whole— 15 minutes Florets— 8 minutes

FRESH VEGETABLE CHART *(continued)*

Vegetable & (Peak Season)	Amount to Buy (4 Servings)	Buying, Storing, Preparing, and Serving Information	Cooking Timetable*
CAULIFLOWER *(continued)*		(or leave head whole) and remove any tough ends from the stems. Wash well under cold running water; drain well. Cook or use raw.	*Pressure Cooker:* Whole— 10 minutes Florets— 1½–3 minutes
		Serve whole, stuffed; plain cooked florets; puréed; with sauces, such as cheese sauce; marinated; or raw with dips.	*Braised:* 15 minutes
			Stir-Fried: 8–10 minutes
			Baked (350°F.): (Pre-cooked) 20 minutes
CELERIAC (Celery Root) (Oct.– Apr.)	1½ pounds (About ½ root per serving)	*Buy* firm, unblemished roots. *Store* in a cool, dry place. *Prepare* by washing well and removing the upper stalks. Since it has a slightly bitter flavor, most people prefer to either soak it 1 hour in water to cover with 2 tablespoons of lemon juice added or to blanch it for 5 minutes in boiling water with 2 tablespoons lemon juice added. Cook or use raw. If cooked, remove from pan or steamer when fork-tender and peel before serving.	*Steamed:* Whole— 50–60 minutes Sliced— 10–12 minutes *Boiled* (in 1½ inches water): Whole— 40–50 minutes Sliced— 5–8 minutes *Braised:* 35–40 minutes *Stir-Fried:* 10–15 minutes
		Serve whole, sliced, diced, julienned, or puréed; hot or cold; marinated raw; in soups; salads; stuffed with other vegetables and baked; or cooked with stock and herbs and served as a side dish.	*Baked* (375°F.) (Blanched, sliced and stuffed): 20–30 minutes

(continued)

FRESH VEGETABLE CHART *(continued)*

Vegetable & (Peak Season)	Amount to Buy (4 Servings)	Buying, Storing, Preparing, and Serving Information	Cooking Timetable*
CELERY (All year)	1 medium bunch	*Buy* firm, green, unblemished stalks with fresh-looking green leaves. *Store* in vegetable crisper or tightly closed plastic bag in refrigerator *or* in ice water in the refrigerator. *Prepare* by washing well and trimming the ends. If using raw, crisp the celery by placing it in cold water. To cook celery, dice, slice, or julienne it first. Use stalks and leaves in soups and stews. *Serve* raw, plain or stuffed with cheese or other spreads; cooked in main dishes, soups, stews, casseroles, and salads; or cooked as a side dish.	*Steamed:* Diced— 25–30 minutes *Boiled* (in ½ inch water): Diced— 15–18 minutes *Pressure Cooker:* 2–3 minutes *Braised:* 30–40 minutes *Baked* (300°F.): ¾–1 hour
CORN ON THE COB (May– Aug.)	4 ears	*Buy* fresh, green husks with silk that is not dry. Look under the husk for kernels that are small and pale yellow. *Store* 1–2 days in husks, uncovered, in the refrigerator. *Prepare* by removing the husks and silk; trim the ends and cook. *Serve* hot on the cob with margarine or strip kernels from the cob and use in chowder, pudding, casseroles, or plain as a side dish.	*Steamed:* 10–15 minutes *Boiled* (drop into large pot of boiling water): 4–6 minutes *Pressure Cooker:* ½–1½ minutes *Baked** (350°F.): 15–20 minutes *Roasted** (over coals): 20–25 minutes

* To bake or roast corn on the cob, sprinkle stripped ears with dots of margarine, salt and pepper, if desired, and wrap in a piece of foil, large romaine lettuce leaf, or return to the husks (without the silk) and cook.

FRESH VEGETABLE CHART *(continued)*

Vegetable & (Peak Season)	*Amount to Buy (4 Servings)*	*Buying, Storing, Preparing, and Serving Information*	*Cooking Timetable**
CUCUMBER (All year— peaks May to July)	2 cucumbers	*Buy* dark green, firm and well-shaped cucumbers. Avoid cucumbers that are very large in diameter because they usually contain lots of seeds. *Store* 3–5 days in the refrigerator. *Prepare* cucumbers to be eaten raw by either peeling them *or* washing them well, trimming the ends, and scoring the peel lengthwise with the tines of a fork. To cook cucumbers, peel them and remove any seeds that are very soft; slice or dice them or halve them lengthwise, remove the seeds, and stuff before baking. *Serve* raw, in slices or sticks, plain or in vinegar, yogurt, or vinaigrette dressing; cooked, plain or with complementary herbs or stuffed with other vegetables, bread crumbs, or cheese.	*Steamed:* 10–12 minutes *Boiled* (in small amount of water): 8–10 minutes *Stir-Fried:* 5–6 minutes *Baked:* (375°F.) 20–25 minutes
EGGPLANT (All year— peaks in Aug.– Sept.)	1 pound (Approx. ½ cup per serving, cooked)	*Buy* firm, smooth, dark-purple eggplant. Avoid those that are poorly colored or soft. *Store* at 60°F.—do not refrigerate as temperatures below 50°F. may cause injury. If stored at room temperature, use within 1 week. *Prepare* for stewing or marinating by peeling and dicing (¾–inch). Prepare for baking and frying by rinsing well and leaving the skin on, if desired. (Most cookbooks advise peeling eggplant, but the skin is quite good when baked or fried and provides another source of fiber.)	*Steamed:* 15–20 minutes *Boiled:* (in 1–2 inches water) 10–20 minutes *Baked:* (Halved and stuffed; baked at 375°F.) 20–25 minutes (Sliced, breaded, and fried first; baked at 350°F.): 20–30 minutes

(continued)

FRESH VEGETABLE CHART *(continued)*

Vegetable & (Peak Season)	Amount to Buy (4 Servings)	Buying, Storing, Preparing, and Serving Information	Cooking Timetable*
EGGPLANT *(continued)*		*Serve* stewed with other vegetables; marinated, cold; baked with cheese and tomato sauce; breaded and fried; or stuffed, whole or halved, with other vegetables and/or ground meat, rice, and herbs.	
ENDIVE, BELGIUM (Also known as French Endive or Witloof Chicory) (Oct.– May)	1 medium head per serving	*Buy* pale, compact, firm heads. *Store* in a plastic bag in the refrigerator. *Prepare* by washing the heads very well under cold running water, separating the leaves and washing in between. Slice into circles, julienne, or cut lengthwise in half. Cook or use raw. *Serve* braised, baked (stuffed or unstuffed), raw in salads (julienned), or halved and stuffed with cold meat, poultry, or fish salad.	*Braised:* 5–8 minutes *Baked* (350°F.): 30 minutes
GREENS *Beet Collard Dandelion Kale Mustard Spinach Swiss Chard Turnip* (All year)	2 pounds (Approx. ¾–1 cup per serving, cooked)	*Buy* crisp, unblemished, bright-green leaves. *Store* 1–2 days in a vegetable crisper or tightly closed plastic bag in refrigerator. *Prepare* by discarding any coarse-looking ribs or stems. Wash greens thoroughly under running tepid water. Cook or use raw. *Serve* plain or seasoned with salt, pepper, margarine, lemon juice, or plain vinegar; also added to mixed dishes, soups, or raw in salads and sandwiches.	*Steamed:* 5–12 minutes *Boiled* (in *small* amount water —about ¼ inch): 3–10 minutes *Pressure Cooker:* 1½–3 minutes *Baked* (350°F.): (Soufflés; casseroles) 25–30 minutes

FRESH VEGETABLE CHART *(continued)*

Vegetable & (Peak Season)	Amount to Buy (4 Servings)	Buying, Storing, Preparing, and Serving Information	Cooking Timetable*
KOHLRABI (June & July)	1 medium bunch	**Buy** firm, unblemished bulbs with fresh green leaves. **Store** in a cool (60°F.) dry place. **Prepare** by trimming the roots and discarding the tops. Wash well. Cut into ¼–½-inch slices, cubes, or julienne. Cook or use raw. **Serve** plain (cut up, riced, or mashed) with seasonings; stir-fried with other vegetables; in casseroles, soups, or stews; stuffed and baked; or raw (thinly sliced or julienned) in salads with a vinaigrette dressing.	*Steamed:* Sliced—15–20 minutes *Boiled* (in small amount water): Diced—10–15 minutes *Stir-Fried:* 10–15 minutes *Baked* (350°F.): 30–40 minutes
LETTUCE (All year) (See page 172 for types.)	1 medium head or 2 small heads	**Buy** fresh, compact heads with bright-green leaves. (Iceberg and romaine lettuce leaves should be crisp; others, such as Bibb, will be softer.) **Store** 1–2 days in a vegetable crisper or tightly closed plastic bag in refrigerator. **Prepare** by washing leaves thoroughly under cold running water. Drain well in colander. Pat dry and crisp in refrigerator (as above) for at least 1 hour before serving. Tear into bite-sized pieces. **Serve** raw in salads and sandwiches or braised.	*Braised:* 4–5 minutes
LEEKS (Oct.–May)	1 bunch	**Buy** firm, unblemished, white bulbs with bright green, firm leaves. **Store** in tightly closed plastic bag in refrigerator.	*Boiled* (in 1½ inches water; sliced): 15 minutes *Braised:* 20–25 minutes *(continued)*

FRESH VEGETABLE CHART *(continued)*

Vegetable & (Peak Season)	Amount to Buy (4 Servings)	Buying, Storing, Preparing, and Serving Information	Cooking Timetable*
LEEKS *(continued)*		*Prepare* by trimming away most of the green leaves and the roots. (Save the greens to make stock.) Peel away the tough outer layer on the bulbs and rinse. Leave whole or slice in ½–1-inch pieces before cooking. *Serve* plain with margarine and seasonings; stuffed with meat, fish, poultry, or vegetable salad (cold or hot); or in soups and stews.	*Baked* (350°F.) (Sautéed first): 30–35 minutes
MUSHROOMS (All year— peaks Nov.– April)	1 pound	*Buy* firm, unblemished caps that are creamy white or light brown. The gills (under the cap, should be light tan or pinkish. *Store* in a tightly closed plastic bag in refrigerator. *Prepare* by wiping them well with a damp cloth or, if very dirty, rinse under cold running water and pat dry. Slice, dice or use whole. Cook or use raw. *Serve* raw in salads with a lemon dressing; stir-fried alone or with other vegetables and/or meats; in soups, stews, casseroles or sauces; or stuffed with bread crumbs, wheat germ, nuts, seeds, and/or cheese and baked or broiled.	*Stir-Fried:* 5–7 minutes *Broiled* (4–5 inches from heat source): 5–7 minutes *Baked* (stuffed caps at 350°F.): 15–20 minutes
OKRA (June– Nov.)	1 pound	*Buy* crisp, unblemished, bright green, small pods (less than 4½ inches). *Store* in plastic bag or vegetable crisper in refrigerator. *Prepare* by washing well and breaking stems away from pods. Leave whole or slice to cook.	*Steamed:* 20 minutes *Blanched* (in water to cover): 5 minutes *Boiled* (in 1½ inches water): 10 minutes

FRESH VEGETABLE CHART *(continued)*

Vegetable & (Peak Season)	Amount to Buy (4 Servings)	Buying, Storing, Preparing, and Serving Information	Cooking Timetable*
OKRA (continued)		Serve plain with seasonings or in soups, stews and other mixed dishes.	Pressure Cooker: (Sliced) 3–4 minutes
ONIONS Bermuda Red Spanish White Yellow (All year)	1 pound (Approx. ½ cup per serving, chopped & cooked)	Buy firm, unblemished onions with dry skins and short necks. Store in open mesh containers at room (or slightly cooler) temperature. Prepare by removing both ends and outer skin. If preparing small white onions, cut an X in the root end to prevent them from bursting while cooking. Use raw or cooked as suggested below. Serve: Small white onions: plain boiled with margarine and seasonings; creamed (in nonfat milk); braised; or in stews. Large yellow or white onions: chopped or sliced and stir-fried with other vegetables and/or meats or stuffed (whole or halves) and baked. Red: raw in salads (soaked in vinegar first if a milder flavor is desired). Spanish or Bermuda: raw, sliced in sandwiches; chopped or sliced in salads.	Steamed: 25–35 minutes Boiled (in 1½ inches water): 15–30 minutes Pressure Cooker: Small—3–4 minutes Large—5–8 minutes Stir-Fried: Sliced—5–6 minutes Baked (Large, whole & stuffed; baked at 350°F.): 40–50 minutes
PARSNIPS (Jan.– March)	1 pound (Approx. ½ cup per serving, cooked)	Buy small, firm, unblemished parsnips. Store in a tightly closed plastic bag in refrigerator. Prepare by trimming both ends and scrubbing parsnips well. Cook whole, halved, quartered, sliced, or julienned; raw, grated.	Steamed: Whole— 30–45 minutes Sliced— 30–40 minutes Boiled (in 1 inch water): Whole— 20–30 minutes Sliced—8–15 minutes

(continued)

FRESH VEGETABLE CHART *(continued)*

Vegetable & (Peak Season)	Amount to Buy (4 Servings)	Buying, Storing, Preparing, and Serving Information	Cooking Timetable*
PARSNIPS *(continued)*		*Serve* plain, boiled, or steamed, in any shape, including mashed, with seasonings; baked in casseroles; added to soups and stews; or raw, finely diced or grated in salads.	*Pressure Cooker:* Whole—9–10 minutes Quartered— 4–8 minutes *Baked* (whole at 350°F.): 30–45 minutes
PEAS March– June)	2 pounds (Approx. ½ cup per serving, shelled & cooked)	*Buy* peas with small, full, green pods. *Store* 1–2 days in plastic bag in refrigerator. *Prepare* by shelling and cooking. *Serve* plain with seasonings; braised or stir-fried with other vegetables, meats, fish, or poultry; added to soups, stews, or other mixed dishes.	*Steamed:* 10–20 minutes *Boiled* (in 1 inch water): 10–15 minutes *Pressure Cooker:* ½ minute *Braised:* 10–15 minutes *Stir-Fried* (blanched 5 minutes first): 1–2 minutes
PEPPERS Sweet Red or Green Bell (All year)	1 stuffed per serving	*Buy* peppers with firm green or red pods. (Red coloring in this type of pepper indicates a mature, sweet pepper.) *Store* 3–5 days in plastic bag or vegetable crisper in refrigerator. *Prepare* by washing and removing the stem and seeds. Leave whole for stuffing or slice, dice, mince, or julienne, depending on use. *Serve* raw or sautéed in mixed dishes; raw in salads, sandwiches, or as appetizer/ snacks; and baked, stuffed.	*Steamed (Whole):* 10–15 minutes *Parboiled* (in boiling water to cover): 5 minutes *Stir-Fried:* 5–6 minutes *Baked* (Parboiled and stuffed first; then baked at 375°F.): 30–40 minutes

FRESH VEGETABLE CHART *(continued)*

Vegetable & (Peak Season)	*Amount to Buy (4 Servings)*	*Buying, Storing, Preparing, and Serving Information*	*Cooking Timetable**
POTATOES Idaho (All year) Round Red or "New" (Spring & summer) Russet (Early summer) Long White (Spring & summer)	1 pound (Approx. ½ cup per serving, cooked)	*Buy* unblemished, firm, well-shaped potatoes. *Store* in a dark, dry, well-ventilated place. Temperature should be 45–50°F. *Prepare* by scrubbing well (preferably with a stiff vegetable brush) and cook with skins on to preserve vitamins susceptible to heat and water. *Serve* plain (whole or mashed; boiled or baked) with margarine and seasonings; scalloped; creamed; added to soups, stews, chowders, and other mixed dishes; or diced cold for salads.	*Steamed:* Whole— 30–45 minutes *Boiled* (in 1 inch water): Whole— 15–20 minutes *Pressure Cooker:* Whole— 8–11 minutes *Baked* (medium, whole at 400°F.): 45–60 minutes
PUMPKIN (Oct.–Dec.)	2 pounds (Approx. ½ cup per serving, cooked)	*Buy* firm, unblemished, deep orange pumpkins. *Store* 1 week at room temperature or, if longer storage is desired, keep at 60°F. *Prepare* by washing and cutting in half with a strong, heavy knife. Remove seeds and strings from center (save the seeds to toast); cut into 1–2-inch pieces. Drain well after cooking. *Serve* plain mashed with seasonings; cut up in stews or casseroles; or puréed in soups, pies, puddings, breads, rolls, and cookies.	*Steamed:* Diced—25–30 minutes *Boiled* (in 1 inch water): Diced—15–20 minutes *Pressure Cooker:* 6–12 minutes *Baked* (350°F.): 40–60 minutes
RADISH (All year—peaks in May–July)	1 bunch	*Buy* smooth, firm, unblemished radishes. *Store* 1–2 weeks in a tightly closed plastic bag or vegetable crisper in the refrigerator.	*Steamed:* 10–15 minutes *Boiled* (in small amount water): 6–10 minutes

(continued)

FRESH VEGETABLE CHART (continued)

Vegetable & (Peak Season)	Amount to Buy (4 Servings)	Buying, Storing, Preparing, and Serving Information	Cooking Timetable*
RADISH (continued)		*Prepare* by washing them well and removing the ends. Use raw (preferably) or cooked. *Serve* raw (whole, sliced, diced, or minced) in salads or alone as snacks; cooked with other vegetables to add an accent flavor.	
RUTABAGA (Oct.– Feb.)	2 pounds	*Buy* firm, hard, unblemished roots. *Store* at 60°F. Do not refrigerate because temperatures less than 50°F. may cause damage. If stored at room temperature, use within 1 week. *Prepare* by peeling (taking care to remove only the skin) and cut into cubes, strips, or slices to cook. *Serve* plain (cut up or mashed) with seasonings; added to casseroles, soufflés, stews, other vegetables (such as mashed with potatoes), and other mixed dishes.	*Steamed:* Diced—25–30 minutes *Boiled* (in 1½ inches water): Diced—15–20 minutes *Pressure Cooker:* 5–8 minutes
SALSIFY (Also called Oyster Plant) (Oct.– Nov.)	8–12 roots	*Buy* unblemished, firm roots. *Store* briefly in plastic bag in refrigerator—best to cook immediately. *Prepare* by scrubbing well, removing ends, peeling, slicing and cooking (with a few drops of lemon juice or vinegar added to the water to prevent discoloration); drain well after cooking. *Serve* plain with seasonings; in stews, soups or casseroles; or with sauces, such as cheese sauce.	*Boiled* (in 1½ inches water): 12–15 minutes

FRESH VEGETABLE CHART *(continued)*

Vegetable & (Peak Season)	Amount to Buy (4 Servings)	Buying, Storing, Preparing, and Serving Information	Cooking Timetable*
SCALLIONS (Green Onions) (All year— peaks in May–Aug.)	1 bunch	*Buy* crisp green tops and firm white bulbs. *Store* 1–2 days in tightly closed plastic bag or vegetable crisper in refrigerator. *Prepare* by washing well and removing root ends and any loose outer layers. Cut into 2–3-inch lengths to cook. *Serve* raw, cup up, in salads; raw, whole, as an appetizer/ snack; sliced or minced for stir-fried dishes, casseroles, quiches, stuffings, and as a garnish on soups and other foods.	*Stir-Fried:* 2–3 minutes
SQUASH, SUMMER Crookneck (yellow) Pattypan (white) Chayote (light green) Striped Cocozelle (green & white) Zucchini (dark green)	2½ pounds (Approx. 1 cup per serving, cooked)	*Buy* firm, smooth, unblemished squash. *Store* in plastic bag in refrigerator 2–3 days. *Prepare* by washing well removing a thin slice from each end and cutting into cubes, slices, or julienne to cook, or thin shreds if to be eaten raw. *Serve* plain with seasonings; stir-fried with other vegetables and meats; added to casseroles, stews, soups, breads; or cut lengthwise, stuffed (with other vegetables, ground meats, grains, cheese, or bread crumbs) and baked.	*Steamed:* Sliced—15–20 minutes *Boiled* (in 1 inch water): Sliced—8–15 minutes *Pressure Cooker:* Sliced—1½–3 minutes *Baked* (blanched 5 minutes, sliced, and baked at 350°F.): 30 minutes

(continued)

FRESH VEGETABLE CHART *(continued)*

Vegetable & (Peak Season)	Amount to Buy (4 Servings)	Buying, Storing, Preparing, and Serving Information	Cooking Timetable*
SQUASH, WINTER Acorn Buttercup (Turban) Butternut Cushaw Green & Gold Banana Green & Blue Hubbard Mammoth	2 whole acorn or buttercup squash (½ squash per serving) or 2 pounds other winter squash (Approx. ½ cup per serving, cooked)	*Buy* firm, heavy, unblemished squash. *Store* at 60°F. Avoid refrigeration because temperatures less than 50°F. may cause damage. If stored at room temperature, use within 1 week. *Prepare* by washing well and cutting in half to remove the seeds and strings. (Save seeds, wash, and toast in oven.) Cut squash into 2–3-inch pieces or leave in halves (if baking them) and cook. *Serve* in shells (if small squash) or with skin removed and mashed with seasonings; or in soups, pies, breads, soufflés, custards, casseroles.	*Steamed:* 25–40 minutes *Boiled* (in 1 inch water): 15–20 minutes *Pressure Cooker:* 6–12 minutes *Baked* (halves at 400°F.): 1 hour or more
SWEET POTATO* and YAM** (Sept.– March)	1⅓ pounds (1 potato per serving)	*Buy* firm, unblemished, well-shaped tubers. *Store* at 60°F. Avoid refrigeration because temperatures below 50°F. may cause damage. If stored at room temperature, use within 1 week. *Prepare* by scrubbing well, trimming the ends, and cooking whole. *Serve* plain, whole, sliced, or mashed with margarine and seasonings; cut up in casseroles and other mixed dishes; in soups; breads; and pies.	*Steamed:* 30–35 minutes *Boiled* (in 1 inch water): 20–30 minutes *Pressure Cooker:* Whole—5–8 minutes *Baked* (whole at 350°F.): 45–60 minutes

* There are two types—one has dry, mealy, pale-yellow flesh; the other has moist, deep-orange flesh that is sweeter than the first variety.
** Although yams are botanically very different from the sweet potato, they are cared for and prepared in similar fashion.

FRESH VEGETABLE CHART *(continued)*

Vegetable & *(Peak Season)*	Amount to Buy *(4 Servings)*	Buying, Storing, Preparing, and Serving Information	Cooking Timetable*
TOMATO (All year—peaks in May–August)	2 pounds (Approx. ¾ cup per serving, cooked, or 1 whole medium tomato per serving)	*Buy* firm, red, vine-ripened tomatoes. *Store* ripe tomatoes, uncovered, in the refrigerator; store unripe tomatoes at room temperature, away from direct sunlight, until they ripen. *Prepare* by washing and removing the shallow core. Slice, quarter, dice, or leave whole. Cook or use raw. *Serve* stewed, baked (plain or stuffed), or raw in salads, alone with a vinaigrette dressing—or nothing.	*Boiled* (stewed): 7–15 minutes *Pressure Cooker:* ½–1 minute *Baked* (whole or halved): 15–30 minutes
TURNIPS	2 pounds (Approx. 1 cup per serving, cooked)	*Buy* firm, unblemished turnips. *Store* in a cool, dry place (same as rutabagas). *Prepare* by peeling, dicing, slicing, or leaving whole and cooking. *Serve* plain, mashed with seasonings; puréed in soufflés; or cut up in soups, stews, casseroles, or other mixed dishes.	*Steamed:* sliced—20–25 minutes *Boiled* (in 1 inch water): Whole—20–30 minutes *Pressure Cooker:* Whole—8–12 minutes Sliced—1½ minutes *Baked* (2-inch pieces at 375°F. in liquid): 30–40 minutes

Rosemary Artichokes

3 tablespoons vegetable oil
1 medium onion, finely
   chopped
1 large carrot, finely
   chopped
1 large garlic clove,
   crushed
2 tablespoons minced fresh
   parsley

½ teaspoon crushed
   rosemary
½ cup vinegar
Salt to taste
1 cup water
4 large fresh artichokes,
   trimmed (see Vegetable
   Chart for instructions)

Heat the oil in a large saucepan. Add the onion, carrot, and garlic; sauté until tender. Add all remaining ingredients—except the artichokes—and bring to a boil.

Lower the heat to simmer and add artichokes; cook about 45 minutes, or until tender. (Check occasionally to be sure that the water level is not too low.) Serve artichokes with sauce remaining in the pan poured on top of them.

Size of Serving: 1 artichoke   Number of Servings: 4
Per Serving: Calories: 80; Protein: 5 g; Total Fat: 4 g; Sodium: 25 mg
Excellent Source of: Vitamin A

Broccoli with Fresh Orange Sauce

1 bunch fresh broccoli
2 tablespoons margarine
2 tablespoons enriched
   all-purpose flour
½ teaspoon grated fresh
   orange rind

½ cup fresh orange juice
   (2 medium oranges)
½ cup plain lowfat yogurt
¼ teaspoon crushed dried
   thyme
Salt to taste
⅛ teaspoon pepper

Wash broccoli; remove large leaves and tough parts of stalks; separate florets and cut into individual spears. Place in large saucepan with ½ inch boiling water or in steamer; cover and simmer 8–10 minutes, or until crisp-tender.

Drain and serve with Orange Sauce.

ORANGE SAUCE:

Melt margarine in small saucepan; blend in flour. Add remaining ingredients and stir over low heat until mixture thickens and comes to a boil.

VARIATION: Use fresh asparagus or Brussels sprouts in place of broccoli.

Size of Serving: 1 stalk with ¼ cup sauce   *Number of Servings:* 4
Per Serving: Calories: 145 (115 with asparagus, 130 with Brussels sprouts);
Protein: 8 g; Total Fat: 9 g; Sodium: 105 mg
Excellent Source of: Calcium, Vitamin A, Thiamin, Riboflavin, and
Vitamin C

Browned Brussels Sprouts

2 pints fresh Brussels
sprouts (or 2 10-ounce
packages frozen
sprouts)

¼ cup margarine
2 tablespoons lemon juice
or the juice from 1
lemon
Salt and pepper to taste

Cook Brussels sprouts in a little water (⅓ cup) until just tender (about
15 minutes for fresh); drain.

Brown margarine slowly in a 10-inch skillet. Add lemon juice, Brussels
sprouts, and salt and pepper. Heat and stir for a minute or two, coating
Brussels sprouts with mixture.

Size of Serving: 1 cup   *Number of Servings:* 4
Per Serving: Calories: 150; Protein: 5 g; Total Fat: 12 g; Sodium: 160 mg
Excellent Source of: Vitamin A and Vitamin C

Cheese Glazed Carrots

4 large carrots, well
scrubbed and trimmed
¼ teaspoon dill weed

1 small onion, finely
chopped
⅔ cup shredded cheddar
cheese

Preheat oven to 400°F.

Cut each carrot into 4 or 5 pieces. Cook in a small amount of boiling
water with the dill weed and onion until tender but still crisp (about
8–10 minutes); drain.

Place in baking dish and sprinkle with cheese. Bake for about 5 minutes,
or until cheese melts.

Size of Serving: 1 carrot   *Number of Servings:* 4
Per Serving: Calories: 115; Protein: 6 g; Total Fat: 6 g; Sodium: 170 mg
Excellent Source of: Calcium and Vitamin A

Puréed Cauliflower (Mock Mashed Potatoes)

For those who have been trained to believe that they dislike cauliflower, this recipe will prove a pleasant surprise. (If necessary it can be served in disguise as mashed potatoes until the non-believers are convinced.)

1 medium cauliflower
1 tablespoon dry sherry
  Garlic powder to taste
  Salt to taste (optional)

½ cup defatted chicken or
  veal stock (see Index or
  use canned)

Prepare and wash cauliflower as in basic instructions on Fresh Vegetable Chart; break into florets. Place in pan with sherry and ½ inch of water; cover and cook until tender (about 8 minutes). Allow to cool slightly.

Transfer to electric blender with cooking liquid. Add seasonings and blend at medium speed, adding stock as needed, until mixture is smooth, with a fine grainy texture. Serve immediately with any veal, chicken, or beef dish.

NOTE: Do not attempt to prepare this more than a few hours in advance of the meal because it does not keep well.

Size of Serving: 1 cup   Number of Servings: 4
Per Serving: Calories: 70; Protein: 6 g; Total Fat: Trace; Sodium: 35 mg
Excellent Source of: Iron, Thiamin, Riboflavin, and Vitamin C

Stir-fried Cauliflower

1 tablespoon vegetable
  oil
1½ cups thinly sliced
  celery
2 cups thinly sliced
  cauliflowerets (about 1
  small head)

1 large sweet red or
  green pepper, thinly
  sliced
1–2 drops hot pepper sauce
  Salt to taste

Heat oil in large skillet or wok. Add celery and cook 2–3 minutes, stirring constantly. Add cauliflower and pepper slices. Continue to stir-fry for 4–5 minutes longer. Add pepper sauce and salt. Mix well, cover, remove from heat and let rest for about 3 minutes before serving.

Size of Serving: 1 cup   Number of Servings: 4
Per Serving: Calories: 35; Protein: 2 g; Total Fat: 2 g; Sodium: 45 mg
Excellent Source of: Vitamin A, Thiamin, and Vitamin C

Sweet Potatoes (or Yams) and Yogurt

Sweet potatoes are often mistaken for yams, but they are two different vegetables—and there's a big difference nutritionally. One sweet potato supplies us with over 11,000 I.U.s of vitamin A, whereas a yam contains only a trace of vitamin A.

2 pounds sweet potatoes,
  unpeeled and scrubbed
1 cup plain lowfat yogurt
¼ cup crushed pineapple
  packed in its natural
  juice

2 tablespoons grated
  orange rind
Salt to taste

Cook sweet potatoes in 1 inch of boiling water for 25–30 minutes, or until tender. Drain well; cool slightly and remove skins. Mash well with a potato masher or fork. Stir in remaining ingredients and mix well; reheat if desired.

Size of Serving: ½ cup   *Number of Servings:* 8
Per Serving: Calories: 110; Protein: 3 g; Total Fat: 1 g; Sodium: 25 mg
Excellent Source of: Vitamin A and Vitamin C

Potato Kugel

8 medium potatoes, peeled
  (save peelings for
  vegetable stock—see
  Index)
1 medium onion
2 large eggs

½ cup enriched all-
  purpose flour
½ teaspoon baking powder
  Salt and pepper to taste
5 tablespoons melted
  margarine

Preheat oven to 350°F. Grease a 9-inch square pan well (or a 9 x 13-inch pan if you prefer a thinner kugel).

Grate the potatoes and onion; combine with eggs and remaining ingredients; beat well. Pour into pan and bake about 1 hour, or until top is brown and crusty.

Size of Serving: 1 cup   *Number of Servings:* 8
Per Serving: Calories: 240; Protein: 6 g; Total Fat: 9 g; Sodium: 130 mg
Excellent Source of: Iron, Thiamin, and Vitamin C

Cheese-Baked Potato

2 large potatoes, baked
⅓ cup skim milk
¾ cup lowfat cottage
    cheese

2 tablespoons fresh
    chopped chives
Salt and pepper to taste
½ teaspoon paprika

Preheat oven to 400°F.

Cut baked potatoes in half lengthwise; scoop out potato and mash with skim milk. Beat in cottage cheese, chives, salt, and pepper. Refill potato shells and sprinkle with paprika.

Return to oven and bake until brown (about 10 minutes).

Size of Serving: ½ potato   *Number of Servings:* 4
Per Serving: Calories: 115; Protein: 9 g; Total Fat: 1 g; Sodium: 125 mg
Excellent Source of: Riboflavin and Vitamin C

Hash Brown Potatoes

2 tablespoons vegetable oil
    or margarine
4 medium unpeeled
    potatoes, scrubbed and
    coarsely grated with
    skins

½ cup finely grated fresh
    carrot
½ cup finely chopped
    onion or thinly sliced
    scallion
Salt and pepper to taste

Heat fat in 10-inch skillet over medium heat; spread fat evenly around pan.

Combine grated potatoes, carrot, and chopped onion and pack into skillet evenly, using spatula. Cover and cook for 5 minutes, then reduce heat lightly and cook for 5 more minutes Remove cover and brown for 2 more minutes to remove some moisture. Add salt and pepper to taste.

Cut into servings with a spatula and serve brown side up.

Size of Serving: 1¼ cups   *Number of Servings:* 4
Per Serving: Calories: 220; Protein: 5 g; Total Fat: 6 g; Sodium: 15 mg
Excellent Source of: Thiamin and Vitamin C

Potatoes and Pseudokraut

½ cup cider vinegar
¼ cup water
¼ teaspoon caraway seeds
    Ground white pepper to
    taste
  4 cups finely shredded
    cabbage

2 medium potatoes, peeled
    and thinly sliced
1 green apple, diced
4 tablespoons melted
    margarine

Preheat oven to 350°F.

Combine vinegar and water in a large saucepan. Add caraway seeds and a dash of white pepper. Bring to a boil. Add cabbage, cover pan, and cook for 5 minutes. Drain.

Oil 1½-quart casserole lightly. Layer ingredients: potatoes, cabbage, apples; repeat. Top with layer of potatoes. Pour melted margarine over top and sprinkle with pepper.

Bake 1 hour, or until top layer of potatoes begins to get crisp.

Size of Serving: 1 cup   *Number of Servings:* 6
Per serving: Calories: 160; Protein: 12 g; Total Fat: 8 g; Sodium: 110 mg
Excellent Source of: Vitamin C

Easy Baked Tomatoes

2 *medium fresh tomatoes*	½ *teaspoon basil or dill*
4 *teaspoons grated*	*weed*
Parmesan cheese	*Salt and pepper to taste*
4 *teaspoons wheat germ*	4 *teaspoons margarine or*
(or toasted bread	*vegetable oil*
crumbs)	

Preheat oven to 400°F.

Cut tomatoes in half crosswise and place in pie plate with cut side up. Sprinkle each tomato half with 1 teaspoon grated cheese and 1 teaspoon wheat germ, ⅛ teaspoon basil or dill, and salt and pepper to taste. Dot with margarine (or dribble with oil) and bake for 15 minutes, or until tomatoes are tender. If desired, brown under broiler 1–2 minutes, watching carefully to avoid burning.

Size of Serving: tomato half   *Number of Servings:* 4
Per Serving: Calories: 80; Protein: 3 g; Total Fat: 5 g; Sodium: 60 mg
Excellent Source of: Thiamin and Vitamin C

Spinach Soufflé

3 *tablespoons margarine*	2 *tablespoons fresh chives*
3 *tablespoons enriched*	*or 2 teaspoons dried*
all-purpose flour	*chives*
1 *cup skim milk*	½ *pound fresh spinach,*
¼ *teaspoon salt*	*cooked, drained,*
¼ *teaspoon pepper*	*squeezed, and chopped*
⅛ *teaspoon marjoram*	3 *large egg yolks, at room*
¼ *teaspoon chervil*	*temperature, beaten*
	4 *large egg whites, at*
	room temperature

(continued)

Preheat oven to 350°F. Grease a 1-quart soufflé dish very well (or use any other pan with smooth sides the mixture can cling to as it rises).

Melt the margarine in a saucepan and combine with the flour. Add the milk, salt, and pepper. Cook over low heat until thickened. Add the seasonings and spinach and allow to cool. Once mixture has cooled, add the beaten egg yolks and mix well.

Beat the egg whites until stiff and carefully fold into the spinach mixture. Pour into greased soufflé dish and bake for 40–50 minutes.

Size of Serving: about ½ cup   *Number of Servings:* 6
Per Serving: Calories: 130; Protein: 7 g; Total Fat: 9 g; Sodium: 230 mg
Excellent Source of: Calcium, Vitamin A, and Riboflavin; (min. 1 cup) Iron, Thiamin, and Vitamin C

Fresh Turnip Casserole

1 pound fresh white turnips	½ cup chopped celery
	Salt to taste
2 tablespoons melted margarine	½ teaspoon sugar
	¼ teaspoon crushed dried sage
¼ cup chopped onion	
1 cup chopped, peeled, fresh tomatoes	⅛ teaspoon pepper

Preheat oven to 350°F. and grease a 1-quart casserole.

Peel the turnips and cut into large chunks. Place in 1 inch of boiling water in a medium-size saucepan and cook, covered, until barely tender (about 10 minutes). Drain well, then cut into cubes (about 2 cups). Place turnip cubes and remaining ingredients in casserole dish and mix well. Cover and bake about 15 minutes, or until vegetables are tender.

Size of Serving: about ⅔ cup   *Number of Servings:* 4
Per Serving: Calories: 100; Protein: 2 g; Total Fat: 6 g; Sodium: 135 mg
Excellent Source of: Vitamin C

Sautéed Fresh Vegetables with Seasoned Yogurt

This succulent blend of fresh vegetable flavors goes with any main dish—
or serve it alone with some chewy whole-grain bread. Delicious hot or
cold.

1 eggplant, diced	1 cup thickly sliced large
¼ cup vegetable oil	fresh mushrooms
1 onion, sliced	Fresh basil (if
2 green peppers, sliced	available)
1 tender zucchini, cut in	¼ cup fresh parsley
strips	Salt to taste
1 tender crookneck	Ground black pepper to
summer squash	taste
(yellow), sliced	1 cup plain lowfat yogurt
lengthwise	1 clove garlic, crushed
2 tomatoes, quartered	

After salting the eggplant, drain for ½ hour, then squeeze and dry slices.

Heat oil in a large skillet. Sauté onion in oil until soft and golden. Add
eggplant, peppers, zucchini, and yellow squash and fry gently about 8–10
minutes, or until tender but still crisp. Add tomatoes, mushrooms, basil,
parsley, salt, and pepper. Simmer to reduce pan juices, being careful not
to scorch. Allow to cool, then chill.

Season yogurt with fresh crushed garlic. Serve yogurt in a small bowl
nestled amidst the vegetables. Use a large flat spoon to serve vegetables
and a small ladle for yogurt.

VARIATION: Any kind of fresh, tender vegetable can be used to create
color and texture, or to increase quantity. Sweet red pepper is especially
nice to replace part of the green pepper.

Size of Serving: 1 cup   *Number of Servings:* 8
Per Serving: Calories: 115; Protein: 3 g; Total Fat: 7 g; Sodium: 25 mg
Excellent Source of: Thiamin, Riboflavin, and Vitamin C

CEREAL GRAINS
AND LEGUMES

Cereal Grains

People are beginning to rediscover the merits of a steaming bowl of whole wheat or oatmeal cereal, the crunchy goodness of a homemade granola, and the satisfying chewiness of a brown rice pilaf or stuffing. In addition to the eating pleasures that they offer, whole cereal grains are important sources of vitamins, minerals, protein, carbohydrate, and fiber. So use them however you wish—for breakfast, in salads, as side dishes or part of the main course, and even as desserts—but do be sure to use them! If you can't find them in your supermarket, check all those bins at the local health food store.

BASIC METHODS FOR COOKING CEREAL GRAINS

Regular Method

1. Rinse grain in cold water and drain.
2. Bring water or stock to a boil in a heavy pan with a tightly fitting cover.* (See Cooking Timetable below for amounts.)
3. Lower the heat to a simmer and pour in the grain slowly, stirring constantly.
4. Bring to a boil again; lower heat to a simmer; cover and cook until

---

* Double boilers and slow cookers can also be used and, for some grains (whole barley, millet, and rice), pressure cookers can be used. However, pressure cookers are not advisable for cracked grains because they are likely to clog the vent. Be sure to follow the manufacturer's instructions for cooking grains in a pressure cooker.

all the liquid is absorbed. (It's best not to stir the grain after it has boiled—this mashes it and promotes a gummy consistency. Also, be sure not to lift the cover while the grain is cooking because steam will escape and the grain might stick.) (See Cooking Timetable.)
5. If the grain is too hard add a small amount of boiling water and simmer as above until it is soft.

Sautéing. This is another way to cook cereal grains and is particularly good for bulgur, rice, or buckwheat groats. However, this method uses fats, which supply about 45 calories per teaspoon. So if keeping calories to a minimum is of major concern, the regular method for cooking grains would be more suitable.

1. Heat 2 tablespoons of margarine or oil in a heavy pan.
2. Add the grain and sauté, stirring constantly, until it is lightly browned (about 5 minutes). Chopped onion, celery, green pepper, garlic, or other vegetables may be sautéed with the grain if desired.
3. Add boiling water or stock; bring to a boil; lower the heat; cover tightly and simmer until all the liquid is absorbed. Deduct 10–15 minutes from Cooking Timetable for grains prepared this way.

TIMETABLE FOR COOKING WHOLE GRAINS

Grain (1 cup dry)	Liquid	Cooking Time	Yield
Barley*	3 cups	1 hour	3½ cups
Buckwheat (kasha)	2 cups	15–20 mins.	2½ cups
Bulgur wheat**	2 cups	15–20 mins.	2½ cups
Cornmeal (yellow or white)	4 cups	25–30 mins.	3 cups
Cracked wheat	2½ cups	20–25 mins.	2½ cups
Millet	3 cups	30–40 mins.	3½ cups
Oats, rolled (old-fashioned)	2 cups	10–15 mins.	1⅔ cups
Rice:			
brown	2 cups	45–50 mins.	3 cups
wild	3 cups	1 hour	4 cups
Whole wheat berries	2¾ cups	1½ hours	2⅔ cups

* Most supermarkets sell quick-cooking barley which only takes 10–15 minutes to cook, but it is not as nutritious as the whole-grain barley found mainly in health food and specialty stores.

** Bulgur can also be prepared by soaking it in warm water for about 1 hour.

Legumes: Dried Beans, Peas, and Lentils

Colorful dried beans, peas, and lentils are as pleasing to look at as they are to eat. Legumes are important sources of carbohydrate, protein, fiber, B vitamins, and minerals (particularly minerals such as iron, magnesium, and zinc that are in short supply in many diets). Dried beans, peas, and lentils have highly individualized nutrient portfolios, however, so it's a good practice to eat a variety of them often to take advantage of their full nutritional range.

Cooked dried beans, peas, and lentils are delicious in many types of recipes—soups, salads, sandwich spreads and dips, stews, and casseroles. Try them with herbs and spices (chili and curry are particularly good); lemon juice or vinegar; chopped vegetables; and in combination with grains, meats, fish, or poultry.

BASIC METHODS FOR COOKING LEGUMES

To Prepare

1. Sort through and remove any discolored legumes and rocks; rinse well and drain.
2. Cover with water to at least 1 inch above the legumes and soak overnight to replace some of the moisture lost during drying and to cut down on the cooking time. (Soybeans need to be refrigerated during soaking to prevent fermentation.)
   or
   Instead of overnight soaking, bring the legumes and water to a boil; simmer for 2 minutes; remove from the heat and allow to stand for 1 hour.

To Cook

TOP OF STOVE METHOD: Cook legumes in a heavy pot in their soaking water (to preserve any water-soluble vitamins that have migrated into the water during soaking).* Add more water, if necessary, to cover.

* Many people avoid eating dried beans because of the discomfort that may occur from gas. Some researchers suggest that the culprits in dried beans are two sugars, stachyose and raffinose, which are not digested properly because the human body does not have the enzymes needed to convert them to simple sugars. So they pass undigested into the lower intestinal tract where they react with bacterial enzymes

Bring to a boil, then lower heat and simmer, partially covered, until tender. Replenish the water during cooking as needed. (See Cooking Timetable.)

PRESSURE COOKER METHOD: Use great caution when cooking legumes in a pressure cooker because they tend to foam and clog the vent. To cut down on this foaming, soak legumes overnight with salt and cooking oil added to the soaking water. Then cook according to the manufacturer's instructions.

SLOW COOKER METHOD: Soak legumes in the slow cooker on low setting overnight. In the morning add any other ingredients and cook on low all day.

TIMETABLE FOR COOKING LEGUMES

Dried Legumes	Cooking Time*
Adzuki beans (small red beans)	3 hours
Black beans	2 hours
Black-eye peas (cowpeas)	1 hour
Fava beans (broad beans)	1½ hours
Garbanzo beans (chickpeas)	3 hours
Kidney beans	1½ hours
Lentils	1 hour
Lima beans	1½ hours
Navy beans (Great Northern)	1½ hours
Pigeon peas	1 hour
Pinto beans	2½ hours
Red beans	1½ hours
Soybeans	3½ hours
Soy grits	15–20 minutes
Split peas	1 hour

Yield from dry legumes:
1 cup dry beans or peas	=	approximately 2 cups cooked
1 cup dry split peas or lentils	=	approximately 2¼ cups cooked

to produce gas. For people with this problem, the following cooking method may be of help. Of course, some of the water-soluble vitamins will be lost using this method, but the protein, carbohydrate, and fiber is still available:
1. Boil the beans in water about five times the amount of the beans for about 10 minutes.
2. Soak 8–10 hours.
3. Drain well; *discard the soaking water.*
4. Continue with the recipe using fresh water in place of the soaking water.
* This does not include the required presoaking time for legumes, which would add anywhere from 1 hour to 8 hours (for overnight soaking) to the total preparation time (see Basic Methods for Cooking Legumes).

Barley Pilaf

2 tablespoons margarine
½ cup whole-grain barley
10 mushrooms, sliced
½ cup chopped onion
¼ teaspoon salt

3 tablespoons chopped
fresh parsley
2 cups defatted chicken
stock (see Index or use
canned)

Preheat oven to 350°F.

Melt 1 tablespoon margarine in a frying pan. Add barley and sauté until lightly browned, stirring constantly. Pour into ungreased 1-quart casserole.

Melt remaining tablespoon of margarine and sauté mushrooms for 2 minutes. Add mushrooms, onion, salt, parsley, and chicken stock to barley, mixing well. Cover tightly and bake about 1 hour, or until barley is tender. Uncover and bake 10–15 minutes longer, if necessary, to absorb all the water.

Size of Serving: 1 cup   *Number of Servings:* 4
Per Serving: Calories: 145; Protein: 5 g; Total Fat: 7 g; Sodium: 240 mg
Excellent Source of: Iron

Bulgur Parsnip Pilaf

2 tablespoons vegetable
oil
¼ cup finely chopped
celery
1 cup finely chopped
parsnip
¼ cup finely sliced
scallion
1 cup raw bulgur wheat

2 cups defatted chicken
stock or vegetable stock
(see Index)
1 bay leaf
1 teaspoon dill weed
Garlic salt to taste
Freshly ground pepper
to taste
¼ cup toasted slivered
almonds (optional)

Heat oil in a heavy, medium-size frying pan. Add celery, parsnip, and scallion; sauté, stirring constantly, for 3–4 minutes. Add bulgur and cook, stirring often, until golden.

Add stock and seasonings. Mix well and bring to a boil; reduce heat and simmer, covered, 15 minutes. If too moist, remove cover and simmer a few more minutes, then remove bay leaf. Add toasted almonds and toss lightly.

Size of Serving: about ¾ cup   *Number of Servings:* 4
Per Serving: Calories: 285 (245 without almonds): Protein: 7 g; Total Fat: 11 g; Sodium: 45 mg
Excellent Source of: Iron and Thiamin

Pignolia Pilaf

Pignolia (or pine) nuts are available in supermarkets and specialty stores.

1 tablespoon margarine
1 small onion, finely
    minced
¾ cup raw long-grain
    brown rice

1½ cups defatted chicken
    stock (see Index)
¼ teaspoon salt
⅛ teaspoon pepper
2 tablespoons pignolia
    nuts

Melt 1 tablespoon margarine in heavy saucepan; add onion and cook until transparent. Add rice and *stir constantly* until rice turns a golden brown. Pour in stock and bring to boil, add salt and pepper. Place several layers of paper towels over the top of the pan and cover tightly with lid (this helps to prevent the steam from escaping). Cook over low heat 25–30 minutes, or until tender.

While rice is cooking, toast pignolia nuts in the oven or broiler, stirring once, until golden brown. (Watch them carefully because they burn easily.) Toss nuts with cooked rice and serve.

Size of Serving: ½ cup   *Number of Servings:* 4
Per Serving: Calories: 215; Protein: 5 g; Total Fat: 9 g; Sodium: 190 mg
Excellent Source of: Iron and Thiamin

Dolmas (Armenian Stuffed Grape Leaves)

⅓ cup olive oil or other
    vegetable oil
2 cups finely chopped
    onion
½ cup raw long-grain
    brown rice
30 fresh or frozen grape
    leaves (1 pint, canned)
½ cup chopped parsley

¼ cup currants or raisins
¼ cup pine nuts or other
    nuts, chopped
¼ cup tomato sauce
½ cup water
¼ teaspoon allspice
¼ teaspoon cinnamon
½ teaspoon salt
¼ teaspoon pepper

Heat oil in a medium-size saucepan; add onion and sauté until soft but not browned. Add rice, cover, and cook ½ hour.

Meanwhile, prepare grape leaves as follows:

Fresh: Wash leaves and remove stems. Blanch leaves in boiling water (to make them pliable).
Canned: Rinse leaves well to remove canning brine.
Frozen: Defrost; blanch if this has not already been done.

After rice has cooked ½ hour, add remaining ingredients; cook 5 minutes and cool mixture slightly.

To assemble dolmas, place a teaspoonful of the rice mixture on the stem end of the bottom side of a grape leaf. Fold in sides and roll up into a neat package.

Line a 3-quart saucepan with whole grape leaves and place dolmas seam side down in lined pan.

Place a large, heatproof plate on top of the dolmas to prevent floating (but small enough to allow water to run over its sides to cover the dolmas). Pour enough boiling water over dolmas to cover. Simmer, with pan uncovered, for ½ hour, or until the rice absorbs enough water to be soft. (Add a small amount of water if necessary—some may be left at the end of the cooking time.) Cool slightly and refrigerate.

Serve cold as an appetizer or hot as a main dish with lemon wedges.

NOTE: Short-grain rice is unsuitable since it becomes mushy.

VARIATION: Long-grain white rice may be used instead of the brown. If so, it's a good idea to add 2 tablespoons soy grits to improve the protein quality.

Size of Serving: 4–5 dolmas   *Number of Servings:* 6
Per Serving: Calories: 295; Protein 5 g; Total Fat: 19 g; Sodium: 315 mg
Excellent Source of: Iron, Vitamin A, Thiamin, and Vitamin C

Spinach Fettucine

3 *eggs*
2 *tablespoons vegetable oil*
¼ *teaspoon salt*
1 *10-ounce package frozen spinach, cooked, squeezed very well to remove all moisture; finely chopped*

1 *cup enriched, all-purpose flour*
1 *cup whole wheat flour*

Beat eggs in a large bowl; add oil, salt, and spinach; mix well. Gradually stir in the flours and mix well. Cover the bowl and let dough rest 30 minutes.

Divide dough into 4 parts. Place on lightly floured surface and roll dough to pie crust thickness. Allow to dry 10–15 minutes and roll again as thinly as possible. Shave off ¼-inch-wide slices; straighten out. Cook immediately *or* dry well at room temperature and store uncooked noodles in tightly sealed plastic bags or large canisters.

Yield: about 12 ounces (approximately 5 cups)
Per ½ Cup: Calories: 145; Protein, 6 g; Total Fat: 6 g; Sodium 90 mg
Excellent Source of: Iron, Vitamin A, and Thiamin

Whole Wheat Noodles

This recipe requires about 4–5 hours to complete, most of which is drying time for the noodles. The actual time involvement for the cook (about 30–40 minutes) is well rewarded in terms of flavor and personal satisfaction.

> 1 *egg, beaten*
> 2 *tablespoons skim milk*
> ¼ *teaspoon salt*
>
> 1 *cup stirred whole wheat flour*

Combine egg, milk, and salt. Stir in flour, cover, and let rest 10 minutes.

On lightly floured surface, roll dough very thin to a 16 x 12-inch rectangle. Let stand 40 minutes, or until surface is fairly dry.

Flour well both top and bottom surfaces. Loosely fold dough in thirds. Cut into ¼-inch slices.

Unroll slices. Spread out and let dry 3 hours or more. If desired, store in container and refrigerate or freeze for later use.

To cook, drop noodles into a large amount of boiling water and cook, uncovered, for 12–15 minutes; drain well.

Yield: 2½–3 cups
Per ½ Cup: Calories: 80; Protein: 4 g; Total Fat: 1 g; Sodium: 100 mg

Whole Wheat Spaetzle with Poppy Seeds

A cross between dumplings and noodles, German spaetzle offer something deliciously different for the dinner table.

> 1¼ *cups whole wheat flour*
> 3 *eggs*
> ¼ *cup skim milk*
> ¼ *teaspoon salt*
> ¼ *teaspoon grated nutmeg*
> 1 *tablespoon margarine*
>
> 1½ *teaspoons poppy seeds (optional)*
> 2 *teaspoons minced fresh parsley*
> *Freshly ground pepper to taste*

Bring a large pot of water to a boil, then turn down to a simmer.

Combine flour, eggs, milk, salt, and nutmeg; beat until smooth. Spread batter on a board or on a piece of waxed paper on a flat surface. Using a spatula, slice off ¼-inch strips of batter directly into the water. The spaetzle will sink to the bottom, then rise to the surface when they are cooked, which will take only 1–2 minutes.

Remove spaetzle from the water with a slotted spoon, drain them well and place in a warm, covered serving dish. Add margarine, poppy seeds, parsley, and pepper. Toss well until spaetzle are coated.

VARIATIONS:
- Use 1–2 tablespoons of Leafy Green Butter or Herb Butter (see Index) in place of margarine and parsley.
- Sprinkle spaetzle with fresh dill, basil, or tarragon in place of parsley.
- Add freshly grated cheese before serving.

Size of Serving: ½ cup   *Number of Servings:* 8
Per Serving: Calories: 110; Protein: 8 g; Total Fat: 5 g; Sodium: 110 mg
Excellent Source of: (min. 1 cup) Protein, Iron, and Thiamin

Spinach Gnocchi

Pronounced "kneeoh-kee," these dumplinglike balls can serve as an appetizer or main dish—alone or in soups.

1 *pound fresh spinach*	3–4 *whole scallions, finely chopped*
1 *cup seasoned bread crumbs*	¼ *teaspoon salt*
1½ *cups partially skimmed ricotta cheese*	1 *garlic clove, minced*
¼ *cup grated Parmesan cheese + extra for sprinkling on top, if desired*	2 *eggs, beaten*
	2–3 *tablespoons enriched all-purpose flour (to roll gnocchi)*

Cook spinach. Drain well and squeeze dry, then chop finely. Combine spinach with bread crumbs, ricotta cheese, Parmesan cheese, scallions, salt, garlic, and eggs; mix well.

Spread the flour on a sheet of waxed paper. Flour the palms of your hands and, taking a small amount of the spinach mixture at a time, form it into a couple of 1½-inch balls. Put the gnocchi in boiling water; if they disintegrate, add 1–2 tablespoons of flour to the spinach mixture. Roll all of the gnocchi and place on a waxed-paper-lined cookie sheet and store, covered with waxed paper, in refrigerator until cooking time.

To cook, bring 2–3 quarts of water to a boil. Drop gnocchi in, about 3–4 at a time. When they rise to the top, remove with a slotted spoon. Drain well and store in a warmed serving dish. Serve sprinkled with extra Parmesan cheese, if desired.

Yield: about 1 dozen gnocchi
Per 2 Gnocchi: Calories: 160; Protein: 16 g; Total Fat: 6 g; Sodium: 350 mg
Excellent Source of: Protein, Calcium, Iron, Vitamin A, Thiamin, Riboflavin, and Vitamin C

Tabouli

½ cup extra-fine bulgur (cracked wheat)

½ cup cooked navy beans

2 cups finely chopped parsley

3 scallions, finely chopped

1 medium tomato, finely chopped

⅓ cup fresh mint (or 1 tablespoon dried mint), minced

¾ teaspoon allspice (or to taste)

½ teaspoon salt

¼ teaspoon freshly ground pepper

¼ cup lemon juice

3 tablespoons vegetable oil

8 large romaine lettuce leaves

Cover the bulgur with cold water and soak for 1 hour. Drain in a sieve or colander lined with cheesecloth; wrap the cheesecloth around the bulgur and squeeze it dry.

Combine the bulgur with the beans, parsley, scallions, tomato, mint, allspice, salt, pepper, and lemon juice. Cover and chill thoroughly to allow flavors to blend. Add oil and correct seasonings before serving on romaine leaves.

Size of Serving: 1¼ cups   *Number of Servings:* 4
Per Serving: Calories: 265; Protein: 9 g; Total Fat: 11 g; Sodium: 275 mg
Excellent Source of: Calcium, Iron, Vitamin A, Thiamin, and Vitamin C

Sesame Seed Rice

½ cup sesame seeds

2 teaspoons vegetable oil

2 whole scallions, thinly sliced

1 cup brown rice

1¾ cups chicken broth (or beef or vegetable broth)

1–2 teaspoons soy sauce (or to taste)

Pepper to taste

Brown the sesame seeds in a 350°F. oven for 8–10 minutes (watch them carefully to avoid burning).

Heat the oil in a medium-size, heavy saucepan with a tight-fitting cover. Add the scallions and rice. Sauté for 5–8 minutes, or until the rice is golden brown.

Add the chicken broth and bring to a boil; lower the heat and simmer, covered, for 30–40 minutes, or until the rice is soft. Add the soy sauce and pepper to taste and toss lightly. Serve with sesame seeds sprinkled on top.

Size of Serving: ¾ cup   *Number of Servings:* 4
Per Serving: Calories: 310; Protein: 10 g; Total Fat: 13 g; Sodium: 430 mg
Excellent Source of: Iron and Thiamin

Vegetarian Couscous

Although this brilliantly constructed dish may appear complicated to the uninitiated, couscous is really quite simple to prepare. Basically, the dish consists of a grain—*also* called couscous (tiny balls of rolled semolina flour)—steamed over a bubbling stew. The steam from the stew swells the couscous and flavors it with its vapors. The stew is often a mixture of vegetables, spices, raisins, almonds, and one or two meats—usually beef or lamb and chicken. This recipe is, as the name suggests, a wonderful mixture of fresh vegetables in a tangy tomato sauce.

THE COUSCOUS:

1 pound dry couscous,
medium or fine textured

THE SAUCE:

1 cup freshly soaked
chickpeas (or use 2 cups
canned)
2 tablespoons vegetable
oil
1 large onion, chopped
2 garlic cloves, crushed
½ teaspoon ground cumin

½ teaspoon ground
coriander
½ teaspoon oregano
¼ teaspoon red pepper
flakes
¼ teaspoon pepper
2 cups tomato sauce
3 cups water
Salt to taste

THE VEGETABLES:

1 small acorn squash,
seeded and peeled
2 zucchini

6 carrots
1 small cabbage
3 medium potatoes

Couscous is usually available in the international department at many supermarkets.

Drain the soaked chickpeas, cover with water, and cook 1 hour.

Sprinkle the couscous with 1½–2 cups cool water; mix thoroughly. Allow to soak up the water while preparing the sauce and vegetables.

Measure the oil into a large, heavy pot; add the onion and garlic; sauté until golden. Add the spices, tomato sauce, chickpeas, and water; cook over medium heat, stirring occasionally, for about 1 hour. (If using canned chickpeas, do not add until later.)

Wash and cut the vegetables into large chunks or wedges. (Small pieces cook too quickly and become mashed.) Add the vegetables to the tomato

(continued)

sauce (and add the canned chickpeas, if used). Add salt, if desired. When the vegetable stew has heated and hot vapor is rising from the pan, place the moist couscous in a wire mesh steaming basket. Place the basket over the simmering stew and cover tightly to trap steam. If available, a couscousier (a two-sectioned couscous pot with steamer basket) can be used instead of a regular pot with steaming basket.

Stir the couscous gently a few times during steaming to ensure even cooking; steam for about ½ hour, or until it is moist and soft (but not mushy and sticky) and separates like well-cooked rice.

To serve, mix about 2 tablespoons of sauce into couscous to give it color, then spread in a mound on a large serving tray. Break apart any lumps.

Arrange vegetables and chickpeas attractively on top of the couscous, reserving sauce. Place sauce in separate serving bowl, to be spooned on at the table as desired.

A salad of shredded cucumber and plain yogurt offers a pleasing contrast to the hot and spicy sauce.

Size of Serving: about 2½ cups vegetables + sauce and 1 cup couscous
Number of Servings: 6
Per Serving: Calories: 570; Protein: 20 g; Total Fat: 8 g; Sodium: 385 mg
Excellent Source of: Protein, Calcium, Iron, Vitamin A, Thiamin, Riboflavin, Niacin, and Vitamin C

Boston Baked Soybeans

2 cups (1 pound) dried soybeans, soaked and cooked according to directions (see Index)	2–3 tablespoons molasses (or to taste)
	1½ teaspoons dry mustard
	¼ cup freshly chopped parsley
1 tablespoon vegetable oil	2–3 drops hot pepper sauce (or to taste)
1 small onion, chopped	
1 garlic clove, crushed	
½ cup tomato sauce	½ teaspoon ground allspice (or to taste)
2 tablespoons tomato paste	
2 tablespoons cider vinegar	¼ teaspoon ground cumin

Preheat oven to 350°F.

Put cooked soybeans (with cooking liquid) into an oiled 2-quart Dutch oven or other heavy casserole.

Heat oil in a small skillet. Add onion and garlic; sauté until onion is translucent, then add to soybeans. Add tomato sauce, tomato paste, vinegar, molasses, mustard, parsley, hot pepper sauce, allspice, and cumin; mix well. Bake 1½ hours, or until soybeans are tender.

Size of Serving: about 1¼ cups   *Number of Servings:* 4
Per Serving: Calories: 250; Protein: 14 g; Total Fat: 12 g; Sodium: 390 mg
Excellent Source of: Calcium, Iron, and Thiamin

Lentil Surprise Stew

2 cups dried lentils, rinsed thoroughly	2 tablespoons vegetable oil
10 cups water or vegetable stock (see Index)	2 bay leaves
1 medium onion, chopped	1 teaspoon salt
2 small carrots, thinly sliced	1½ teaspoons vinegar
3 stalks celery, thinly sliced	8 ounces Brie or Camembert cheese

Mix all ingredients, except vinegar and cheese, in a large pot and cook until lentils are very soft—about 45 minutes. Add vinegar.

Place 1 ounce of cheese in each soup bowl. Pour hot soup over the cheese and serve.

Size of Serving: 1½ cups   *Number of Servings:* 8
Per Serving: Calories: 300; Protein: 18 g; Total Fat: 12 g; Sodium: 300 mg
Excellent Source of: Protein, Iron, Vitamin A, Thiamin, and Riboflavin

Brazilian Black Beans with Rice

This is a classic example of how rice and beans form a higher-quality protein coalition.

½ pound dried black beans (1¼ cups)	4 whole cloves
4 cups water	2 tablespoons vegetable oil
½ teaspoon salt	1 medium onion, diced
2 large garlic cloves, crushed	1 large green pepper, diced
½ teaspoon allspice	1 cup uncooked brown rice
1 medium onion, peeled and left whole	1 cup Salsa (see Index)

In a 2-quart heavy pan, soak the beans in the water, covered, for 8–10 hours in the refrigerator.

Add salt to beans, and bring to a boil. Reduce heat and simmer, covered, 1 hour. Add garlic, allspice, and whole onion with cloves poked into it. Mix well and cook, covered, ¾–1 hour. (Look at beans often and add more water if liquid gets halfway down the thickness of beans.)

(continued)

Meanwhile, heat oil in a medium-size skillet. Add diced onion and green pepper; sauté, stirring often, until onions are golden. Cook rice according to directions at beginning of this chapter.

Remove whole onion from beans and discard; add sautéed onion and green pepper to beans and cook 5 minutes.

Serve bean sauce over rice with Salsa (see Index).

Size of Serving: 1½ cups beans and rice   *Number of Servings:* 4
Per Serving: Calories: 440; Protein: 17 g; Total Fat: 9 g; Sodium: 275 mg
Excellent Source of: Protein, Calcium, Iron, Thiamin, Riboflavin, and Vitamin C

Soybean Walnut Loaf with Cheese

½ cup dried soybeans
2 pints warm water
½ cup uncooked brown
   rice
¼ cup chopped onion
¾ cup finely diced carrots
½ cup finely diced celery
¼ cup canned tomatoes
1 garlic clove, crushed
¼ teaspoon cumin

¼ teaspoon thyme
1 bay leaf
½ teaspoon salt
⅛ teaspoon pepper
½ cup wheat germ
1 egg, slightly beaten
½ cup chopped walnuts
½ cup shredded cheddar
   cheese

Soak soybeans in water overnight.

Bring to a boil; cover and cook for 2 hours. Mash in the water at end of cooking time.

Meanwhile, cook brown rice according to package directions or directions at beginning of this chapter. Add onion, carrots, celery, tomatoes, garlic, cumin, thyme, bay leaf, salt, and pepper. Simmer for ½ hour, then remove bay leaf.

Preheat oven to 375°F.

Mix together wheat germ, cooked brown rice mixture, beaten egg, and walnuts; blend thoroughly. Pour into well-greased 9 x 5 x 3-inch loaf pan and bake for 50 minutes. After baking, allow loaf to set for 5 minutes. Remove from pan and place on ovenproof platter. Sprinkle with cheese; melt under broiler for 1 minute.

Size of Serving: ¾ cup   *Number of Servings:* 8
Per Serving: Calories: 220; Protein: 12 g; Total Fat: 12 g; Sodium: 215 mg
Excellent Source of: Calcium, Iron, Vitamin A, and Thiamin

Soybean Salad

1½ pounds soybeans,
    cooked
    Lemon juice to taste
1 cup minced celery
8 teaspoons mayonnaise
    (or low-calorie
    mayonnaise)

Salt to taste
4 large romaine lettuce
    leaves
1 cup shredded carrots
8 tomato wedges

Grind soybeans in blender with the lemon juice. Mix with celery, mayonnaise, and salt. Chill. Serve on lettuce leaves, topped with shredded carrots and surrounded with tomato wedges.

Size of Serving: 1 cup   *Number of Servings:* 4
Per Serving: Calories: 315; Protein: 21 g; Total Fat: 18 g; Sodium: 155 mg
Excellent Source of: Protein, Calcium, Iron, Vitamin A, Thiamin, Riboflavin, and Vitamin C

Chili Sin Carne (Meatless Chili)

2 tablespoons vegetable oil
1 medium onion, chopped
1 small green pepper,
    chopped
1 medium stalk celery,
    chopped
1 28-ounce can tomatoes,
    undrained
1 tablespoon chili powder
1 teaspoon cumin

1 1-pound can kidney
    beans, undrained (or 1
    pound cooked, dried
    beans)
½ cup uncooked ditalini,
    tubetti, or other tiny
    macaroni
¼ pound cheddar cheese,
    coarsely shredded

In a heavy 2½-quart saucepan, heat the oil and add the onion, green pepper and celery. Sauté until tender but not brown. Add tomatoes, chili powder, and cumin and simmer, uncovered, about 30 minutes. Add kidney beans and uncooked macaroni; simmer 12–15 minutes, stirring frequently, or just until macaroni is tender.
    Served topped with cheese.

Size of Serving: 1½ cups   *Number of Servings:* 4
Per Serving: Calories: 695; Protein: 16 g; Total Fat: 18 g; Sodium: 430 mg with canned kidney beans (245 with cooked, dried beans)
Excellent Source of: Protein, Calcium, Iron, Vitamin A, Thiamin, Riboflavin, Niacin, and Vitamin C

FISH AND SHELLFISH

Although often regarded as second best to meat, fish has several advantages that have made it an all-time favorite with people interested in getting high nutritional value for their calories. Like meat, fish is an excellent source of high quality protein; however, most fish is lower in fat, and therefore lower in calories, than meat. And the fat in most fish is higher in polyunsaturated fatty acids than meats, which contain more saturated and monounsaturated fatty acids (see discussion on fats on page 23). Fish are also an important source of B vitamins and several minerals, including iodine (seafood), copper, zinc (particularly oysters), fluoride (seafood), phosphorus, and calcium (oysters and small fish eaten with the bones).

Overcooking, heavy seasonings, and rich sauces can easily defeat the delicate, subtle flavor and texture of fish. All fish requires is a short time in the skillet, oven, or poacher with a few seasonings and some lemon or lime juice to enhance its natural goodness.

There are over 160 species of lake, stream, and ocean fish to choose from, so enjoy the benefits of fish often. Serve fish as appetizers, salads, sandwiches, soups, and entrées, and at any meal—breakfast and lunch as well as dinner.

HOW TO STORE FISH

Fish should be stored in the coldest part of the refrigerator and cooked as soon as possible to retain its fresh flavor. Keep prepackaged fish in the original packaging—otherwise keep it in foil or plastic wrap or place it in a tightly covered container. Fish can be stored in the freezer wrapped in moistureproof freezer paper, foil, or plastic wrap or, if already frozen, it can be stored in the original packaging. The following are recommended storage times for fish:

	In refrigerator (35°F. to 40°F.):	In freezer (0°F.):
Fresh fish	1–2 days	4–6 months
Cooked fish	3–4 days	2–3 months
Salted or smoked fish	Several weeks	
Lox	3–4 days	

TO THAW FISH

· It is best not to thaw fish at room temperature—keep it in the refrigerator for a day or submerge it in cold water.
· To avoid deterioration of quality, do not refreeze fish once it has been thawed.
· Usually frozen breaded fish products should not be thawed; they should be cooked in the frozen state.

HOW TO COOK FISH

Fish is cooked when it has lost its translucent appearance; it becomes an opaque white and flakes easily when tested with a fork. The following methods are recommended for cooking fish:

To Bake: Place cleaned dressed whole fish, or fish steaks or fillets, in a foil-lined or lightly greased baking dish. Season and bake in a preheated moderate oven (about 350°F.) until fork-tender (see Cooking Time-table). Whole fish may be stuffed and baked; or stuffing may be put on top of fillets, which can then be rolled, secured with a skewer, and baked. If fish begins to look dry during cooking, moisten with liquid,* or dot with margarine, if you can afford the extra calories.**

To Broil: Place thick fillets, fish steaks, or smaller whole fish on a preheated, foil-lined broiler pan. The pan needs to be 2–3 inches from the heat, or 4–5 inches for very thick fish. Add seasonings and cook according to Cooking Timetable. Most fillets will not need to be turned. Thicker whole fish and fish steaks need to be browned on one side, then turned, seasoned if desired, and browned on the other side. If the fish appears to be drying out during cooking, baste with liquid* or with melted margarine** during cooking.

---

* Skim milk, tomato juice, vegetable juice, clam broth, or vegetable broth are all low-calorie liquids to use for basting fish to prevent it from drying out while cooking.
** 1 tablespoon of margarine = 100 calories (and 1 tablespoon of vegetable oil = 120 calories!)

To Poach: Place fish in a fish poacher or in a wide shallow pan with sides. The fish is easier to handle if it is tied in a piece of cheesecloth. Cover the fish with liquid,* add seasonings, and bring to a boil over moderate heat. Reduce heat and simmer until the fish flakes easily (see Cooking Timetable). The remaining liquid is good to use as a fish stock or as a base for a sauce to serve with the fish.

To Steam: Place fish in a steaming basket or on a perforated rack that will fit inside a deep pot with a tight-fitting cover. (The rack needs to sit high enough from the bottom of the pan to allow the fish to be held above the liquid level of 1½–2 inches.) Add seasonings to the fish, if desired. Pour 1½–2 inches of water into the pot and bring to a boil. Place the basket or rack with the fish above the water level and cover the pot tightly. Steam the fish according to the Cooking Timetable until it flakes easily with a fork.

TIMETABLE FOR COOKING FISH AND SHELLFISH

Type	Amount	Baking (350°F.)	Broiling	Poaching	Steaming
FISH					
chunks	2 pounds	30–40 mins.	————	15–20 mins.	————
dressed	3 pounds	45–60 mins.	————	25–35 mins.	25–35 mins.
fillets,					
steaks	2 pounds	20–25 mins.	10–15 mins.	5–10 mins.	5–10 mins.
pan-dressed	3 pounds	25–30 mins.	10–15 mins.	8–10 mins.	8–10 mins.
CLAMS					
live	3 dozen	10–15 mins. (450°F.)	4–5 mins.	————	5–10 mins.
shucked	2 pounds	8–10 mins.	4–5 mins.	————	————
CRABS					
King	4 pounds	8–10 mins.	————	————	————
Blue	2 dozen	————	————	12–15 mins.	12–15 mins.
Dungeness	3 crabs	————	————	15–20 mins.	15–20 mins.
LOBSTERS					
live	6 pounds	20–25 mins. (400°F.)	15–20 mins.	15–20 mins.	15–20 mins.
Spiny Tails	2 pounds	20–25 mins.	10–15 mins.	10–15 mins.	10–15 mins.
OYSTERS					
live	3 dozen	10–15 mins. (450°F.)	4–5 mins.	————	————
shucked	2 pounds	8–10 mins.	4–5 mins.	————	————
SCALLOPS					
shucked	2 pounds	20–25 mins.	6–8 mins.	3–5 mins.	3–4 mins.
SHRIMP					
headless	2 pounds	20–25 mins.	8–10 mins.	3–5 mins.	3–4 mins.

Based on: The American Home Economics Association, *Handbook of Food Preparation*, 7th ed., 1975.

Baked Stuffed Fish

2 pounds whole rock cod, red snapper, or striped bass
3 ounces cooked shrimp (fresh, canned, or frozen)
6 oysters (fresh or canned), well drained
1 tablespoon fresh parsley
1 tablespoon thinly sliced yellow onion

½ teaspoon crushed dried tarragon or 1 teaspoon chopped fresh tarragon
Juice of ½ lemon
1 teaspoon salt
⅓ cup fine dry bread crumbs
2 tablespoons vegetable oil
Freshly ground pepper
Fresh lemon wedges for garnish

Preheat oven to 475°F.

Wash the cleaned, whole fish (head can be left on) in cold running water and dry well.

Mix all the remaining ingredients lightly to make a stuffing for the fish.

Lightly oil or grease a double thickness of aluminum foil large enough to completely wrap up the fish. Place foil in long, shallow casserole. Place fish in center of foil and stuff with prepared mixture. Fold the foil over the fish and seal with a lengthwise fold, being sure fish is completely sealed.

Bake fish on top shelf of oven for 40–45 minutes. Allow fish to rest 5–10 minutes in sealed foil, then place on serving platter in foil; cut away excess foil but do not remove from underneath fish. Garnish with lemon wedges and serve.

VARIATIONS: Cooked rice, bulgur wheat, or wild rice may be substituted for bread crumbs in stuffing.

Size of Serving: 6 ounces   *Number of Servings:* 4
Per Serving: Calories: 285; Protein: 35 g; Total Fat: 13 g; Sodium: 420 mg
Excellent Source of: Protein, Iron, and Riboflavin

Watercress Dressing for Fish

This is delicious with poultry and pork as well as fish.

¼ cup margarine
¾ cup finely chopped onion
¾ cup finely chopped celery
1 bunch watercress, finely chopped

Salt to taste
⅛ teaspoon freshly ground pepper
¾ cup dry whole wheat bread crumbs

Melt margarine in skillet, remove 2 tablespoons, and save. Add onion and celery to skillet; sauté until soft. Add watercress, salt, and pepper; cook until liquid has evaporated. Stir in bread crumbs and remaining melted margarine. Toss well.

Yield: 2 cups
Per ½ Cup: Calories: 150; Protein: 2 g; Total Fat: 12 g; Sodium: 345 mg
Excellent Source of: Vitamin A

Baked Fish au Naturel

Cooking this in a foil package encourages the fish and vegetable juices to be released and blend into a delicious sauce.

- 1 *cup sliced fresh mushrooms*
- 1 *medium onion, sliced*
- 4 *tablespoons chopped fresh parsley*
- 4 *tablespoons lemon juice, fresh or bottled*
- 2 *tablespoons vegetable oil*

- ½ *teaspoon dill seed*
- 1 *pound thick, white, flaky fish, such as haddock or sea bass, cut into 4 equal serving pieces*
- *Pepper to taste*
- 4 *small pieces bay leaf*
- 4 *thick slices fresh tomato*

Preheat oven to 425°F.

Mix mushrooms, onion, parsley, lemon juice, oil, and dill seed. Spread half the mixture on a sheet of foil large enough to encase the fish. Add fish; sprinkle with pepper. Place 1 piece bay leaf and tomato slice on each serving of fish. Cover each piece of fish with remaining vegetable mixture.

Cover with foil; bake about 40 minutes, or until fish flakes with fork. Remove bay leaf and serve juices as a sauce.

Size of Serving: 3¼ oz., cooked (4 oz., raw)   *Number of Servings:* 4
Per Serving: Calories: 250; Protein: 19 g; Total Fat: 13 g; Sodium: 190 mg
Excellent Source of: Protein

Marinated Salmon

- 1 *1-pound can salmon, drained*
- 1 *cup plain lowfat yogurt*
- 2 *tablespoons lemon juice*
- ¼ *cup minced red onion*

- ¼ *cup minced scallion*
- 2 *tablespoons chopped parsley*
- ¼ *teaspoon freshly ground black pepper*

Arrange chunks of salmon in serving bowl.

Mix together yogurt, lemon juice, and red onion; pour over salmon. Garnish with scallion, parsley, and pepper.

(continued)

Store in the refrigerator, covered, for several hours so flavors will blend.

Size of Serving: ¾ cup   *Number of Servings:* 4
Per Serving: Calories: 220; Protein: 29 g; Total Fat: 9 g; Sodium: 150 mg
Excellent Source of: Calcium, Thiamin, Riboflavin, and Niacin

Gudrun's Scandinavian Scrod Salad

For those who have become steadfastly limited to the ubiquitous tuna fish salad, it's time to join the northern Europeans who have long enjoyed the pleasure of a wide variety of cold fish salads.

2 cups cooked scrod or other firm-fleshed white fish with bones and skin removed
¼ cup mayonnaise (or low-calorie mayonnaise)
¼ cup plain lowfat yogurt (or more to taste)
¼–½ teaspoon curry powder (or to taste)

1 teaspoon dill weed
2 tablespoons capers (optional)
Salt to taste
Freshly ground pepper to taste
4 small red potatoes, cooked in skins and diced into ½-inch pieces
4 romaine or Boston lettuce leaves
¼–½ teaspoon paprika

Carefully separate fish into bite-size pieces (handling the fish as little and as gently as possible to maintain the integrity of the pieces and to keep the salad from being mushy).

In a separate bowl, combine the mayonnaise, yogurt, curry, dill, capers, salt, and pepper; mix well. Add potatoes and mix lightly—just enough to coat the potatoes. Add to fish and mix briefly with a rubber spatula, taking care not to mash the fish.

Serve salad on lettuce leaves; sprinkle with paprika. This is delicious served with caraway rye bread.

Size of Serving: 1 cup   *Number of Servings:* 4
Per Serving: Calories: 225; Protein: 19 g; Total Fat: 5 g; Sodium: 88 mg
Excellent Source of: Protein, Thiamin, and Vitamin C

Steamed Clams

4 dozen medium to large softshell, Littleneck, cherrystone, or razor clams

Clams that ingest large amounts of sand, such as the softshell and razor, need to purge themselves before cooking. To allow this, place them in a container of clean seawater (to cover) with 1 cup of cornmeal *or* a salt solution (⅓ cup salt to 1 gallon of water)—fresh water will not work. Allow them to "spit" sand for at least ½ hour.

Discard any clams that will not close when touched—if they stay open they are dead and not safe to eat.

Rinse clams in cold water and, if necessary scrub them under running water with a brush to remove seaweed or other clinging material. Place in a clam steamer or other deep pot that has a tightly fitted lid. Add about 1½ inches of water. Cover, steam until clam shells open (about 10–15 minutes).

Strain clam broth through cheesecloth-lined strainer. Serve this broth with the clams.

Refrigerate or freeze any leftover broth to use in fish recipes that call for clam broth.

NOTE: Steamers are usually served with melted butter to use for dunking. The butter introduces excessive calories and saturated fat to an otherwise low-calorie, low-fat food. True clam lovers can do without the butter, using the clam broth for dipping the clams before eating.

Size of Serving: 1 dozen (3 ounces without shells)   *Number of Servings:* 4
Per Serving: Calories: 95; Protein: 15 g; Total Fat: 2 g; Sodium: 215 mg
Excellent Source of: Iron

White Clam Sauce

2 pounds fresh cherrystone clams (or 2 7½-ounce cans baby clams)
2 tablespoons olive oil or other vegetable oil
1 garlic clove, sliced
¼ cup dry white wine
Salt to taste
Freshly ground pepper to taste
2 tablespoons minced fresh parsley

Scrub and wash clams thoroughly.

Put a small amount of water in a large saucepan; add clams and sauté over high heat until they open their shells. Remove them from pan and cool enough to shuck; coarsely chop clams.

Strain juices left in pan through a fine sieve or cheesecloth-lined sieve and save.

Heat oil in large skillet; add garlic and sauté until golden brown. Discard garlic. Add chopped clams, the strained clam juice, and wine; cook over medium heat for 2–3 minutes. Add salt, pepper, and parsley; simmer 3–4 minutes.

Serve with vermicelli (very thin spaghetti) or linguini.

(continued)

VARIATION: *Red Clam Sauce:* Omit the wine and add 2 cups of peeled, diced fresh plum tomatoes and the salt; cook (bubbling), uncovered, for 10–15 minutes, or until juices have reduced slightly and thickened. Add ½ teaspoon hot pepper seeds or ⅛ teaspoon crushed red pepper and the parsley. Cook for 2–3 minutes. Serve as with White Clam Sauce.

Size of Serving: 3½–4 ounces   *Number of Servings:* 4
Per Serving (White Clam Sauce): Calories: 170; Protein: 16 g; Total Fat: 9 g; Sodium: 215 mg
Excellent Source of: Protein, Calcium, Iron, and Riboflavin

Per Serving (Red Clam Sauce): Calories: 170; Protein: 16 g; Total Fat: 9 g; Sodium: 215 mg
Excellent Source of: Protein, Calcium, Iron, Riboflavin, and Vitamin C

Egg Puffs with Crab Sauce

EGG PUFFS:

> 3 *large eggs*
> 6 *tablespoons enriched all-purpose flour*
> ¾ *teaspoon baking powder*
>
> ¾ *cup shredded sharp cheddar cheese (3 ounces)*

Using an electric mixer, beat eggs until thick (about 5–7 minutes) in a medium-size bowl.

Sift together flour and baking powder; gradually add to eggs, beating only until blended. Fold in cheese.

Cook immediately after mixing: drop ¼ cup batter on oiled griddle or frying pan at 400°F. When lightly browned on the bottom, turn and cook on other side until lightly brown. *Do not overcook.*

Cook as many puffs at one time as your griddle will hold. Keep puffs warm by covering with aluminum foil on a plate. Serve with Crab Sauce.

CRAB SAUCE:

> 1½ *teaspoons sliced scallion*
> 1 *tablespoon margarine*
> 1 *tablespoon enriched all-purpose flour*
>
> ¼ *teaspoon paprika*
> ½ *teaspoon dry mustard*
> ¾ *cup skim milk*
> 3 *ounces frozen crab meat, defrosted*

Sauté scallion in margarine until tender but not brown. Stir in flour, paprika, and dry mustard. Gradually stir in milk. Cook over medium heat until thick and bubbly. Add defrosted crab meat and heat through but do not boil. Serve with Egg Puffs.

VARIATION: Swiss or cottage cheese may be used in place of cheddar. Shrimp, tuna, or lobster may be used instead of crab.

Size of Serving: 2 puffs and ¼ cup Crab Sauce   *Number of Servings:* 4
Per Serving: Calories: 265; Protein: 18 g; Total Fat: 14 g; Sodium: 540 mg
Excellent Source of: Protein, Calcium, Iron, Vitamin A, and Riboflavin

MUSSELS

To Prepare for Cooking:
Fresh mussels should be alive when they're cooked. Since live mussels keep their shells tightly closed, discard any mussels with open or cracked shells. If the shell is rigid when lightly squeezed in your hand, the mussel is alive and okay to use; if the shell moves, the mussel is probably not fresh and should be discarded.

Scrub mussels well with a stiff brush under cool running water. Remove any bits of seaweed, barnacles, or other debris, and pull off the "beard" (a threadlike seam where the mussel was attached to the rocks). Rinse mussels well.

To Steam Mussels:
Place mussels in a large pot with just enough water to cover the bottom of the pot. Cover the pot tightly and bring the water to a boil; reduce the heat and simmer for 5–6 minutes, or until the shells open wide. (If any mussels do not open their shells, be sure to discard them because this is not normal behavior for a fresh mussel; the mussel may have been dead before cooking.)

Moules the French Way

1 tablespoon margarine	1 bay leaf
3 shallots, finely chopped	⅛ teaspoon freshly ground
1 cup dry white wine	pepper
2 tablespoons chopped	4 dozen fresh mussels,
fresh parsley	cleaned
2 sprigs chopped fresh	
thyme (or ¼ teaspoon	
dried thyme)	

Melt margarine in a large saucepan; add shallots and sauté until translucent. Add wine and seasonings; simmer 10 minutes. Add mussels; steam, covered, shaking the pan often, until mussel shells open. Place in a heated serving dish.

Quickly reduce cooking liquid to half by boiling; pour over the mussels.

Size of Serving: 1 dozen (3–4 ounces, shucked)   *Number of Servings:* 4
Per Serving: Calories: 85; Protein: 9 g; Total Fat: 5 g; Sodium: 35 mg
Excellent Source of: Calcium

Marinated Mussels

2 dozen mussels, scrubbed
½ cup dry white wine
1 cup water
½ cup olive oil or other vegetable oil
3 tablespoons lime juice
¼ cup chopped fresh parsley

1 large garlic clove, crushed
2 shallots, minced
2 dashes hot pepper sauce
½ teaspoon dry mustard
Freshly ground pepper to taste
1–2 limes, sliced into wedges

Place mussels in a large pot with wine and water and bring to a boil. Lower the heat and cook, covered, about 5–6 minutes, or until mussel shells open wide.

Discard unopened mussels; place shell halves containing mussels in a single layer in a large dish.

Combine remaining ingredients in blender and whirl until well mixed; pour this over the mussels; cover. Allow mussels to marinate 2–3 hours in refrigerator; serve garnished with lime wedges.

Size of Serving: 3 mussels   *Number of Servings:* 8
Per Serving: Calories: 180; Protein: 6 g; Total Fat: 15 g; Sodium: 125 mg

Low-Cal Coquilles

1 pound shucked fresh scallops
2 tablespoons lemon juice
¼ teaspoon pepper
3–4 tablespoons bottled clam juice
3 tablespoons minced shallots (or scallions)
1 garlic clove, crushed
¼ cup minced fresh parsley

½ cup dry French vermouth
1 lemon, cut into wedges
4 large scallop shells (optional)
1 tablespoon margarine (optional)
4 teaspoons finely shredded Swiss cheese (optional)

Dry scallops; then sprinkle with lemon juice and pepper.

Heat clam juice in frying pan (a non-stick one works well for this); add scallops and cook, stirring often, for 5 minutes. Add shallots, garlic, parsley, and vermouth; toss lightly and simmer, covered, about 2–3 minutes. Uncover and boil 1–2 minutes to reduce juices slightly. Scallops may be served as is, garnished with lemon wedges, or as follows:

Coat scallop shells with 2 teaspoons of margarine and spoon scallops and sauce into them. Sprinkle each with 1 teaspoon of Swiss cheese and dot with ¼ teaspoon margarine. Place under broiler until cheese and margarine have melted and are lightly browned. Serve immediately garnished with lemon wedges.

Size of Serving: 2½–3 ounces   *Number of Servings:* 4
Per Serving: Calories: 160; Protein: 18 g; Total Fat: 4 g; Sodium: 330
Excellent Source of: Protein, Calcium, Iron; (with lemon garnish) Vitamin C

Bouillabaisse

While some purists may claim that true bouillabaisse cannot be properly constructed without twelve special types of fish native only to the Mediterranean, the fact is that any available fresh fish and shellfish can be combined to produce a spectacular local version. Here is a delicious example which, like most bouillabaisse recipes, is low in calories for such elegant fare due to the low fat content of the fish and shellfish.

1½ tablespoons vegetable oil
1 medium onion, chopped
1 garlic clove, crushed
½ teaspoon fennel seeds (optional)
1 cup chopped celery
1 bay leaf
2 16-ounce cans stewed tomatoes (or 2 pounds fresh tomatoes, peeled and chopped)
1 cup dry white wine
3 cups fish stock (or bottled clam broth or defatted chicken stock —see Index)

¼ teaspoon crushed thyme or basil
Pepper to taste
1 pound cod or other firm-fleshed fish
½ pound Alaskan King crab legs (optional)
½ pound shucked scallops
1 dozen clams, in shell (optional)
1 dozen mussels, in shell (optional)
½ pound fresh or frozen shrimp, skinned and deveined
½ cup chopped fresh parsley

Heat oil in a large, heavy pot. Add onion, garlic, fennel, and celery; sauté until slightly soft. Add bay leaf, tomatoes, wine, stock, thyme, and pepper; simmer, covered, 30 minutes. Add the cod and crab; simmer 10 minutes. Add scallops, clams, mussels, and shrimp, in that order; cook just until

(continued)

the shrimp redden and the clams and mussels open—avoid overcooking.

Serve sprinkled with chopped parsley and accompanied by crusty, chewy hot bread.

Size of Serving: about 2½ cups (including 3½ ounces seafood)   *Number of Servings:* 8
Per Serving: Calories: 250 (325 with optional ingredients added); Protein: 33 g (45 with optional ingredients); Total Fat: 7 g (8 with optional ingredients); Sodium: 380 mg (620 with optional ingredients)
Excellent Source of: Protein, Calcium, Iron, Vitamin A, Thiamin, and Vitamin C

Spanish Shrimp Rice Salad

2½ cups defatted chicken stock (see Index or use canned)

½ teaspoon crushed saffron

¾ cup uncooked brown rice

1 tablespoon chopped fresh tarragon or ½ teaspoon crushed dried tarragon

⅓ cup cider or wine vinegar

¼ teaspoon dry mustard

¼ teaspoon garlic salt

1½ cups cooked, shelled, and deveined shrimp

½ cup cooked green peas

¼ cup thinly sliced scallion

⅓ cup finely diced celery

¼ cup finely diced sweet red pepper

¼ cup vegetable oil

8 leaves flat escarole, Swiss chard, romaine, or other crisp leafy green

1–2 ripe tomatoes, quartered

4–8 Spanish olives (optional, particularly for those watching their weight)

Bring chicken stock to a boil in medium-size saucepan. Remove ½ cup of the hot stock and dissolve the saffron in it; pour it into the rest of the stock.

While stock is still boiling, stir in the rice and mix well. Reduce heat and simmer, covered, about 40–50 minutes, or until rice is tender and all liquid has been absorbed. Put rice in a large bowl to cool.

Combine tarragon, vinegar, mustard, and garlic salt; mix well and pour over rice; toss lightly. Add shrimp, peas, scallion, celery, sweet red pepper, and oil; toss lightly to coat shrimp and vegetables with the dressing.

Cover and refrigerate 2–3 hours before serving to allow flavors to blend. Remove from refrigerator 20 minutes before serving. Serve on escarole or other greens garnished with tomato wedges and olives, if desired.
NOTE: This dish may also be served hot.

Size of Serving: 1–1¼ cups   *Number of Servings:* 4
Per Serving: Calories: 270; Protein: 16 g; Total Fat: 15 g; Sodium: 230 mg
Excellent Source of: Protein, Calcium, Iron, and Vitamin C

Quick Crab Quiche

1 9-inch whole wheat or rye pie crust or Low-Cal Crust for Quiche (see Index)

2 tablespoons vegetable oil

2 tablespoons margarine

1 medium onion, finely chopped

1 cup sliced raw zucchini (cut slices in half if zucchini is large)

1 cup sliced raw mushrooms

1 cup cooked crab meat or shrimp (with all cartilage or shells removed)

4 large eggs

1 cup plain lowfat yogurt

1½ cups shredded Swiss cheese (about 4 ounces)

½ teaspoon salt

⅛ teaspoon pepper

Prepare pie crust.

Preheat oven to 400°F.

Heat the oil in a large skillet; add the margarine and melt. Add the onion and zucchini; sauté about 5–6 minutes, or until zucchini is slightly soft. Add mushrooms; sauté over moderate heat, stirring, for about 5 minutes. Add crab meat or shrimp and simmer until most of the liquid has evaporated. (If there is a great amount of liquid, drain off some of it.)

Place sautéed ingredients in bottom of pie shell, spreading them out evenly to cover the bottom.

Beat together the eggs and yogurt; add the cheese, salt, and pepper; mix well. Pour over the sautéed vegetables; mix slightly.

Place pie on a piece of foil (to catch any overflow) in the oven and bake for about 45 minutes, or until a knife inserted in the center comes out clean. Remove pie from oven and let it sit for 5–10 minutes before cutting.

NOTE: The amounts of zucchini, mushrooms, and seafood can be altered— any combination will work, just as long as you use 3 cups total.

Number of Servings: 6   *Size of Serving:* one-sixth of 9-inch pie
Per Serving (with Whole Wheat Crust): Calories: 360 (295 with Low-Cal Crust for Quiche); Protein: 18 g; Total Fat: 25 g; Sodium: 520 mg
Excellent Source of: Protein, Calcium, Iron, Vitamin A, and Thiamin

Marinated Squid Salad

2 cups thinly sliced,
cleaned, and cooked
squid (sliced about ½
inch wide)

½ cup diced sweet red
pepper

½ cup thin green pepper
strips

½ cup thinly sliced celery

¼ cup finely diced carrot

¼ cup thinly sliced
scallion

2 tablespoons minced
fresh parsley

2 teaspoons dill seed

¼ teaspoon freshly ground
pepper

¼ cup Low-Calorie
Vinaigrette (see Index)

Combine all ingredients thoroughly; cover and chill in refrigerator for
4–5 hours before serving.

This also works well as an appetizer (serve it with toothpicks).

Size of Serving: 1 cup   *Number of Servings:* 4
Per Serving: Calories: 190; Protein: 9 g; Total Fat: 15 g; Sodium: 45 mg
Excellent Source of: Vitamin A and Vitamin C

MEATS

Many of us have grown up with a respect for meat second to no other food. This is due in part to its number-one place at the supermarket and on the dinner table. Many restaurants have earned their reputations based on the size of their steaks and thickness of their roast beef—a serving of which is often large enough to feed an entire family of four! While it's true that meat has rightfully earned respect because it is an excellent source of high-quality protein, vitamins, and minerals (particularly iron), most of us could decrease our meat consumption considerably and still get more than enough to help meet our nutritional needs. And with inflation affecting the price of meats and the knowledge that excess meat consumption may negatively affect our health (as described in Part I), people are becoming more concerned with the need to cut down on meat.

Since most meats (especially pork, beef, and lamb) are high in calories, saturated fats, and cholesterol, it is recommended that their use be limited not only by switching to fish, shellfish, poultry, and veal (which is from young animals and is lower in fat), but also by eating *much* smaller portions of all of these foods. We can fill the empty space on our plates with more grains and vegetables. Also, in place of meats, fish, and poultry, we can substitute more of the non-meat protein sources, such as legumes, lowfat cheeses, milk, and yogurt.

With over 300 cuts of meat available, the meat counter becomes a confusing place for most shoppers. So it's certainly worth spending some time to become well versed in the different cuts of meat—particularly the less expensive cuts—and how they are best prepared.

Generally, the more tender cuts of meat come from the least exercised parts of the animal (such as the loin, sirloin, and rib areas). These are also the most heavily marbled cuts of meat, meaning that they have a greater amount of fat interspersed throughout the lean part of the meat. Marbling increases the flavor, tenderness, and juiciness of the meat—as well as the cholesterol and calories from fat, and this is mainly *saturated* fat. The only advantage with tender cuts of meat is that they usually will be tender no matter how they are cooked; and they are best cooked in dry heat (by roasting or broiling) since the marbling creates sufficient moisture to prevent them from drying out. So it doesn't make sense to pay premium prices for all that extra fat if the recipe calls for moist cooking and a less tender, less expensive cut will do perfectly well.

Fortunately, meat doesn't have to be heavily marbled to taste good. The less tender cuts of meat from the chuck (arm, blade, and shoulder cuts), shank, brisket, round, and flank areas can be prepared so that they often end up tasting more delicious than the higher-priced cuts. Less tender meats are most successfully prepared by tenderizing them to break down their muscular structure. This is best done by either cooking them slowly in liquid, as with braising (good for steaks and chops), stewing (for smaller pieces of meat), and pot roasting (best for larger cuts of meat); *or* by marinating the meat in an acidic liquid (such as wine or lemon, orange, or tomato juice) with seasonings (herbs, garlic, and onion) for several hours before cooking. This makes them not only more tender, but juicier and more flavorful as well. Marinating is particularly good for broiled steaks and chops or small pieces of meat to be cooked on skewers, but it can also be used to increase the tenderness and flavor of braised meats and pot roasts.

MEAT STORAGE

Meat should be stored in the coldest part of the refrigerator or in the freezer as soon as possible after shopping. If meat is to be kept longer than a few days, it should be frozen. If necessary, wipe the meat with a damp cloth before storing it—but never wash meat because too much moisture will increase the chance of bacterial growth. If the meat has not been prepackaged, wrap it loosely in aluminum foil or waxed paper to prevent it from drying out. Packaged meat can be stored in its own wrapper. Meat that is to be frozen is best divided into small quantities that can be used easily and then wrapped in moistureproof paper to keep air out and prevent freezer burn. Aluminum foil, plastic wrap, tightly sealed plastic bags, or freezer paper are all good to use as freezer wrappings. If you freeze a lot of meat, be sure to label it with the date and weight for future reference. Use meats within the storage times recommended below. All meats should be thawed in the refrigerator to prevent bacterial contamination.

Meat	Refrigerator Storage Time (36° to 40°F.)	Freezer Storage Time (0°F. or lower)
Beef, fresh	2 to 3 days	6 to 12 months
Veal, fresh	2 to 3 days	6 to 9 months
Pork, fresh	2 to 3 days	3 to 6 months
Lamb, fresh	2 to 3 days	6 to 9 months
Ground beef, veal, lamb	1 to 2 days	3 to 4 months
Ground pork	1 to 2 days	2 to 3 months
Variety meats	1 to 2 days	3 to 4 months
Sausage, fresh pork	1 week	2 months
Smoked ham	1 week	2 months
Ham slices	3 to 4 days	2 months
Leftover cooked meat	4 to 5 days	2 to 3 months

MEAT CUTS CHART

BEEF—Recommended Cooking Methods

ROUND CUTS:
1. Standing Rump Roast (braise; cook in liquid)
2. Round Steak (braise; cook in liquid; pan-fry)
3. Sirloin Tip Roast or Steak (braise; cook in liquid; roast)
4. Top Round Steak (braise; cook in liquid; broil; pan-broil; pan-fry)
5. Top Round Roast (roast)
6. Bottom Round Steak or Roast (braise; cook in liquid)
7. Eye of Round Roast (braise; cook in liquid; roast)
8. Eye of Round Steak (braise; cook in liquid; pan-broil; pan-fry)
9. Heel of Round Roast (braise; cook in liquid)
10. Ground Beef (broil; pan-fry; pan-broil; bake)

SIRLOIN CUTS: (broil; pan-broil; pan-fry)

LOIN CUTS:
1. All Steaks (broil; pan-broil; pan-fry; roast)
2. Tenderloin (Filet Mignon) Roast (broil; roast; pan-broil; pan-fry)

RIB CUTS:
1. Standing Rib Roast (roast)
2. Rib Steaks (broil; pan-broil; pan-fry)

CHUCK CUTS: (braise; cook in liquid)

FORE SHANK:
1. Shank Cross Cuts (braise; cook in liquid)
2. Beef for Stew (braise; cook in liquid)

BRISKET (fresh or corned): (braise; cook in liquid)

SHORT PLATE: (braise; cook in liquid)

FLANK: (braise; cook in liquid)

LAMB—Recommended Cooking Methods

LEG CUTS:
1. Leg (roast)
2. Leg Chop or Steak (broil; pan-broil; pan-fry)

SIRLOIN CUTS:
1. Sirloin Roast (roast)
2. Sirloin Chop (broil; pan-broil; pan-fry)

LOIN CUTS:
1. Loin Roast (roast)
2. Loin Chops (broil; pan-broil; pan-fry)

RIB CUTS (HOTEL RACK):
1. Rib Roasts (roast)
2. Rib Chops (broil; pan-broil; pan-fry; roast)

CHUCK CUTS (SHOULDER):
1. Square Shoulder (roast)
2. Arm or Blade Chops (broil; pan-broil; pan-fry)
3. Neck Slices (braise)
4. Cubes for Kabobs—may be made from other cuts also (broil)

FORE SHANK: (braise; cook in liquid)

BREAST: (roast; braise)

FLANK:
1. Ground Lamb—may come from any cut (bake; broil; pan-broil; pan-fry)
2. Lamb for Stew—may come from any cut (braise; cook in liquid)

HIND SHANK: (braise; cook in liquid)

PORK—Recommended Cooking Methods

LEG (HAM) CUTS:
1. Ham Butt Portion (roast; cook in liquid)
2. Ham Shank Portion (roast; cook in liquid)
3. Smoked Ham, Center Slice (broil; pan-broil; pan-fry)
4. Rolled Leg—Fresh Ham (roast)

LOIN CUTS:
1. Loin and Sirloin Roasts (roast)
2. Blade, Rib, Loin, and Sirloin Chops (braise; broil; pan-broil; pan-fry)
3. Tenderloin (roast; braise; pan-fry)

BOSTON BUTT (BOSTON SHOULDER) CUTS:
1. Boston Butt (Blade Boston) Roasts (roast)
2. Blade Steak (braise; pan-fry)
3. Pork Cubes (broil; braise; cook in liquid)

PICNIC SHOULDER CUTS:
1. Fresh Arm Picnic (roast)
2. Smoked Arm Picnic (roast; cook in liquid)
3. Arm Roast (roast)
4. Arm Steak (braise; pan-fry)
5. Fresh or Smoked Hock (braise; cook in liquid)
6. Ground Pork—may also be made from Boston Shoulder, Loin, or Leg (bake; pan-broil; pan-fry)

VEAL Recommended Cooking Methods

ROUND (LEG) CUTS:
1. Rump and Round Roasts (roast; braise)
2. Round Steak (braise; pan-fry)
3. Cutlets (braise; pan-fry)

SIRLOIN (LEG) CUTS:
1. Sirloin Roast (roast)
2. Sirloin Chop (braise; pan-fry)
3. Cube Steak—can be made from any thick, solid veal cut (braise; pan-fry)

LOIN CUTS:
1. Loin Roast (roast)
2. Loin and Kidney Chops (braise; pan-fry)

RIB CUTS:
1. Rib Roast (roast)
2. Rib Chops (braise; pan-fry)

SHOULDER CUTS:
1. Arm, Blade, and Shoulder Roasts (roast; braise)
2. Arm and Blade Steaks (braise; pan-fry)
3. Veal for Stew—may be made from any cut (braise; cook in liquid)

SHANK CUTS: (braise; cook in liquid)

BREAST CUTS:
1. Breast (roast; braise)
2. Riblets (braise; cook in liquid)

VARIETY MEATS

Brains, heart, kidney, liver, sweetbreads, tongue, and tripe are often lower in cost because so few people know what to do with them. They are all exceptionally high in nutrients. Liver is the real star with its valuable supply of iron, phosphorus, riboflavin, niacin, pantothenic acid, biotin, folacin, vitamin B-12, vitamin A and, of course, protein. The size of variety meats varies depending on which animal they come from—the largest come from cattle, medium-size ones from pigs and calves, and the smallest from lamb.

Variety Meats	*Recommended Cooking Method*
BRAINS	Precook in water with a little lemon juice or vinegar to keep them white and firm; then pan-fry.
HEART—beef, pork, lamb, or veal	Slow cook in moisture.
KIDNEYS	
beef	Cook with moist heat.
pork, lamb or veal	Broil or pan-fry.
LIVER	
beef, pork, lamb, or veal	Cook with moist heat. Broil or pan-fry.
SWEETBREADS—thymus gland from calf or lamb	Precook in water with a little lemon juice or vinegar to keep them white and firm; then pan-fry.
TONGUE—fresh, pickled, smoked, or corned from beef, veal, pork or lamb	Cook slowly in liquid.
TRIPE—stomach lining of cattle; may be fresh, pickled, or canned	Cook in liquid (usually partially cooked when purchased).

HOW TO COOK MEAT

Roasting: Roasting is one of the dry-heat cooking methods. Generally, this method is used for larger, tender cuts of meat.

1. Preheat oven to 300–325°F. (check Timetable for Roasting Meat).
2. Rub seasonings into the meat, if desired.
3. Place meat on rack in shallow roasting pan with fat side up. *Do not* add water to the pan and *do not* cover the pan because this will steam the meat, and roasting requires dry heat.
4. About ½ hour before the meat is scheduled to come out of the oven, insert a meat thermometer into the thickest part of the meat. (It should not touch the bone.) This will give the internal temperature of the meat—check the Timetable for the temperature correlating with the

degree of doneness (rare, medium or well done) desired. Remove the
meat from the oven when it is 5 degrees below the desired internal
temperature; is will continue to cook for a short time outside the oven.

5. Roasts should set for 15 minutes after they come out of the oven
   so they will be easier to carve.

Broiling: Broiling is another dry-heat cooking method that is best for
tender steaks, chops, and ground meat patties.

1. Preheat the broiler; trim meat of all excess (visible) fat.
2. Place meat on broiler rack about 2–4 inches from the heat, depending
   on the thickness of the meat.
3. Broil until the top of the meat is browned; then season that side, if
   desired.
4. Turn meat over, brown other side, and season.

Pan-broiling: Tender meats that are 1 inch thick or less are suitable for
pan-broiling. Generally, this applies to steaks and chops.

1. Cook meat in a heavy skillet.
2. *Do not* add water or cover the pan since this is a dry-heat method of
   cooking. There should be enough fat in the meat to prevent sticking.
3. Cook slowly using moderate heat and turning the meat to brown it
   evenly on each side. Pour off the fat as it accumulates.
4. Season the meat after it is cooked.

Pan-frying and Stir-frying: Meats can be pan-fried in a small amount of
oil or margarine (sautéed) or stir-fried either without fat or with a very
small amount of oil or margarine. (The quick, continual stirring action
during stir-frying helps to keep the meat from sticking.) Deep-fat frying
is not recommended because of the large number of calories from fat
that are introduced.

To Pan-fry or Sauté

1. Use thin pieces of tender meat; add a small amount of oil or margarine
   to the pan (this is particularly necessary if the meat has been breaded).
   If the meat has sufficient natural fat, do not add fat but allow a small
   amount of the fat from the meat to accumulate in the pan.
2. *Do not* cover the pan during cooking because this will prevent the
   meat from being crisp.
3. Cook over moderate heat. Turn the meat occasionally so that it will
   brown and cook evenly.
4. Season the meat *after* it has been browned.
5. Remove the meat with a slotted utensil to allow excess fat to drain off.

To Stir-fry

1. Put a small amount of oil in a wok or skillet with high sides and place over high heat. (Or try using no fat, particularly if the pan has been seasoned or has a no-stick coating.)
2. Add meat that has been cut into small pieces of uniform size.
3. When oil is hot (but not smoking), add the meat and stir it constantly while it cooks. Cooking generally takes only 3–5 minutes, depending on the thickness of the meat and the quantity being cooked.

Braising: This is a good way to cook less tender cuts of meat. Slow cooking in moisture helps to tenderize the meat and add flavor.

1. Add a small amount of oil or margarine to a heavy skillet or Dutch oven (fat does not need to be added if the meat has enough of its own) and place over moderately low heat on top of the stove.
2. Add the meat and brown slowly on all sides.
3. Remove the meat from the pan; pour off the fat; return the meat to the pan.
4. Add a small amount of liquid to the pan, such as defatted stock (see Index or use canned), vegetable juice, wine or water, and seasonings.
5. Cover tightly and cook over low heat or in 300–325°F. oven until meat is tender. (See cooking timetable.) If vegetables are to be added, follow the timetable on the Vegetable Chart for individual vegetables (see Index).

Cooking in Liquid: Large cuts of less tender meats can be cooked whole in liquid or cut up in stews.

Large whole cuts
1. Add a small amount of oil to a Dutch oven or other large, heavy pan (oil is not necessary if the meat has enough fat of its own).
2. Brown the meat on all sides (do not brown cured meats).
3. Drain off all the fat, season the meat, and cover the meat with liquid. Cut-up vegetables may be added for extra flavor.
4. Cover the pan and simmer until the meat is tender. Add more liquid during cooking if necessary. Cook vegetables according to their individual timetables on the Vegetable Chart (see Index).
5. If the meat needs to be cooled before serving, it's best to let it cool in the cooking liquid so that the meat will be moist; this will also reduce the amount of shrinkage.

Stews
1. Trim all fat off the meat and cut into 1½-inch cubes or strips.
2. Brown the meat evenly in a heavy Dutch oven or other large, heavy

pan (use a small amount of oil if necessary to prevent sticking); drain off all excess fat after the meat is browned.

3. Add seasonings and enough liquid to cover the meat.
4. Cover the pan and simmer the meat until it is fork-tender; add more liquid, if necessary. (This will take about 1½ hours.)
5. Add vegetables during the latter part of cooking time and cook according to their individual timetables on the Vegetable Chart (see Index) so they won't be overcooked.
6. If desired, thicken the stew after it is cooked by puréeing 1–2 cups of the vegetables with some of the cooking liquid in a blender, then mix this into the stew.

TIMETABLE FOR ROASTING MEAT

Cut of Meat	Ready-to-Cook Weight	Approximate Roasting Time at 325°F.	To Reach Internal Temp. of
BEEF:			
rib roasts	4 to 6 lb	2 to 2½ hrs	140°F. (rare)
		2½ to 3½ hrs	160°F. (medium)
		2¾ to 4 hrs	170°F. (well done)
steaks (1½ inches thick)	2 lb	1 to 1¼ hrs	140°F. (rare)
		1½ hrs	160°F. (medium)
		1½ to 2 hrs	170°F. (well done)
LAMB:			
chops		½ hr	180°F. (well done)
roasts	3 to 5 lb	2 to 3 hrs	150°F. (medium)
		2¼ to 3¼ hrs	180°F. (well done)
PORK:			
chops		¾ to 1 hr	
loin roasts	4 to 6 lb	2¼ to 3½ hrs	170°F. (well done)
		3½ to 4 hrs	185°F. (well done)
VEAL:			
chops		1 hr	170°F. (well done)
roasts	3 to 5 lb	2 to 3 hrs	170°F. (well done)

TIMETABLE FOR BROILING MEAT

Cut of Meat	Total Cooking Time*
Beef:	
ground patties	8 to 15 minutes
steaks (1 inch thick)	10 to 25 minutes
Kabobs (beef or lamb)	20 minutes
Lamb chops (¾ to 1 inch thick)	12 to 18 minutes
Liver (½ inch thick)	12 minutes
Pork chops (¾ to 1 inch thick)	20 to 25 minutes

* Broil for about half the time indicated in timetable; turn meat and broil for remainder of time.

Timetable based on: The American Home Economics Association, *Handbook of Food Preparation,* 7th ed., 1975.

Oven Pot Roast

3 pounds boneless chuck roast
1 cup dry red wine
1 garlic clove, crushed
½ teaspoon salt
¼ teaspoon pepper
3 whole cloves
½ teaspoon ground allspice
1–2 tablespoons vegetable oil
1 cup vegetable stock (see Index) or water
1 Bouquet Garni (see Index)
4 stalks celery, sliced
1 large onion, sliced
8 carrots

Prick the roast all over with a fork. Combine the wine, garlic, salt, pepper, cloves, and allspice; pour over the meat and let it marinate 20–30 minutes.

Preheat oven to 325°F.

Heat oil in a large, heavy pot and brown roast on all sides; drain off excess oil. Add marinade to roast along with stock, Bouquet Garni, celery, onion, and carrots. Cook, covered, in oven for 2½–3 hours (3½–4 hours if meat is frozen).

NOTE: Pot roast can also be cooked on top of the stove, if desired.

Size of Serving: about 4 ounces *Number of Servings:* 8
Per Serving: Calories: 410; Protein: 32 g; Total Fat: 24 g; Sodium: 250 mg
Excellent Source of: Protein, Iron, Vitamin A, Thiamin, Riboflavin, and Niacin

Meat Loaf Pot Roast

This meat loaf is unique because it is cooked on top of the stove rather than baked in the oven.

1½ pounds lean ground beef
½ cup dry whole wheat bread crumbs
½ cup water
1 egg
¼ teaspoon salt
¼ teaspoon pepper
1–2 tablespoons chopped onion
1 teaspoon Worcestershire sauce
1 teaspoon dry mustard
1 cup vegetable stock (see Index) or water
3 cups cut-up raw vegetables in season, such as potatoes, rutabagas, carrots, onions, turnips, green beans, celery, and parsnips

Mix together thoroughly the ground beef, dry bread crumbs, ½ cup water, egg, salt, pepper, onion, Worcestershire sauce, and dry mustard. Shape the mixture into one big loaf. Brown loaf on all sides in a Dutch oven or heavy pan with a lid.

Add stock and vegetables. Simmer, covered, 45 minutes to 1 hour, or until meat is done and vegetables are tender.

Make gravy from rich pot juice, if desired, by puréeing ½ cup of the vegetables and ½ cup liquid in a blender and stirring sauce into the rest of the vegetables.

Size of Serving: 4 ounces   *Number of Servings:* 6
Per Serving: Calories: 280; Protein: 27 g; Total Fat: 13 g; Sodium: 280 mg
Excellent Source of: Protein, Iron, Vitamin A, Thiamin, Riboflavin, Niacin, and Vitamin C

Kim's Zucchini Meat Loaf

2 tablespoons vegetable oil
2 small zucchini, chopped or grated
2 medium onions, chopped
3 medium fresh tomatoes, chopped (or 4 small)
¼ cup skim milk
2 slices whole wheat bread, finely crumbled
2 eggs, slightly beaten
2 garlic cloves, crushed
1 tablespoon Worcestershire sauce
¼ teaspoon salt
½ teaspoon pepper
¼ pound lean ground beef
1 pound lean ground pork

(continued)

Preheat oven to 325°F.

Heat oil in large pan or skillet. Add zucchini and onions and sauté until onions are translucent. Add tomatoes and simmer slightly.

Heat milk to lukewarm in a separate pan. Add bread, eggs, garlic, Worcestershire sauce, salt, and pepper.

Combine all ingredients, including the ground meat, in a large bowl; mix together well. Pack into a loaf pan or shape into a loaf and place in an ungreased baking dish. Bake 1 hour. For easier slicing, cool 10 minutes before serving.

Size of Serving: 3½ ounces   *Number of Servings:* 6
Per Serving: Calories: 255; Protein: 23 g; Total Fat: 15 g; Sodium: 170 mg
Excellent Source of: Protein, Iron, Thiamin, Riboflavin, and Vitamin C

Spinach Meatballs

1 pound lean ground beef	¼ cup whole wheat
¼ cup minced onion	bread crumbs
1 garlic clove, crushed	1 egg, slightly beaten
¼ teaspoon thyme	1 cup tomato sauce (see
¾ 10-ounce package	Index or use canned)
frozen chopped spinach,	1½ cups water
thawed	½ teaspoon dry oregano
	½ teaspoon dry basil

Combine beef, onion, garlic, thyme, spinach, and bread crumbs. Add egg and mix well. Shape into balls, using about a tablespoonful of the mixture for each ball. Broil, until brown, turning once.

Combine tomato sauce, water, oregano, and basil in medium-size saucepan. Heat to boiling. Add broiled meatballs to sauce, lower heat, cover, and simmer 30 minutes. Skim off any fat that rises to the top. Cool slightly and serve.

Size of Serving: 1 cup meat and sauce   *Number of Servings:* 4
Per Serving: Calories: 270; Protein: 28 g; Total Fat: 13 g: Sodium: 375 mg
Excellent Source of: Protein, Iron, Vitamin A, Thiamin, Riboflavin, Niacin, and Vitamin C

Stir-Fry Beef with Kiwi

2 tablespoons soy sauce
2 tablespoons dry sherry
1 garlic clove, crushed
1 teaspoon sugar
½ teaspoon ground ginger
1 pound flank or round
  steak, thinly and
  diagonally sliced
¼ cup vegetable oil
1 sweet red pepper, cut
  into strips

1 6-ounce can water
  chestnuts, drained and
  sliced
1 cup cold vegetable stock
  (see Index) or water
2 tablespoons cornstarch
1 scallion, chopped
2 ripe kiwifruit, peeled and
  sliced, or 1½ cups
  chopped honeydew
  melon

In bowl, stir together soy sauce, sherry, garlic, sugar, and ginger. Add beef; cover and marinate at least 1 hour.

In large skillet or wok, heat oil. Add beef, reserving marinade, and stir-fry 2 minutes, or until browned. Add red pepper and water chestnuts and stir-fry for 2 minutes.

Combine cold stock or water with cornstarch and marinade; add to skillet. Stirring constantly, bring to a boil over medium heat and boil 1 minute. Stir in scallions and kiwifruit or honeydew melon.

Size of Serving: about 1 cup   *Number of Servings:* 4
Per Serving: Calories: 445; Protein: 25 g; Total Fat: 28 g; Sodium: 750 mg
Excellent Source of: Protein, Iron, Thiamin, Riboflavin, Niacin, and Vitamin C

Stir-Fried Beef with Peas and Cashew Nuts

¼ pound flank steak or
  round steak, cut into
  small pieces
1 garlic clove, crushed
1 teaspoon soy sauce
1 tablespoon cornstarch
2 tablespoons water
6 tablespoons vegetable
  oil

1 10-ounce package
  frozen peas, thawed
¼ cup water
2 tablespoons oyster
  sauce
1 cup roasted cashew nuts
  (about 3½ ounces)
Salt to taste

Place meat and garlic in small bowl; mix in soy sauce, cover and set aside.

Mix the cornstarch and 2 tablespoons water in a small bowl; set aside.

Heat large skillet or wok; add ¼ cup oil and heat until it just begins to smoke. Add meat; stir-fry until the pink coloring is gone. Remove meat from skillet and drain on paper towels.

(continued)

Add more oil to pan to make 2 tablespoons. Stir-fry peas for about 1 minute; add ¼ cup water; cover and cook for 1 minute.

Return meat to skillet; mix well. Re-stir cornstarch mixture and add along with oyster sauce. Stir over medium heat until thickened; shut off heat. Mix in cashew nuts and salt to taste, if necessary. Remove to a warm platter and serve hot.

NOTE: A wok is preferable because its shape makes it easy to stir-fry. Either the skillet or wok should be constructed from metals that conduct heat evenly and quickly.

Peanut oil is preferred because of its higher smoke-point and bland flavor.

Oyster sauce may be found in any Oriental grocery store.

VARIATIONS:
· Substitute ½ whole chicken breast, skinned, for steak.
· Substitute walnuts or roasted almonds for cashew nuts.

Size of Serving: ¾ cup   *Number of Servings:* 4
Per Serving: Calories: 500; Protein: 16 g; Total Fat: 40 g; Sodium: 560 mg
Excellent Source of: Protein, Iron, Thiamin, and Riboflavin

Speedy Supper Pie

1 *pound lean ground beef*	½ *teaspoon salt*
2 *tablespoons chopped onion*	*Pinch marjoram*
	Pinch sage
¼ *teaspoon salt*	*Pinch oregano*
½ *teaspoon chili powder*	2 *tablespoons nonfat dry milk*
½ *cup tomato sauce*	
1 *cup enriched all-purpose flour*	1 *egg*
	⅓ *cup hot tap water*
1 *package active dry yeast*	1 *tablespoon vegetable oil*
1 *tablespoon sugar*	

Fry ground beef in non-stick frying pan until lightly browned; drain off accumulated fat. Add chopped onion, salt, chili powder, and tomato sauce; simmer 5 minutes.

While meat is simmering, prepare dough: mix flour, yeast, sugar, salt, herbs, and dry milk and stir until blended. Beat egg and add water and oil. Add to dry ingredients and mix well.

Spread beef mixture in a 9-inch square pan and spread dough over the top. Let it rise for 30 minutes in a warm place.

Preheat oven to 350°F.

Bake for 25–30 minutes. Cut into 6 squares and invert to serve.

Size of Serving: 1 square (approximately 1 cup)   *Number of Servings:* 6
Per Serving: Calories: 280; Protein: 21 g; Total Fat: 11 g; Sodium: 400 mg
Excellent Source of: Protein, Iron, Thiamin, Riboflavin, and Niacin

Fresh Oven Stew

1½ pounds beef stew meat, cut into 2-inch cubes
¼ teaspoon salt
⅛ teaspoon pepper
1 small garlic clove, crushed
4 small onions
½ teaspoon crushed dried thyme
1 bay leaf
¼ cup chopped fresh parsley
1¼ cups vegetable stock (see Index) or water
2 whole cloves (3 cloves if a spicier dish is desired)
4 carrots, peeled and cut into 2-inch pieces
3 medium potatoes, washed and cut into 2-inch pieces
1½ cups rutabaga or turnip, peeled and cut into 2-inch pieces
¼ pound fresh mushrooms, cut in half
1½ teaspoons cornstarch

Preheat oven to 500°F.

Place meat cubes in a layer in a large Dutch oven or heavy flameproof casserole. Sprinkle with salt and pepper, add garlic. Chop 2 onions, add to beef, and mix well; cover.

Bake for 20 minutes. Remove from oven. Stir in thyme, bay leaf, parsley, and add stock or water.

Reduce oven temperature to 350°F. Bake casserole, covered, 40 minutes more.

Stick cloves into the two remaining whole onions and add both onions to stew with carrots, potatoes, and rutabaga. Bake, covered, 45 minutes. Add mushrooms and bake 10 minutes longer.

Remove from oven, mix cornstarch with a little cold water (just enough to dissolve it), and stir into liquid. Simmer 2–3 minutes on top of range, or until gravy thickens slightly, adding more cornstarch if necessary.

NOTE: For even cooking, cut carrots, potatoes, and rutabaga into uniform-size pieces.

Size of Serving: 1½ cups   *Number of Servings:* 6
Per Serving: Calories: 395; Protein: 24 g; Total Fat: 23 g; Sodium: 195 mg
Excellent Source of: Protein, Calcium, Iron, Vitamin A, Thiamin, Riboflavin, Niacin, and Vitamin C

Texas Chili

This is delicious served with hot cornbread or tortilla chips.

1 pound lean ground beef
1 large onion, finely chopped
1 sweet red pepper (or green pepper), finely chopped
2 large garlic cloves, crushed
2 tablespoons chili powder (or more to taste)
1 teaspoon ground cumin (or more to taste)
⅛ teaspoon freshly ground pepper
Pinch cayenne
2 1-pound cans red kidney beans, including liquid (or prepare from dried kidney beans—see Index)
1 1-pound can tomatoes plus half the liquid (save the rest)
Salt to taste
1 cup shredded romaine lettuce
1 cup shredded Jack cheese
1 cup chopped onion

Sauté the beef, onion, and red pepper in a non-stick frying pan (or use 1 tablespoon oil in a regular frying pan) until the meat is browned and the onion soft. Drain off excess fat.

Add the garlic, chili, cumin, pepper, and cayenne; sauté over low heat 2 minutes. Add the kidney beans, tomatoes, and salt, mashing the tomatoes into small pieces with a spoon. Bring to a boil, then reduce heat and simmer, *uncovered* (to prevent it from getting too soupy), 30 minutes. (Add reserved tomato liquid if the chili gets too thick.)

Serve chili in bowls and shredded lettuce, cheese, and chopped onion in small serving bowls on the side to be added to the chili, if desired, at the table.

Size of Serving: 1 cup   *Number of Servings:* 8
Per Serving: Calories: 285; Protein: 23 g; Total Fat: 10 g; Sodium: 600 mg (230 with cooked, dried beans)
Excellent Source of: Protein, Calcium, Iron, Vitamin A, Thiamin, Riboflavin, and Vitamin C

Broiled Avocados with Chili

2 ripe avocados, halved, peeled, and seeded
Lemon juice
1 15-ounce can chili with beans or 2 cups homemade chili
2 fresh tomatoes, chopped
4 ounces Jack cheese, shredded

Prepare avocados according to directions in Vegetable Chart, page 67. Sprinkle lemon juice on avocados to prevent discoloration.

Meanwhile, heat chili thoroughly. Add tomatoes. Spoon mixture into avocados and top each half with shredded cheese. Place under broiler briefly until cheese melts.

Size of Serving: ½ avocado stuffed with ½ cup chili mixture *Number of Servings:* 4
Per Serving: Calories: 450; Protein: 17 g; Total Fat: 35 g; Sodium: 750 mg
Excellent Source of: Protein, Calcium, Iron, Vitamin A, Thiamin, Riboflavin, Niacin, and Vitamin C

Cowboy Steak with Lima Beans

1 pound dried lima beans	1 large onion, sliced
6 cups water	1 18-ounce can tomato
4 tablespoons margarine	juice
or vegetable oil	1 tablespoon brown sugar
2 pounds round steak,	¾ teaspoon salt
cut into 1-inch strips	1 teaspoon dry mustard
¼ cup enriched	⅛ teaspoon pepper
all-purpose flour	

Rinse beans and place in a large saucepan. Add water and bring to a boil; simmer 2 minutes. Remove from heat and let stand, covered, for 1 hour; *do not drain.* (Or soak beans overnight in refrigerator.) Bring beans to boil. Reduce heat and simmer, covered, for 25 minutes; drain, reserving liquid.

Preheat oven to 325°F.

Heat margarine or oil in a Dutch oven or other large, heavy pan. Coat beef with flour (by shaking the two together in a bag); place in pan and brown. Add beans, onion, tomato juice, brown sugar, salt, mustard, and pepper. Cover and bake 1½ hours; add bean liquid if additional liquid is needed.

Size of Serving: Approximately 4 ounces beef + 1 cup beans and liquid
Number of Servings: 8
Per Serving: Calories: 515; Protein: 36 g; Total Fat: 22 g; Sodium: 430 mg
Excellent Source of: Protein, Iron, Thiamin, Riboflavin, and Niacin

Spaghetti Pie

6 ounces spaghetti,
  uncooked
2 tablespoons margarine
½ cup grated Parmesan
  cheese
2 eggs, well beaten
1 pound lean ground beef
½ cup chopped onion
8 ounces canned
  tomatoes, cut up
4 ounces canned
  mushrooms, drained

6 ounces canned tomato
  paste
1 teaspoon sugar
1 teaspoon oregano
½ teaspoon garlic salt
1 cup lowfat cottage
  cheese
½ cup shredded, partially
  skimmed mozzarella
  cheese

Preheat oven to 350°F.

Cook spaghetti until tender and drain. Stir in margarine, Parmesan cheese, and eggs. Form spaghetti mixture into a "crust" in a buttered 12-inch pie plate.

Cook ground beef and onion in non-stick frying pan until beef is browned; drain off fat. Stir tomatoes, mushrooms, tomato paste, sugar, oregano, and garlic salt into beef mixture; heat through.

Spread cottage cheese over bottom of spaghetti crust. Add tomato mixture. Bake, uncovered, for 20 minutes. Sprinkle mozzarella cheese on top and bake 5 more minutes, or until cheese melts.

NOTE: Spaghetti Pie can be frozen before baking.

Size of Serving: one-eighth of a 12-inch pie   *Number of Servings:* 8
Per Serving: Calories: 320; Protein: 26 g; Total Fat: 14 g; Sodium: 420 mg
Excellent Source of: Protein, Calcium, Iron, Vitamin A, Thiamin, Riboflavin, Niacin, and Vitamin C

Zucchini "Lasagne"

½ pound lean ground beef
½ cup chopped onion
1 large garlic clove, crushed
½ cup chopped green pepper
1 8-ounce can tomatoes
1 8-ounce can tomato sauce
4 tablespoons minced fresh parsley (or 2 tablespoons dried parsley flakes)
Salt to taste

1 teaspoon crushed oregano
1 teaspoon crushed basil
1½ cups lowfat cottage cheese
1 egg
1 large zucchini or 2 medium, cut lengthwise into 9 full-length slices, about ¼ inch thick
4 ounces partially skimmed mozzarella cheese, shredded

Preheat oven to 350°F.

Cook and stir ground beef, onion, garlic, and green pepper in large saucepan until meat is brown and vegetables are tender; drain off all fat. Add tomatoes and break up with fork; stir in tomato sauce, 2 tablespoons parsley, salt, oregano, and basil. Heat to boiling, stirring occasionally; reduce heat and simmer, uncovered, 1 hour, or until mixture is thick.

Mix cottage cheese, egg, and remaining 2 tablespoons parsley together.

In ungreased 8 x 8 x 2-inch baking pan, spread thin layer of meat sauce. Layer one-third each of zucchini slices, remaining meat sauce, mozzarella cheese, and cottage cheese mixture. (If desired, lasagne can be covered and refrigerated several hours at this point.)

Bake, uncovered, 45 minutes. (Allow additional 10–15 minutes if lasagne has been refrigerated.) For easier cutting, let stand 15 minutes after removing from oven.

VARIATIONS: Cooked lasagna noodles may be used instead of, or in addition to, the zucchini. However, the noodles are much higher in calories (200 calories/1 cup cooked) than the zucchini (22 calories/1 cup cooked). Add 1–2 teaspoons fennel seed to vary the flavor.

Size of Serving: 1 8-inch square   *Number of Servings:* 4
Per Serving: Calories: 330; Protein: 35 g; Total Fat: 15 g; Sodium: 530 mg
Excellent Source of: Protein, Iron, Vitamin A, Thiamin, Riboflavin, Niacin, and Vitamin C

Steak Stroganoff

1 pound lean round or
  flank steak, ¼–½-inch
  thick
  Salt and pepper to taste
1 teaspoon paprika
2 teaspoons cornstarch
  mixed with ¼ cup water
1 teaspoon sugar

1 cup vegetable stock (see
  Index or use defatted,
  canned beef broth)
1 small onion, grated
½ cup plain lowfat yogurt
1 tablespoon tomato paste
1 teaspoon chopped
  parsley
¼ cup mushroom pieces

Broil steak lightly on rack; season with salt, pepper, and paprika; cut into 1-inch strips and place in frying pan.

In 1-quart saucepan, dissolve cornstarch and sugar in stock and simmer, stirring constantly, until thickened. Add onion, yogurt, tomato paste, parsley, and mushrooms; stir until blended and add to steak slices in frying pan. Simmer for about 15 minutes and serve hot.

Size of Serving: about 1 cup   *Number of Servings:* 4
Per Serving: Calories: 255; Protein: 24 g; Total Fat: 15 g; Sodium: 100 mg
Excellent Source of: Protein, Iron, Riboflavin, and Niacin

Hot Monterey Salad

1 teaspoon vegetable oil
¾ pound lean ground
  beef
1 garlic clove, crushed
  Salt to taste
6–8 drops hot pepper sauce
2 teaspoons lemon juice
½ cup mayonnaise (or
  low-calorie
  mayonnaise)

2 cups cooked rice
1 cup sliced celery
½ cup chopped onion
½ cup chopped green
  pepper
2 medium fresh tomatoes,
  cut in wedges
½ teaspoon pepper
⅔ cup crushed baked
  tortillas

Preheat oven to 375°F.
Heat oil in large skillet. Cook beef and garlic in oil about 10 minutes, or until meat is almost done. Add salt, pepper sauce, lemon juice, and mayonnaise; mix well.

Stir in remaining ingredients, except tortilla chips; turn into a lightly greased shallow 1½-quart casserole. Top with crushed tortilla chips. Bake 25–30 minutes.

Size of Serving: 1½ cups   *Number of Servings:* 4
Per Serving: Calories: 400; Protein: 22 g; Total Fat: 18 g; Sodium 275 mg (with plain, unsalted tortillas)
Excellent Source of: Protein, Iron, Thiamin, Riboflavin, Niacin, and Vitamin C

Machaca

1 recipe Salsa (Mexican   Salt to taste
    Relish—see Index)   ⅛ teaspoon pepper
1 pound flank steak

Prepare Salsa; cover and chill for 2 hours.

Preheat oven to 300°F.

Score the steak against the grain of the muscle with a sharp knife, making cuts at about 1-inch intervals (cut just deep enough to break the muscle fibers). Place steak in a 9 x 12-inch baking pan; cover with foil and bake for 1½ hours. Remove steak from oven; leave in pan and, using two forks in a scissorlike motion, shred it into 1-inch strands.

Add Salsa, salt and pepper; mix well. Return to oven and bake, uncovered, about 5 minutes, or until heated through.

Size of Serving: about 4 ounces   *Number of Servings:* 4
Per Serving (with ½ cup Salsa): Calories: 240; Protein: 28 g; Total Fat: 9 g; Sodium: 230 mg
Excellent Source of: Protein, Iron, Vitamin A, Thiamin, Riboflavin, Niacin, and Vitamin C

Anticuchos Teriyaki (Marinated Barbecued Beef Hearts)

THE MARINADE:

½ cup wine vinegar   1 garlic clove, crushed
2 small dried hot chilis or   1 teaspoon cumin
    ½ teaspoon ground hot   ¼ teaspoon pepper
    chili   1 tablespoon vegetable oil

1 pound beef heart, cut into 1-inch cubes

THE TERIYAKI:

⅛ cup soy sauce (or more   2 teaspoons sugar
    to taste)   ¼ teaspoon pepper
1 garlic clove, crushed   1 tablespoon vegetable
2 tablespoons wine   oil
    vinegar

Put ingredients for marinade in blender and whirl until smooth. Coat heart cubes with marinade and refrigerate for at least 1 hour.

Skewer meat and broil over charcoal or in oven broiler for 5 minutes, or until meat is done but still pink. (This will ensure that the meat will be tender.)

Serve with teriyaki. Dip the cubes in teriyaki sparingly, since it is high

(continued)

in sodium. (Each tablespoon soy sauce = 1320 milligrams of sodium.)
NOTE: The oil is necessary in the marinade to keep the meat moist, since
it is low in fat and can be dry.

Size of Serving: 3¾ ounces   *Number of Servings:* 4
Per Serving: Calories: 260; Protein: 37 g; Total Fat: 13 g; Sodium: 780 mg
Excellent Source of: Protein, Iron, Thiamin, Riboflavin, and Niacin

Stuffed Cabbage Rolls

⅓ cup uncooked brown
    rice
1 2½-pound head of
    cabbage
1½ pounds lean ground
    beef
1 large egg
¼ cup chopped parsley
1 teaspoon salt
¾ teaspoon crushed
    thyme leaves

¼ teaspoon ground black
    pepper
3 cups peeled, cored,
    coarsely chopped
    tomatoes
½ cup sliced onion
1 tablespoon honey
1 tablespoon lemon juice
½ teaspoon ground
    allspice

Cook brown rice according to directions on package or see Index.

Place cabbage in a colander and wash thoroughly under cold running
water; remove any exceptionally tough outer leaves. Place cabbage in a
large pot with about 1 inch of boiling water. Cover and steam for about 10
minutes, or until the leaves can be separated easily from the head; drain
thoroughly and cool.

While cabbage is cooking, combine the beef, cooked rice, egg, parsley,
½ teaspoon salt, thyme, and pepper; mix well.

Remove cabbage leaves from head and cut out large center rib with
a sharp paring knife. Place approximately ¼ cup of meat mixture in the
center of each cabbage leaf; fold the sides of the leaves over the stuffing;
roll up leaves to form plump cylinder-shaped rolls.

Combine the tomatoes, onion, honey, lemon juice, allspice, and remaining ½ teaspoon of salt. Mix well and spoon about half of this mixture into
a large, heavy pot.

Arrange cabbage rolls, seam sides down in the pot, stacking them
neatly. Add remaining tomato mixture; cover and simmer for 2 hours.

Remove cabbage rolls to a covered serving dish; boil remaining tomato
sauce until it is reduced to about 2 cups. Spoon sauce over cabbage rolls
before serving.

Size of Serving: 2 large cabbage rolls   *Number of Servings:* 6
Per Serving: Calories: 330; Protein: 29 g; Total Fat: 13 g; Sodium: 636 mg
Excellent Source of: Protein, Calcium, Iron, Vitamin A, Thiamin, Ribo-
flavin, Niacin, and Vitamin C

Smoked Leg of Lamb

⅔ cup wine vinegar
½ cup vegetable oil
2 small onions, chopped
2 garlic cloves, crushed
½ teaspoon ground dried
　chili peppers

1 teaspoon ground
　coriander
1 4-pound leg of lamb,
　trimmed of excess fat

Combine vinegar, oil, onions, garlic, chili peppers, and coriander in a blender and blend until smooth. (If a blender is not available, just chop the onions very finely and mix well.)

Marinate lamb in vinegar mixture for 6–24 hours.

Cook in a *covered* barbecue for 30 minutes a pound. (Lamb should sit on a sheet of heavy aluminum foil to hold drippings, and charcoal should be pulled away from the center. The lamb should not fry. It needs to bake—and smoke. Put on fresh wild cherry or other leaves from time to time to make smoke.)

Size of Serving: about 4 ounces   *Number of Servings:* 8
Per Serving: Calories: 340; Protein: 32 g; Total Fat: 21 g; Sodium: 85 mg
Excellent Source of: Protein, Iron, Thiamin, and Riboflavin

Moussaka (Greek Lamb, Eggplant, Tomato Casserole)

1 medium eggplant,
　peeled and cut into
　¼-inch slices
½ teaspoon salt
2 tablespoons vegetable
　oil
2 garlic cloves, crushed
1 large onion, chopped
1 pound lean ground
　lamb
½ cup tomato sauce
¼ cup dry red wine
2 tablespoons chopped
　fresh parsley
½ teaspoon dried thyme
½ teaspoon dried oregano
½ teaspoon ground
　nutmeg (or more to
　taste)

½ teaspoon ground
　cinnamon (or more to
　taste)
Salt to taste
Freshly ground pepper
　to taste
3 tablespoons margarine
3 tablespoons enriched
　all-purpose flour
1½ cups heated skim milk
2 egg yolks
¼ teaspoon salt
⅛ teaspoon pepper
1 whole egg
½ cup wheat germ or fine
　whole wheat bread
　crumbs
2 large tomatoes, sliced
1½ tablespoons grated
　Parmesan cheese

(continued)

Spread eggplant slices out in a single layer on top of paper towels; sprinkle with salt. Cover with another layer of paper towels and put heavy weight over all (a heavy skillet works well). This helps to remove excess water from the eggplant.

Heat the oil in a skillet: add garlic, onion, and lamb; sauté until onion is translucent and meat is browned. Drain off excess fat. Add tomato sauce, wine, parsley, thyme, oregano, nutmeg, and cinnamon; simmer about 20 minutes. Add salt and pepper to taste.

Meanwhile, prepare "cream" sauce topping by melting margarine in a medium-size saucepan; add flour gradually, mixing well and stirring constantly. Slowly add hot milk, stirring until it thickens; remove from heat and beat in egg yolks, salt, and pepper.

When meat has cooked, remove from heat and allow to cool slightly. Add whole egg and ¼ cup wheat germ; mix well.

Rinse eggplant and pat dry; place eggplant slices on broiler pan and brown lightly on both sides (they will shrivel up slightly).

Preheat oven to 350°F.

Grease a 9 x 13-inch baking dish or a 3-quart casserole; then sprinkle the bottom with remaining ¼ cup wheat germ. Line the bottom of the pan with eggplant slices, spread lamb mixture over eggplant, place tomato slices on top of meat, pour "cream" sauce on top, and sprinkle with Parmesan cheese. Bake 45 minutes; serve hot.

VARIATION: Lean ground beef may be substituted for lamb.

Size of Serving: 3 x 4-inch square   *Number of Servings:* 8 medium (or 6 large)
Per Serving: Calories: 306; Protein: 22 g; Total Fat: 17 g; Sodium: 410 mg
Excellent Source of: Protein, Calcium, Iron, Vitamin A, Thiamin, Riboflavin, Niacin, and Vitamin C

Lamb and Cucumber Salad

2 cups cooked lamb cut in
  ¼-inch julienne strips
1 cup cooked fresh peas,
  drained, or ½ 10-ounce
  package frozen peas,
  cooked
1 cup diced cucumber
½ cup thinly sliced sweet
  red pepper strips

½ cup thinly sliced celery
¼ teaspoon dill seed
¼ cup Low-Calorie
  Vinaigrette Dressing
  (see Index)
  Freshly ground pepper
  to taste
8 Boston lettuce leaves
  (or other leafy green)

Combine lamb with vegetables in a large bowl; sprinkle with dill seed. Cover and chill 30 minutes.

Pour vinaigrette over salad and toss lightly; add pepper to taste. Serve on leafy greens.

Size of Serving: 1¼ cups   *Number of Servings:* 4
Per Serving (with dressing): Calories: 205; Protein: 23 g; Total Fat: 9 g; Sodium: 95 mg
Excellent Source of: Protein, Iron, Thiamin, Riboflavin, Niacin, and Vitamin C

Indian Shepherd's Pie

2 tablespoons vegetable oil
1 onion, chopped
1½ pounds lean ground lamb
1 teaspoon paprika + ½ teaspoon for topping
½ teaspoon pepper
1 tablespoon Worcestershire sauce
1 teaspoon garlic powder
¼ cup dry red wine
3–4 medium fresh tomatoes, diced, or 1 8-ounce can whole tomatoes, drained

1–2 teaspoons dill weed
1 teaspoon basil
½ teaspoon sage
3–4 parsnips, sliced in ½-inch pieces (these are a must)
2–3 carrots, sliced in ½-inch pieces
½ sweet red pepper, diced
½ cup chopped celery
1 teaspoon caraway seed
1–2 teaspoons curry powder (or to taste)
6 medium cooked potatoes mashed with small amount milk

Heat oil in a large Dutch oven or other heavy pan; add onion and lamb and sauté 5 minutes. Drain off excess fat. Add paprika, pepper, Worcestershire sauce, and garlic powder. Cook, *uncovered* (to prevent it from being too soupy), over low heat until meat is cooked.

Add wine, tomatoes, dill, basil, sage, parsnips, and carrots. Cook, uncovered, about 5 minutes. Add red pepper and celery. Cook, uncovered, 10 minutes. Add caraway and curry; cook, uncovered, 10 minutes. Taste and adjust seasonings, if necessary.

Cover with mashed potatoes and sprinkle with paprika; broil until lightly browned and crisp on top.

Size of Serving: 1½ cups   *Number of Servings:* 8
Per Serving: Calories: 335; Protein: 26 g; Total Fat: 13 g; Sodium: 90 mg
Excellent Source of: Protein, Iron, Vitamin A, Thiamin, Riboflavin, Niacin, and Vitamin C

Liver Creole

¼ cup margarine
1 pound raw beef or
   calves' liver, cut in
   cubes or strips
1 onion, chopped
1 garlic clove, crushed
1 8-ounce can tomato
   sauce

1 28-ounce can tomatoes
2 stalks celery, sliced
1 green pepper, chopped
2 teaspoons chili powder
1 teaspoon oregano
  Salt to taste

Melt margarine in a deep 10-inch skillet. Add liver, onion, and garlic; cook until onion is tender. Add the other ingredients and simmer 10–15 minutes. Serve over cooked rice, bulgur, or noodles.

Size of Serving: 1½ cups   *Number of Servings:* 4
Per Serving: Calories: 350; Protein: 33 g; Total Fat: 17 g; Sodium: 675 mg
Excellent Source of: Protein, Iron, Vitamin A, Thiamin, Riboflavin, Niacin, and Vitamin C

Tuscan Roast Pork

3 pounds boneless loin of
   pork (trimmed of excess
   fat)
2 large garlic cloves,
   thinly sliced
1 tablespoon minced
   fresh rosemary or 1
   teaspoon crushed dried
   rosemary (or use
   tarragon)
⅛ teaspoon ground cloves
⅛ teaspoon ground
   allspice
¼ teaspoon ground
   marjoram

⅛ teaspoon ground
   cardamom
⅛ teaspoon ground
   nutmeg
⅛ teaspoon freshly
   ground pepper
1–2 tablespoons vegetable
   oil
½ cup plain wheat germ
½ cup finely crushed
   whole-grain bread
   crumbs
½ teaspoon crushed sage
2–3 tablespoons Dijon-style
   mustard

Make several slits in the pork and insert garlic slices and rosemary or tarragon.

Combine cloves, allspice, marjoram, cardamom, nutmeg, and pepper. Gradually mix in just enough oil to make a thick paste with the spices. Rub mixture over the surface of the pork. Cover and refrigerate 4–5 hours, or overnight if possible.

Preheat oven to 325°F.

Place pork on a rack in a shallow baking pan and roast 1 hour.

Combine wheat germ, bread crumbs, and sage; mix well.

After pork has roasted for the first hour, remove from oven, coat lightly with mustard, then roll in wheat germ mixture. Return to oven and roast for another ½–1 hour, or until meat thermometer registers 170°F. and crust is golden brown.

Size of Serving: about 3¼ ounces   *Number of Servings:* 8
Per Serving: Calories: 300; Protein: 30 g; Total Fat: 16 g; Sodium: 165 mg
Excellent Source of: Protein, Iron, Thiamin, Riboflavin, and Niacin

Pork in Cider

3 *pounds boneless loin of pork (trimmed of excess fat)*	4 *medium potatoes, halved*
1 *teaspoon salt*	4 *medium onions, halved*
¼ *teaspoon pepper*	1 *cup unsweetened cider*
4 *baking apples, cored*	1 *tablespoon flour*
	¼ *cup sherry*

Preheat oven to 350°F.

Rub pork with salt and pepper; place on rack in 10 x 13-inch roasting pan. Roast for 45 minutes; pour off fat.

Arrange apples, potatoes, and onions around the pork, and add ½ cup of the cider; roast 45 minutes longer, basting frequently.

Place pork, apples, potatoes, and onions on a serving platter; cover with foil to keep warm.

Skim fat from the gravy; place pan on direct low heat and stir in the flour, mixing well. Gradually add the sherry and remaining ½ cup of cider, stirring constantly and scraping the bottom. Cook over low heat about 5 minutes, or until slightly thickened. Serve gravy on the side with pork and vegetables.

Size of Serving: about 3¼ ounces   *Number of Servings:* 8
Per Serving: Calories: 350; Protein: 29; Total Fat: 13 g; Sodium: 210 mg
Excellent Source of: Protein, Iron, Thiamin, Riboflavin, Niacin, and Vitamin C

Apple-Raisin-Apricot Stuffing

This is delicious in a boneless rolled pork roast or pork chops.

1 tablespoon margarine	1½ cups white bread
¼ cup chopped scallions	crumbs
1¼ cups finely chopped	½ teaspoon crumbled
onion	sage
½ cup sliced celery	¼ teaspoon ground
3 cups finely diced	ginger
baking apples	¼ teaspoon ground
1 cup finely diced	nutmeg
cooked apricots,	½ cup defatted chicken
drained	stock (see Index or use
½ cup chopped seedless	canned)
raisins	Salt to taste
1½ cups whole wheat	
bread crumbs	

Melt margarine in large saucepan. Add scallions, onion, and celery and sauté until tender. Stir in apples. Continue cooking 5–7 minutes, stirring constantly.

Combine onion-celery-apple mixture in saucepan with apricots and raisins. Add bread crumbs and seasonings; toss well. Add stock until mixture is evenly moistened.

Size of Serving: ½ cup   *Number of Servings:* 8
Per Serving: Calories: 140; Protein: 3 g; Total Fat: 2 g; Sodium: 30 mg

Acorn Squash Bake

2 large acorn squash	2 cups finely shredded
2 tablespoons slivered	green cabbage
almonds	Salt to taste
½ pound lean fresh	¼ teaspoon pepper
sausage meat, crumbled	1 teaspoon finely
2 tablespoons margarine	crumbled dried sage
1 medium onion, chopped	½ teaspoon crushed dried
1 large unpeeled red	thyme
apple, cored and diced	

Preheat oven to 400°F.

Cut squash in half lengthwise; scoop out seeds and fibers. (Wash the seeds and toast in oven for squash seed snacks.) Place squash halves in baking pan, cut side down, in ½ inch hot water. Bake 40 minutes.

While the squash is baking, place almonds in a single layer on a baking sheet and toast in oven about 5 minutes, or until lightly browned.

Brown sausage meat in a large skillet; drain off excess fat; add margarine and melt. Add onion, apple, cabbage, and almonds to skillet; cook over medium heat until vegetables are tender. Add seasonings and mix well.

Turn squash halves cut side up and fill centers with cabbage mixture. Return to oven and bake 20–25 minutes longer, or until squash is tender when pierced with a fork.

Size of Serving: ½ stuffed squash   *Number of Servings:* 4
Per Serving: Calories: 450; Protein: 9 g; Total Fat: 21 g; Sodium: 325 mg
Excellent Source of: Calcium, Iron, Vitamin A, Thiamin, Riboflavin, and Vitamin C

Quick-Cook Vegetables and Pork

¼ cup vegetable oil
½ pound boneless lean pork loin, cut into ¼-inch strips
½ pound fresh broccoli, cut into florets (2 cups)
½ pound fresh mushrooms, sliced (2 cups)
½ pound fresh carrots, cut into 2-inch strips (2 cups)
1 medium yellow onion, thinly sliced (½ cup)
¼ teaspoon salt

¼ teaspoon ground black pepper
½ teaspoon grated lemon rind
½ teaspoon crushed dried oregano
½ teaspoon crushed dried tarragon
½ teaspoon dry mustard
1 cup defatted chicken stock (see Index or use canned)
1 tablespoon cornstarch
Salt to taste

In large skillet or wok heat 2 tablespoons of the oil over medium high heat. Add pork strips; brown quickly on both sides. Remove pork and set aside.

Add remaining oil to skillet. Add broccoli, mushrooms, carrots, and onions. Cook, stirring constantly, 5 minutes, or until vegetables are tender-crisp. Add pork, salt, pepper, lemon rind, oregano, tarragon, and dry mustard; stir together.

Mix chicken stock and cornstarch until smooth, then add to vegetable mixture. Bring to boil over medium heat, stirring constantly, and boil 1 minute. Salt to taste.

Size of Serving: 1 cup   *Number of Servings:* 4
Per Serving: Calories: 315; Protein: 20 g; Total Fat: 22 g; Sodium: 240 mg
Excellent Source of: Protein, Iron, Vitamin A, Thiamin, Riboflavin, Niacin, and Vitamin C

Fruit Stuffed Pork Chops

4 dried figs, cut into small
pieces
1 large apple, cored and
diced
⅛ teaspoon nutmeg
6 pork chops, with pocket
cut in sides

½ teaspoon onion powder
Salt and pepper to taste
⅔ cup defatted chicken
stock (see Index or use
canned)

Mix fruits with nutmeg and stuff into pockets of pork chops. Sprinkle with onion powder, salt, and pepper.

Brown both sides of chops in large skillet. Reduce heat; add stock, cover, and simmer for 35–45 minutes, or until meat is done.

NOTE: Use kitchen scissors to cut figs easily. Dipping figs in hot water before cutting helps prevent stickiness.

VARIATION: Fresh pear can be used instead of apple.

Size of Serving: 1 chop + 2–3 tablespoons fruit stuffing   *Number of Servings:* 6
Per Serving: Calories: 180; Protein: 15 g; Total Fat: 7 g; Sodium: 40 mg
Excellent Source of: Iron and Thiamin

Braised Veal Shanks

4 small veal shanks, cut
into 2–3-inch pieces (or
leave on bone while
cooking)
1–2 tablespoons vegetable
oil
1 large onion, thinly
sliced
4 carrots, sliced
lengthwise into
2 x ¼-inch pieces

½ cup dry white wine
½ cup tomato purée
2–3 garlic cloves, crushed
4 stalks celery, sliced
lengthwise into
2 x ¼-inch pieces
¼ cup chopped fresh
parsley
Grated rind of ½
lemon

Brown veal in oil in skillet. Add all ingredients except the parsley and lemon rind. Cook for 30–40 minutes over moderate heat. Add parsley and lemon rind; cook another 10 minutes.

Size of Serving: 1½ cups   *Number of Servings:* 4
Per Serving: Calories: 185; Protein: 24 g; Total Fat: 15 g; Sodium: 260 mg
Excellent Source of: Protein, Iron, Vitamin A, Thiamin, Riboflavin, and Vitamin C

Dijon-Style Veal

4 veal chops or cutlets
2 tablespoons vegetable oil
½ pound sliced mushrooms
¼ cup chopped fresh parsley
⅛ teaspoon freshly ground pepper
¼ cup dry white wine
½ cup defatted veal or chicken stock (see Index or use canned)
1–2 shallots, finely minced
1–2 tablespoons Dijon-style mustard (or to taste)

In a frying pan, brown the veal in oil; then remove to plate. Add mushroom, half the parsley, and pepper to the pan; sauté 2–3 minutes. Return the veal to pan, cover, and cook 15–20 minutes, or until veal is tender.

Remove the veal and mushrooms—keep warm in foil-covered plate. Add wine, stock, and shallots to pan and boil down until there is about ⅓ cup liquid left. Add mustard and mix quickly with wire whisk over low heat. Add remaining parsley and spoon sauce over veal.

Size of Serving: 1 chop or cutlet + ⅓ cup sauce   *Number of Servings:* 4
Per Serving: Calories: 280; Protein: 24 g; Total Fat: 18 g; Sodium: 135 mg
Excellent Source of: Protein, Iron, Thiamin, Riboflavin, and Niacin

POULTRY

"A chicken in every pot" sums up the status of poultry as an internationally favorite food. Its popularity no doubt results from its versatility, mild succulence, and low cost (relative to other sources of animal protein). It is delicious plain or enhanced by wine, herbs, spices, yogurt, fruits, vegetables, seeds, nuts, and an endless variety of dressings.

Nutritionally, poultry is high in protein, B vitamins, and minerals and relatively low in calories *if* the visible fat is not eaten. Fortunately, much of this fat is neatly packaged in and around the skin, making it easy to remove before cooking.

With all of its nutritional pluses, good taste, and low cost, poultry is clearly one of the better buys at the marketplace.

BUYING AND PREPARING POULTRY

Most of the poultry sold in retail stores has been inspected and stamped by the U.S. Department of Agriculture (USDA). Inspection is required for poultry that is shipped interstate. Inspected poultry may also be graded, but this is done on a voluntary basis. Grades for poultry, established by the USDA as A, B, or C, appear in a shield mark either on a wing tag or on the outer wrapping. Poultry classifications have also been set up based on age, sex, and weight as follows:

Type of Poultry	Approximate Retail Weight	Recommended Cooking Method
CHICKEN:		
broiler or fryer (young chickens, 8–12 weeks old)	¾ to not over 3½ pounds	broiled, baked, barbecued
roaster (older chickens, 12 weeks–4 months)	2½ to over 5 pounds	roasted, barbecued
stewing chicken or fowl (mature hens, usually over 10 months old, that are flavorful but less tender than other chickens. They require a longer cooking time in moisture.)	2½ to over 5½ pounds	stewed
capon (desexed young male chickens that are very flavorful and have a good supply of tender meat)	4–8 pounds	roasted
Rock Cornish game hen (cross between Plymouth Rock chickens and Cornish game hens, a special breed of very small chicken)	not over 2 pounds	roasted, broiled (split), barbecued (on rotisserie)
TURKEY:		
fryer or roaster (very young)	4–8 pounds	roasted, broiled
larger turkeys (may be young or mature)	8–24 or more pounds	roasted
DUCK*		
broiler-fryer or roaster duckling	3 to over 5 pounds	roasted, broiled
mature duck	3 to over 5 pounds	roasted
GOOSE*		
young or mature goose	4 to over 14 pounds	roasted

* Duck and goose have a much higher fat content than the other types of poultry; therefore they are higher in calories. Goose, for example, has a total fat content that is about three times higher than that of light-fleshed chicken or turkey. Duck and goose are also higher in saturated fat and cholesterol than light-fleshed chicken or turkey.

STORING POULTRY

To Store Poultry in Refrigerator: Fresh, unfrozen poultry should be wrapped loosely to allow air to circulate. Remove giblets; wrap and store by themselves. Use refrigerated poultry within 1–2 days.

Cooked poultry should be wrapped loosely and refrigerated as soon as possible after it has cooled. Be sure to remove any stuffing from the bird before refrigerating and store stuffing (and gravy) separately in covered containers in the refrigerator.

To Store Poultry in Freezer: Store raw or cooked poultry in the freezer in moisture/vaporproof wrapping, such as plastic wrap. (Remove stuffing before storing.)

Store previously frozen poultry in its original wrapping.

Store Poultry in 0°F. Freezer	*up to:*
chicken, turkey	1 year
cooked poultry	6 months
raw duck or goose	6 months
giblets	3 months

To Thaw Poultry:

1. Keep poultry wrapped and thaw in the refrigerator for 1–4 days, depending on the size of the bird. A chicken will take about a day to defrost this way, whereas a turkey will take up to 3–4 days.

APPROXIMATE THAWING TIME FOR POULTRY

Weight as Purchased	*To Thaw in Refrigerator*
2–4 pounds	1 day
4–8 pounds	1½–2 days
8–12 pounds	2 days
12–16 pounds	2–3 days
16–24 pounds	3–4 days

2. Keep poultry in freezer wrapping and submerge in cold water for 2–12 hours, depending on the size of the bird. (For example, a 10-pound turkey takes 6–8 hours.)
3. Place wrapped poultry in a heavy double paper bag or wrap it in 2 to 3 layers of newspaper. Close tightly and thaw at room temperature. Figure on about 1 hour of thawing time for each pound of poultry.

Once thawed, remove the wrapping and giblets. Cover loosely with paper or foil and refrigerate immediately. Cook within a few hours.

NOTE: Do not thaw commercially frozen *stuffed* poultry. Cook it from the frozen state according to package directions.

HOW TO COOK POULTRY

To Roast: Preheat oven to 325°F. Wash poultry and pat it dry. (Leave the skin on during roasting because the extended cooking time during roasting can cause poultry to dry out; remove the skin after cooking if you are concerned about the extra calories and saturated fat located in the skin.)

Stuff the cavity, if desired, just before cooking; then truss.

To Truss:

1. Close the cavity by securing the neck skin with a skewer or poultry pins or by sewing with a needle and thread. (Turkeys often have a band of skin that can be slipped over the legs to hold the cavity closed.)
2. Fold the wings under the back, placing the tips against the back.
3. Tie the legs together close to the body and attach the string to the tail for support.

Place on a rack in a shallow roasting pan with the breast side up. Roast, uncovered, according to the following timetable:

TIMETABLE FOR ROASTING POULTRY

Type of Poultry	Ready-to-Cook Weight	Approximate Roasting Time at 325°F.
Chicken, broilers/fryers	1½–2½ pounds	1–2 hours
roasters, stuffed	2½–4½ pounds	2–3½ hours*
Capon, stuffed	5–8 pounds	2½–3½ hours*
Duck	4–6 pounds	2–3 hours
Goose	6–8 pounds	3–3½ hours
	8–12 pounds	3½–4½ hours
Turkey, fryers or roasters (very young)	6–8 pounds	3–3½ hours
roasters (fully grown), stuffed	8–12 pounds	3½–4½ hours*
	12–16 pounds	4½–5½ hours*
	16–20 pounds	5½–6½ hours*
	20–24 pounds	6½–7 hours*
halves, quarters, and half breasts	3–8 pounds	2–3 hours
	8–12 pounds	3–4 hours
boneless turkey roasts	2–10 pounds	2–4 hours (internal temperature will be 170° to 175°F.)

* Poultry without stuffing will take less time.

Based on: The American Home Economics Association, *Handbook of Food Preparation*, 7th ed., 1975.

Large birds, such as turkeys, that require a long cooking time will need to be basted occasionally with oil, melted margarine, or the pan drippings to prevent drying. Many supermarkets now carry self-basting turkeys. However, the fat used is frequently coconut oil, which is highly saturated. When poultry turns golden brown before it is fully cooked, cover it loosely with aluminum foil to prevent excessive browning.

Test poultry for doneness by one of the following methods:
- Insert a thermometer at the center of the inner thigh muscle. This will register 180° to 185°F. when the bird is done. If the bird is stuffed, the thermometer should register 165°F. or higher when inserted into the center of the stuffing.
- Move one of the drumsticks; it will move easily when fully cooked.
- Test the flesh on a drumstick; it will be fork-tender when fully cooked.

To Broil: Wash the poultry and pat dry. Remove the skin if you are concerned about excess calories and saturated fat.

Place the poultry on the broiler pan and season as desired. Broil 4–5 inches from the heat for 20 minutes; turn and season again, if desired, and broil 15–20 minutes, or until fork-tender.

To Bake: Preheat the oven to 350°F. Remove the skin, wash and pat dry. If desired, dip the poultry in skim milk and then in seasoned bread crumbs or flour.*

Place pieces in a single layer in a foil-lined or lightly oiled baking pan; or wrap each piece completely in foil. Bake for 30 minutes; turn and cook 20–30 minutes longer, or until fork-tender.

To Braise: Preheat oven to 325°F. (unless the poultry is to be cooked on top of stove). Remove the skin; wash poultry and pat dry. If desired, dip the pieces in skim milk and dredge in seasoned bread crumbs or flour.*

Pour just enough oil in a heavy skillet to lightly cover the bottom. Brown the poultry in the hot oil; remove pieces from skillet and drain off all excess oil.

Return poultry to the skillet and add 1 cup of defatted chicken stock (see Index or use canned) or water. Cover and cook in oven (or over low to medium heat on top of the stove) for 1½–2½ hours, or until fork-tender. Add vegetables toward the last part of cooking time, if desired; cook vegetables according to timetable in Vegetable Chart (see Index).

To Stew: Remove skin and wash poultry.

Place poultry in a deep pot, such as a Dutch oven; add water to cover and seasonings. Bring to boil; reduce heat; simmer, covered, 1½–2 hours, or until fork-tender.

---

* Each ¼ cup of bread crumbs or flour adds about 100 extra calories to the poultry.

Baked Lemon Chicken with Tarragon

3 tablespoons each wheat germ and fine whole wheat bread crumbs (or use 6 tablespoons wheat germ or bread crumbs)
1 tablespoon crushed tarragon
½ teaspoon garlic powder
¼ teaspoon salt
¼ teaspoon freshly ground pepper
2 chicken breasts, split and skinned
2–3 tablespoons skim milk
2 tablespoons lemon juice
4–8 lemon wedges

Preheat oven to 350°F.

Combine the wheat germ, bread crumbs, tarragon, garlic powder, salt, and pepper; mix well.

Dip the chicken in milk; shake off any excess. Roll chicken in dry ingredients and place in baking dish. Sprinkle with lemon juice.

Bake, uncovered, 45 minutes, or until chicken is fork-tender and coating is lightly browned. Serve garnished with lemon wedges.

Size of Serving: ½ chicken breast   *Number of Servings:* 4
Per Serving: Calories: 200; Protein: 28 g; Total Fat: 6 g; Sodium: 250 mg
Excellent Source of: Protein, Iron, Riboflavin, and Niacin

Brown Rice Poultry Stuffing

This quick-to-fix dressing will stuff 2 Rock Cornish game hens or 1 roasting chicken. Double the recipe for a small turkey.

1 tablespoon vegetable oil
1 large onion, finely chopped
½ cup celery, finely chopped
1 cup defatted chicken stock (see Index or use canned)
⅓ cup uncooked brown rice
½ cup raisins
½ teaspoon sage
½ teaspoon poultry seasoning
¼ teaspoon pepper
½ cup sliced almonds

Heat oil in medium-size saucepan; add onion and celery and sauté until slightly soft. Add stock, rice, and raisins; simmer, covered, until most of the liquid is absorbed (about 5 minutes). Add seasonings and almonds; mix thoroughly.

Yield: 3 cups
Per ½ Cup: Calories: 165; Protein: 4 g; Total Fat: 10 g; Sodium: 25 mg
Excellent Source of: (min. 1 cup) Calcium, Iron, and Thiamin

East Indian Chicken

2 tablespoons vegetable
  oil
1 garlic clove, crushed
1½ teaspoons chili powder
½ teaspoon ground
  coriander
¼ teaspoon crushed
  saffron

⅛ teaspoon freshly ground
  pepper
¼ teaspoon salt
½ cup plain lowfat yogurt
2 whole chicken breasts,
  split and skinned
1 lime, cut into wedges

Heat the oil in a small skillet over moderate heat; add the garlic, chili powder, coriander, and saffron. Cook, stirring constantly, 2 minutes; remove spices from heat and allow to cool slightly. When cooled, add pepper, salt, and yogurt.

Meanwhile, pierce the chicken breasts all over with a fork and place in foil-lined pan. Spoon yogurt mixture over the chicken, covering it well. Cover and place in refrigerator for at least 2 hours to marinate.

Remove cover and broil chicken about 4 inches from heat for about 15–20 minutes on each side, basting often with the marinade. Serve garnished with lime wedges.

Size of Serving: ½ chicken breast   *Number of Servings:* 4
Per Serving: Calories: 245; Protein: 27 g; Total Fat: 12 g; Sodium: 235 mg
Excellent Source of: Protein, Riboflavin, and Niacin

Chutney Baked Chicken

2 pounds broiler-fryer
  chicken, cut into 8 small
  serving pieces and
  skinned

2 tablespoons soy sauce
3 tablespoons chutney,
  commercial or
  homemade (see Index)

Preheat oven to 350°F.

Rinse chicken and pat dry. Place in a large, foil-lined baking dish and brush chicken all over with soy sauce. Let the chicken soak up the soy sauce for about 10 minutes, turning the pieces once or twice to baste them in any sauce at the bottom.

Brush chicken with chutney on top side only. Bake uncovered, for 1 hour, or until fork-tender.

Size of Serving: 2 pieces chicken   *Number of Servings:* 4
Per Serving: Calories: 155; Protein: 25 g; Total Fat: 4 g; Sodium: 735 mg
Excellent Source of: Protein, Iron, Thiamin, Riboflavin, and Niacin

Basil Chicken with Zucchini

1 tablespoon vegetable oil
2 garlic cloves, peeled and
  sliced
4 small zucchini, quartered
  and cut into pieces about
  2 inches long
4 chicken drumsticks,
  skinned

4 chicken thighs, skinned
¼ teaspoon salt
⅛ teaspoon pepper
½ cup dry white wine
⅔ cup defatted chicken
  stock (see Index or use
  canned)
2 teaspoons basil

Heat oil in Dutch oven or other large, heavy pot. Add garlic and cook 2–3 minutes, or until brown; remove garlic and save. Add zucchini and cook 2–3 minutes, or until bright green; remove from pan and save.

Add more oil to the pot if necessary and brown chicken all over; pour off all fat. Sprinkle chicken with salt and pepper. Add wine and reserved garlic; cover and cook 30 minutes, or until chicken is tender. Discard garlic.

Add stock to skillet drippings; heat until blended.

Spoon zucchini over chicken and sprinkle with basil. Cover and cook about 3–4 minutes, or until zucchini is cooked but still crisp. Serve with Pignolia Pilaf (see Index) and sliced fresh tomatoes.

Size of Serving: 2 pieces of chicken and 1 small zucchini   *Number of Servings:* 4
Per Serving: Calories: 290; Protein: 29 g; Total Fat: 13 g; Sodium: 520 mg
Excellent Source of: Protein, Iron, Riboflavin, Niacin, and Vitamin C

Hungarian Chicken Paprikash

Made with lowfat yogurt in place of the traditional sour cream, this paprikash is extra high in protein, calcium, and riboflavin and low in saturated fats and calories.

2 pounds chicken
  breasts, thighs, and
  drumsticks, skinned
2 tablespoons enriched
  all-purpose flour
2–3 tablespoons Hungarian
  paprika (this is a must)
¼ teaspoon salt
2 tablespoons vegetable
  oil

1 cup chopped onion
1 cup defatted chicken
  stock (see Index or
  use canned) or water
2 teaspoons crushed basil
1 bay leaf
1 cup plain lowfat yogurt
  (or more if desired)

Rinse chicken and pat dry. Combine flour, paprika, and salt in a bag; add chicken, a few pieces at a time, and shake to coat.

Heat oil in a large Dutch oven or other heavy pan. Add onion and sauté until soft. Add chicken and brown lightly on all sides (about 10–15 minutes). Add stock or water, basil, and bay leaf; simmer, covered, for about 25–30 minutes, or until chicken is tender. (Add more water or chicken broth if necessary.) Remove bay leaf.

Add yogurt and more paprika to taste; stir while it heats. Serve with Whole Wheat Noodles or Whole Wheat Spaetzle (see Index).

Size of Serving: 2 pieces of chicken and ½ cup sauce   *Number of Servings:* 4
Per Serving: Calories: 300; Protein: 34 g; Total Fat: 13 g; Sodium, 265 mg
Excellent Source of: Protein, Calcium, Iron, Vitamin A, Riboflavin, and Niacin

Chicken and Fresh Tomato Sauce

6 large tomatoes, peeled, seeded, and chopped
1 medium onion, chopped
⅓ cup chopped celery
2 tablespoons chopped fresh parsley
Juice of 1 fresh lemon
¼ teaspoon salt
1 teaspoon sugar
⅛ teaspoon pepper
1 tablespoon margarine
2 pounds broiler-fryer chicken, cut in serving pieces and skinned

Preheat oven to 350°F.
Combine first 8 ingredients in medium saucepan; simmer over medium heat 10 minutes.
While sauce is simmering, melt margarine in a large skillet and brown chicken pieces all over. Place chicken in a 2-quart casserole or baking dish. Pour sauce over chicken and bake 1 hour, or until chicken is tender.
VARIATION: Substitute pork chops for chicken.

Size of Serving: 1½ cups   *Number of Servings:* 4
Per Serving: Calories: 220; Protein: 27 g; Total Fat: 7 g; Sodium: 260 mg
Excellent Source of: Protein, Iron, Vitamin A, Thiamin, Riboflavin, Niacin, and Vitamin C

Chicken and Broccoli Casserole

2 10-ounce packages frozen chopped broccoli
2 tablespoons vegetable oil
1 pound raw chicken breasts, skinned, boned, and cut into ½-inch strips
1 tablespoon enriched all-purpose flour
¾ cup defatted chicken stock (see Index or use canned)
¼ cup dry white wine
Salt and pepper to taste
½ cup canned mushroom pieces
½ cup canned water chestnuts
Paprika

(continued)

Preheat oven to 350°F.

Heat broccoli, drain, and place in 1-quart casserole dish.

Heat oil in heavy frying pan and sauté chicken strips quickly on both sides. Place chicken on top of broccoli in casserole.

Stir flour into any remaining oil in frying pan, then gradually add chicken stock and wine, stirring until thickened; season to taste. Pour sauce over the chicken and broccoli in casserole dish. Scatter mushrooms and water chestnuts on top of the casserole. Bake for 45 minutes. Sprinkle with paprika before serving.

NOTE: This casserole can be made ahead and frozen.

VARIATION: Asparagus may be used in place of broccoli.

Size of Serving: 1½ cups   *Number of Servings:* 4
Per Serving: Calories: 220; Protein: 21 g; Total Fat: 11 g; Sodium: 175 mg
Excellent Source of: Protein, Iron, Vitamin A, Thiamin, Riboflavin, Niacin, and Vitamin C

Marsala Chicken with Herbs

⅓ cup vegetable oil
2 pounds chicken, skinned and cut into small pieces
¼ cup chopped onion
1 teaspoon chopped garlic
½ cup Marsala wine
2 tablespoons margarine
1 28-ounce can tomatoes (Italian-style preferred)
¼ teaspoon pepper
1 tablespoon chopped fresh parsley
½ teaspoon crushed basil leaves
8 ounces uncooked egg noodles (½ pound)
2–3 tablespoons freshly grated Parmesan cheese

Heat oil in a large skillet and brown chicken on all sides. Add onion and garlic; cook until lightly browned. Add Marsala and margarine and cook until wine is completely reduced. Add tomatoes, pepper, parsley, and basil. Simmer, uncovered, about 25 minutes, stirring occasionally, until sauce begins to thicken.

Meanwhile, cook noodles in boiling water until tender; drain in colander. Return noodles to pot. Pour in sauce from chicken and mix well.

Put noodles in large heated serving dish and top with chicken. Sprinkle with Parmesan cheese.

Size of Serving: 1½ cups   *Number of Servings:* 4
Per Serving: Calories: 660; Protein: 34 g; Total Fat: 31 g; Sodium: 420 mg
Excellent Source of: Protein, Iron, Vitamin A, Thiamin, Riboflavin, Niacin, and Vitamin C

Arroz con Pollo (Spanish Chicken Casserole)

2 pounds chicken fryer, skinned and cut into pieces

1 teaspoon dried oregano leaves

¼ teaspoon freshly ground pepper

¼ teaspoon salt

¼ cup vegetable oil

½ cup chopped onion

1 garlic clove, crushed

1 small green pepper, cut into lengthwise strips ¼-inch wide

1 small bay leaf

⅛ teaspoon crushed red pepper (optional)

½ teaspoon saffron threads

1 cup converted raw white rice

1 pound fresh tomatoes, quartered (or canned, undrained)

½ cup defatted chicken stock (see Index or use canned)

5 ounces frozen green peas (½ 10-ounce package)

¼ cup sliced pimiento-stuffed green olives

1 2-ounce can pimientos, drained and cut into ¼-inch strips

Wash chicken pieces under cold running water; drain well; wipe dry with paper towels. Combine oregano, pepper, and ⅛ teaspoon salt. Srinkle chicken all over with mixture and rub in well; let stand 10 minutes.

In 6-quart Dutch oven or other heavy ovenproof pot, heat oil over medium heat. Brown chicken, a third at a time, until golden brown all over, using tongs to turn the pieces. Remove chicken as it browns.

Preheat oven to 350°F.

To drippings in Dutch oven, add onion, garlic, green pepper, bay leaf, and red pepper; sauté, stirring over medium heat until onion is tender (5 minutes).

Using back of spoon, crush saffron threads on small piece of foil, or use a mortar and pestle. Add saffron, ⅛ teaspoon salt, and the rice to Dutch oven; cook, stirring, until rice is lightly browned (about 10 minutes). Add tomatoes and chicken stock. Arrange browned chicken pieces over rice mixture. Bring just to boiling, uncovered; then cover tightly and bake in oven 1 hour.

Remove from oven; add ½ cup water (do not stir). Sprinkle peas and olives and arrange pimiento strips attractively over top. Bake, covered, 20 minutes longer, or until chicken is tender, peas are cooked, and rice has absorbed all liquid. Remove from oven.

Let stand, covered, 10 minutes. Serve right from Dutch oven.

NOTE: Saffron threads can be purchased in the spice section of most major chain food stores.

Size of Serving: 1½ cups   Number of Servings: 4
Per Serving: Calories: 500; Protein: 31 g; Total Fat: 19 g; Sodium: 435 mg
Excellent Source of: Protein, Iron, Vitamin A, Thiamin, Riboflavin, Niacin, and Vitamin C

Mexican Chicken Stew

¼ cup vegetable oil
2 pounds broiler-fryer
  chicken, skinned and
  cut up into 8–12 pieces
1½ cups chopped onion
2 garlic cloves, crushed
1 16-ounce can tomatoes
1½ tablespoons enriched
  all-purpose flour

½ teaspoon chili powder
½ teaspoon ground cloves
2 medium green peppers,
  sliced
¾ cup sherry
⅓ cup raisins
⅓ cup sliced stuffed olives

Heat oil in a large heavy skillet. Add chicken and brown on all sides. Add onion, garlic, and tomatoes. Blend in flour, chili powder, and cloves. Bring to boil and cook 5 minutes.

Reduce heat; add green pepper, sherry, and raisins. Simmer, covered, 15 minutes, or until chicken is tender. Add olives just before serving.

Size of Serving: approximately 2–3 pieces chicken and 1 cup sauce
Number of Servings: 4
Per Serving: Calories: 495; Protein: 27 g; Total Fat: 19 g; Sodium: 410 mg
Excellent Source of: Protein, Iron, Vitamin A, Thiamin, Riboflavin, Niacin, and Vitamin C

Stir-Fried Chicken with Fresh Vegetables

2 whole chicken breasts,
  skinned, boned, and
  cut into 2–3-inch
  pieces
1 tablespoon cornstarch
1 egg white
1 tablespoon Chinese rice
  wine or light dry sherry
¼ teaspoon salt
2 tablespoons vegetable
  oil

¼ pound fresh mushrooms,
  sliced
2 cups fresh snow peas
  with tips and strings
  removed
1 slice fresh ginger root,
  1 x ½-inch thick
1 tablespoon cold,
  defatted chicken stock
  (see Index or use
  canned) or water

Dust chicken lightly with 2 teaspoons of cornstarch in a bowl. Mix egg white, wine, and salt thoroughly and add to chicken, coating it well.

Heat 1 tablespoon oil in wok or large frying pan; add mushrooms and snow peas and stir-fry for about 1 or 2 minutes. Transfer to plate and set aside.

Add second tablespoon of oil and ginger; cook about 1 minute and discard ginger. Add chicken and stir-fry for about 5 minutes, or until chicken is firm and white. Add mushrooms and snow peas. Mix remaining teaspoon cornstarch with 1 tablespoon cold broth or water and add to chicken mixture, stirring constantly; cook about 1 minute and serve.

VARIATIONS: Substitute regular green peas, broccoli, romaine, or Chinese cabbage for Chinese snow peas.

Size of Serving: 1½ cups   *Number of Servings:* 4
Per Serving: Calories: 305; Protein: 32 g; Total Fat: 12 g; Sodium: 230 mg
Excellent Source of: Protein, Iron, Thiamin, Riboflavin, Niacin, and Vitamin C

Chicken Godo Godo

This West African recipe takes peanut butter out of the sandwich league to a place of distinction among international recipes.

½ head Boston lettuce, chopped	1 cup hot Peanut Sauce (recipe follows)
2 cups shredded cooked chicken	

Arrange a bed of lettuce on a serving platter. Cover with shredded chicken. Pour hot peanut sauce over chicken and let stand for ½ hour before serving.

Size of Serving: ½ cup chicken and ¼ cup sauce   *Number of Servings:* 4
Per Serving (with Peanut Sauce): Calories: 245; Protein: 24 g; Total Fat: 14 g; Sodium: 395 mg
Excellent Source of: Iron and Niacin

PEANUT SAUCE:

This high-protein sauce is delicious when served over Chicken Godo Godo, but it can also be used with vegetables such as broccoli, asparagus, or green beans, or as a dip for a fresh vegetable tray.

1 tablespoon vegetable oil	4 tablespoons cider vinegar
2 tablespoons grated fresh ginger (or 1 teaspoon ginger powder)	2 tablespoons soy sauce (or more to taste)*
1 teaspoon crushed dried hot pepper	1 cup peanut butter (ground peanuts without added salt, oil, or other ingredients)
2 tablespoons chopped scallions	
2 tablespoons brown sugar	1 cup (or more) vegetable stock (see Index)

Heat oil. Add ginger and dried pepper; cook 1 minute. Add scallions. sugar, vinegar, and soy sauce. Gradually stir in peanut butter. Add vegetable stock to desired consistency.

* 1 tablespoon soy sauce = 1320 milligrams of sodium

(continued)

NOTE: The sauce tends to thicken, so add more stock as needed.

Yield: 3 cups
Per ¼ Cup: Calories: 150; Protein: 6 g; Total Fat: 12 g; Sodium: 355 mg
Excellent Source of: Iron and Niacin

Papaya Stuffed with Curried Chicken Salad

¼ cup plain lowfat yogurt
2 tablespoons fresh lime
    juice
1 teaspoon curry powder
2 cups cooked chicken
    cut into bite-size pieces

1 cup chopped celery
¼ cup thinly sliced
    scallions
2 small ripe papayas
    Lettuce (optional)
4 lime wedges

In small bowl, mix yogurt, lime juice, and curry powder.

Place chicken, celery, and scallions in medium bowl and add yogurt mixture. Mix well. Cut papayas in half and scoop out seeds; pack curried chicken salad into papaya half-shells.

Serve on lettuce, garnished with lime wedges.

Size of Serving: ½ papaya   *Number of Servings:* 4
Per Serving: Calories: 195; Protein: 24 g; Total Fat: 3 g; Sodium: 95 mg
Excellent Source of: Protein, Vitamin A, Riboflavin, Niacin, and (with lime) Vitamin C

Orange Chicken Salad with Walnuts

2 tablespoons vegetable
    oil
2 chicken breasts,
    skinned, boned, and
    cut into 1-inch pieces
    Dash nutmeg
4–6 cups torn fresh escarole
    leaves (or romaine)

3 oranges, peeled and
    sliced
¼ cup chopped walnuts
⅓ cup fresh orange juice
    Salt and pepper to taste

Heat 1–2 tablespoons oil in skillet; sauté chicken until tender and lightly browned.

Sprinkle chicken with nutmeg, cover, and chill.

Combine chicken with remaining oil and other ingredients.

Size of Serving: 2–2¼ cups   *Number of Servings:* 4
Per Serving: Calories: 340; Protein: 28 g; Total Fat: 17 g; Sodium: 80 mg
Excellent Source of: Protein, Calcium, Iron, Vitamin A, Thiamin, Riboflavin, Niacin, and Vitamin C

Chicken Livers, Mushrooms, and Barley

¼ cup margarine
1 medium onion, minced
½ pound fresh mushrooms,
   sliced
½ green pepper, diced
1 cup whole-grain barley

2 cups defatted chicken
   stock (see Index
   or use canned)
Marjoram, rosemary, or
   basil, to taste
Salt and pepper to taste
1 pound chicken livers

Melt 2 tablespoons margarine in large skillet; add onion and sauté until lightly browned. Add mushrooms and green pepper; sauté 4–5 minutes. Add barley and brown lightly. Add stock and bring to boil; lower heat. Add seasonings and simmer, covered, about 45 minutes, or until barley has absorbed the broth and is soft.

Meanwhile, melt remaining 2 tablespoons of margarine and sauté chicken livers until tender. Combine cooked livers with cooked barley. Simmer for 5–10 minutes before serving.

Size of Serving: 1¾ cups   *Number of Servings:* 4
Per Serving: Calories: 485; Protein: 36 g; Total Fat: 18 g; Sodium: 220 mg
Excellent Source of: Protein, Iron, Vitamin A, Thiamin, Riboflavin, Niacin, and Vitamin C

Chicken Liver Stroganoff

2 tablespoons margarine
1 medium onion, finely
   chopped
1 pound chicken livers,
   halved
1 4-ounce can sliced
   mushrooms

2 teaspoons paprika
¼ teaspoon salt
Dash pepper
1 tablespoon
   instant-blending flour
½ cup orange juice
½ cup plain lowfat yogurt

Melt margarine in a large skillet; add onions and sauté until translucent. Add chicken livers, undrained mushrooms, paprika, salt, and pepper. Cook, covered, over low heat for 8–10 minutes, or until livers are cooked, stirring frequently.

Blend flour with orange juice and yogurt; stir into liver mixture. Heat thoroughly, without boiling.

Size of Serving: ¾ cup   *Number of Servings:* 4
Per Serving: Calories: 280; Protein: 32 g; Total Fat: 11 g; Sodium: 310 mg
Excellent Source of: Protein, Iron, Vitamin A, Thiamin, Riboflavin, Niacin, and Vitamin C

Turkey-Rice Salad with Grapes

3 tablespoons mayonnaise (or low-calorie mayonnaise)
2 teaspoons lemon juice
½ teaspoon onion powder
½ teaspoon finely crushed dried tarragon
Salt to taste
⅛ teaspoon pepper

2 cups diced cooked turkey (or chicken)
1 cup cooked rice
½ cup whole green seedless grapes
¼ cup chopped walnuts or cashews
4 large romaine or Boston lettuce leaves or escarole

Mix mayonnaise, lemon juice, onion powder, tarragon, salt, and pepper. Fold in turkey, rice, grapes, and nuts. Cover and chill well.

Serve on lettuce leaves.

Size of Serving: 1 cup   *Number of Servings:* 4
Per Serving: Calories: 260; Protein: 26 g; Total Fat: 9 g; Sodium: 280 mg
Excellent Source of: Protein Iron, and Niacin

Top of the Stove Turkey Casserole

2 tablespoons margarine
1 pound fresh ground turkey
1 medium onion, chopped
½ cup chopped green pepper
6 ounces noodles, uncooked (whole wheat noodles are higher in nutritional value)

1 cup shredded cheddar cheese (about 4 ounces)
¼ teaspoon salt
Pepper to taste
2 teaspoons poultry seasoning
1 28-ounce can tomatoes, broken up
½ cup thawed frozen peas

Melt margarine in a large skillet; sauté turkey until lightly browned. Stir in onions and green pepper. Arrange dry noodles over mixture; sprinkle with cheese and seasonings. Pour tomatoes over all—do not stir.

Cover and bring to a boil; reduce heat and simmer for 45 minutes. Add peas and continue to simmer for 15 minutes.

Size of Serving: 1½ cups   *Number of Servings:* 6
Per Serving: Calories: 360; Protein: 27 g; Total Fat: 13 g; Sodium: 525 mg
Excellent Source of: Protein, Calcium, Iron, Vitamin A, Thiamin, Riboflavin, Niacin, and Vitamin C

SALADS AND
SALAD DRESSINGS

Salads today contain just about any type of food. This makes them highly versatile not only as side dishes, but as appetizers, desserts (such as fruit salad), or as the meal itself. Salads can be eaten any time of the day—for breakfast, lunch, or dinner—and they also make great snacks. Success with salads depends on your wildest imagination; use of unusual combinations, special attention to contrasts in color, texture, and flavor; and the use of lots of crisp, fresh ingredients. Of course, the nutritional and caloric value of salads depends on how carefully you select what goes into, as well as onto, them. Salad vegetables in general can be important sources of vitamins, minerals, and fiber. For example, raw dark leafy salad greens provide us with a valuable source of vitamins A and C, folacin, and other B vitamins. And subtle touches can vastly improve the nutritional value of a salad, for example . . .

- Fresh parsley is a welcome flavor to many salads, and ½ cup of chopped parsley adds about 2550 I.U.s of vitamin A and 50 milligrams of vitamin C to the salad bowl. It's well worth the small area it takes to grow in your garden or on your windowsill.
- Another nutritious salad treat is sweet red pepper. One cupful supplies an additional 6700 I.U.s of vitamin A and 300 milligrams of vitamin C to a salad, as well as a truly unique and natural sweetness.
- To add extra crunch and nutrients to your salads, try tossing in a handful or two of seeds, nuts, or croutons. These will add some protein, fiber, iron, and B vitamins, as well as appeal. Some favorites are walnuts, pine nuts (pignolias), sunflower seeds, pumpkin

seeds, slivered almonds, croutons made from pumpernickel, rye, or whole wheat bread and flavored with garlic or onion.
- To turn a vegetable salad into a higher-protein main dish, try adding cheese—cubed, grated, or thinly sliced; slivers of chicken, turkey, meat, or fish; sliced or quartered hard-cooked egg; cooked, marinated beans (garbanzo, pinto, or kidney) and lentils.

Salad Greens
Basic to most salads are the greens. Try any of the different varieties:

Belgian or French endive
Bibb or Kentucky Limestone lettuce
Boston or butterhead lettuce
Cabbage—green or Savoy
Chicory or curly endive
Chinese cabbage or Chinese celery
Escarole—flat or curly (flat is less bitter)
Iceburg, crisphead, or Simpson lettuce
Parsley
Red leaf or salad bowl lettuce
Romaine or cos lettuce
Spinach leaves
Swiss chard
Watercress and garden cress

Whatever the type of greens you decide to use, be sure to treat them with care:

- Wash them thoroughly under cold running water.
- Drain in a colander if possible, shaking them well to remove excess water.
- Dry gently with a cloth or paper towel.
- Store in the refrigerator in a crisper or plastic bag until ready to use—they will keep this way for 3–4 days.

Other salad vegetables should be washed, prepared, and chilled until serving time. Cooked vegetables are best if they're still crunchy. For a top-quality salad, assemble ingredients as close to serving time as possible. Some favorite salad ingredients:

alfalfa sprouts
anchovies
artichoke hearts
fresh asparagus, lightly cooked
avocado
fresh broccoli buds, raw
capers
fresh carrots, grated or thinly sliced
fresh raw cauliflower, thinly sliced
celery
fresh Chinese pea pods
cucumbers
tart green apples
green pepper
white part of leeks, thinly sliced
fresh mushrooms, thinly sliced or quartered
black or green olives
orange or grapefruit sections
red cabbage, shredded
red onions
scallions
cherry tomatoes or quartered whole tomatoes
zucchini, thinly sliced

Salad Herbs

Most salads benefit immensely from complementary herbs. Fresh herbs can be minced and added directly to the salad or to the dressing. Crushed dried herbs can be rolled in your palms or in a mortar with a pestle and then added to the salad dressing so that they will have an opportunity to become moistened. (See Herb and Spice Chart.)

Tofu Waldorf Salad

2 medium apples, chopped	1 tablespoon honey
⅓ cup orange juice	½ teaspoon cinnamon
1 cup well-drained tofu	3 tablespoons white wine
3 tablespoons partially skimmed ricotta cheese	¾ cup chopped celery
	¼ cup raisins
	¼ cup walnuts

Prepare apples and cover with 2–3 tablespoons of the orange juice to prevent discoloration.

Blend tofu, ricotta, remaining juice, honey, cinnamon, and wine in a blender until smooth.

Mix apples with celery, raisins, and walnuts and pour tofu mixture over this. Mix well.

NOTE: Tofu is available in some regular supermarkets, Asian markets, and health food stores.

VARIATION: Apple juice can be used in place of orange juice but it is lower in vitamin C. If apple juice is used, sprinkle lemon juice over the chopped apples to prevent them from browning.

Size of Serving: 1¼ cups *Number of Servings:* 4
Per Serving: Calories: 210; Protein; 4 g; Total Fat: 8 g; Sodium: 70 mg
Excellent Source of: Calcium, Iron, and Vitamin C

Cottage Cheese Sprout Salad

1 cup fresh sprouts (mung bean, alfalfa, or any other sprouts)	1 pound lowfat cottage cheese
2 whole scallions, thinly sliced	1 small piece fresh ginger, grated (optional)

Rinse and drain the sprouts thoroughly. Combine sprouts, scallions, and cottage cheese. Cover and chill well. Serve garnished with freshly grated ginger.

Size of Serving: ¾ cup *Number of Servings:* 4
Per Serving: Calories: 110; Protein: 20 g; Total Fat: —; Sodium: 330 mg
Excellent Source of: Protein, Calcium, and Riboflavin

Orange Dressed Spinach Salad

3 tablespoons vegetable
  oil
1 teaspoon grated orange
  rind
3 tablespoons orange
  juice
½ teaspoon sugar
½ teaspoon soy sauce

Salt to taste
6 cups fresh spinach,
  washed and drained
  (½ pound)
1 cup sliced celery
½ cup sliced red onion
⅓ cup whole wheat or rye
  croutons (optional)

To make dressing: in small bowl, stir together oil, orange rind, orange juice, sugar, soy sauce, and salt.

In large bowl, toss together spinach, celery, onion, and croutons. Pour dressing over greens; toss to coat.

Size of Serving: 1½ cups   *Number of Servings:* 4
Per Serving: Calories: 125; Protein: 2 g; Total Fat: 10 g; Sodium: 80 mg (without added salt)
Excellent Source of: Vitamin A and Vitamin C

Curried Caraway Coleslaw

4 cups shredded raw
  cabbage
2 large carrots, shredded
3 celery stalks, finely
  diced
1 sweet red pepper, finely
  diced
1 small half sour pickle,
  finely diced
1 teaspoon caraway seeds
1 teaspoon dried dill weed
  (or 2 tablespoons fresh)

1 tablespoon fresh
  chives
½ teaspoon curry powder
½ teaspoon paprika
2 tablespoons
  mayonnaise* (or just
  enough to moisten)
½ teaspoon lemon juice
1 teaspoon Dijon-style
  mustard
1–2 tablespoons currants
  (optional)

Combine all ingredients; mix well.

* Substitute low calorie mayonnaise if you are dieting.

Size of Serving: 1¼ cups   *Number of Servings:* 8
Per Serving: Calories: 40; Protein: 1 g; Total Fat; 2 g; Sodium: 105 mg
Excellent Source of: Vitamin A and Vitamin C

Kaleidoscope Coleslaw

½ small head cabbage,
   coarsely shredded
½ medium unpeeled
   apple, cored and diced
½ cup grapes, halved and
   seeded

2 tablespoons raisins
1 11-ounce can mandarin
   orange sections, drained
¾ cup Creamy-Style
   Cottage Cheese
   Dressing (see Index)

In a large bowl, combine the cabbage and apple; sprinkle with lemon juice (to prevent discoloration). Add grapes, raisins, and half the orange sections. Pour the dressing over the cabbage and fruits and toss to coat. Garnish with the remainder of orange sections and serve.

Size of Serving: 1⅓ cups   *Number of Servings:* 4
Per Serving: Calories: 145; Protein: 5 g; Total Fat: 6 g; Sodium: 90 mg
Excellent Source of: Vitamin C

Red Cabbage Caraway Slaw

4 cups coarsely sliced red
   cabbage
2 scallions, sliced in ¼-
   inch pieces
1 cup fresh
   cauliflowerets (small
   pieces)

¼ cup caraway seeds
   Low-Cal Vinaigrette
   Dressing to taste (see
   Index)
4 large romaine lettuce
   leaves

Mix all ingredients together well. Serve chilled on lettuce.

Size of Serving: 1¼ cups   *Number of Servings:* 4
Per Serving (without dressing): Calories: 35; Protein: 2 g; Total Fat: —;
Sodium: 30 mg
Excellent Source of: Vitamin C

Grapefruit, Orange, and Red Onion Salad

1 large grapefruit
2 large oranges
2 small red onions, thinly
   sliced
¼ cup vegetable oil
2 tablespoons grapefruit
   juice
2 tablespoons plain low-
   fat yogurt

1 teaspoon honey
   Salt to taste
   Freshly ground pepper,
   to taste
8 romaine lettuce leaves
¼ cup pitted black olives
   (optional)

(continued)

Peel grapefruit and oranges; remove seeds and membranes. Place citrus sections in bowl with onion.

Mix oil, grapefruit juice, yogurt, honey, salt, and pepper with a wire whisk; pour over citrus/onion mixture; toss lightly. Cover and allow flavors to blend for 15–20 minutes before serving.

Serve on romaine lettuce; garnish with olives, if desired.

Size of Serving: 1¼ cups   *Number of Servings:* 4
Per Serving: Calories: 210; Protein: 2 g; Total Fat: 14 g; Sodium: 10 mg
Excellent Source of: Iron and Vitamin C

Turkish Cucumber Salad

1 *large cucumber, peeled*
1 *small onion, minced*
2 *tablespoons raisins*
2 *tablespoons chopped*
   walnuts
¼ *teaspoon pepper*

1 *tablespoon minced*
   fresh mint or 1 teaspoon
   dried mint
1 *cup plain lowfat yogurt*
   Salt to taste

Grate cucumber and squeeze out excess water. Combine cucumber with remaining ingredients; mix well. Cover and chill before serving.

Size of Serving: ¾ cup   *Number of Servings:* 4
Per Serving: Calories: 85; Protein: 4 g; Total Fat: 4 g; Sodium: 40 mg

Black, White, and Red All Over Salad

1 *large head cauliflower*
⅔ *cup chopped parsley*
¼ *cup black olives*
   (canned)
¼ *cup chopped pimiento*

¼ *cup Low-Cal*
   Vinaigrette Dressing
   (or to taste—see Index)
   Freshly ground pepper
   to taste
   Salt to taste

Rinse cauliflower and cut off individual florets. If they are very large, cut them again through the stem so they are bite-size. Put florets into vigorously boiling water and boil them for just about 4 minutes, or until they are barely tender but still crisp. Drain and refrigerate.

Put the cold florets in a wooden salad bowl with parsley, black olives, pimiento, dressing, pepper, and salt. Toss until all florets are lightly coated.

Size of Serving: approximately 1 cup   *Number of Servings:* 4
Per Serving: Calories: 85; Protein: 6 g; Total Fat: 3 g; Sodium: 105 mg
Excellent Source of: Iron, Vitamin A, Thiamin, Riboflavin, and Vitamin C

Italian Basil-Tomato Salad

The success of this salad depends very much on the flavor of vine-ripened tomatoes and fresh basil.

> 4 medium vine-ripened
> fresh tomatoes
> 5–6 fresh basil leaves,
> chopped
> 2 tablespoons vegetable
> oil

> 3 tablespoons wine vinegar
> Salt to taste
> Freshly ground pepper
> to taste

Cut the tomatoes either in thin wedges or slices and spread them out in a wide, shallow bowl.

Combine remaining ingredients and sprinkle over tomatoes. Baste the tomatoes with the dressing by tilting the dish and spooning it over the tomatoes repeatedly. Marinate 20–30 minutes before serving.

Size of Serving: ¾ cup   *Number of Servings:* 4
Per Serving: Calories: 80; Protein: 1 g; Total Fat: 7 g; Sodium: 3 mg (unsalted)
Excellent Source of: Vitamin C

The Salad Experience

> 1 zucchini, sliced
> 1 small head romaine
> lettuce
> 1 small head Boston
> lettuce
> 6 whole scallions, thinly
> sliced
> 4–6 radishes, thinly sliced
> 6 large mushrooms,
> thinly sliced
> 16 cherry tomatoes, cut in
> half, or 2 large
> tomatoes, cut in
> eighths

> ¼ cup coarsely chopped
> walnuts
> Handful parsley,
> chopped
> Vegetable oil to taste
> Salt and freshly ground
> pepper to taste
> Garlic powder to taste
> 2 teaspoons fresh lemon
> juice
> 2 teaspoons red wine
> vinegar

Boil zucchini until barely tender; drain and cool.

Wash lettuce under cold water, drain, and gently dry it. Tear into bite-size pieces and put into large wooden bowl.

Arrange scallions, radishes, and mushrooms attractively over lettuce.

(continued)

Arrange zucchini and tomatoes in a large circle around outside edge of lettuce. Sprinkle walnuts in center. Sprinkle parsley over all.

At the table, add the dressing and do the tossing: Pour oil over the salad and toss until each piece of lettuce is very lightly coated and glistening. (Lettuce must be rather dry). Add salt, pepper, and garlic powder to taste; toss and taste for seasoning *before* adding lemon and vinegar. Add about 2 teaspoons of wine vinegar and freshly squeezed lemon juice, toss, and taste again.

VARIATIONS:

· Add fresh spinach in season, or replace lettuce with spinach altogether. Use other types of lettuce when available.
· Use watercress instead of parsley.

Size of Serving: 1½ cups   *Number of Servings:* 8
Per Serving: Calories: 55 (without oil); Protein: 3 g; Total Fat: 3 g (without oil); Sodium: 10 mg (unsalted) (For each tablespoon of oil, add 120 calories and 14 grams fat.)
Excellent Source of: Vitamin A and Vitamin C

Crudités

The French deserve credit for these colorful, crispy fresh vegetables cut at various angles. The recipe has been doubled to satisfy any between-meal cravings.

> 1 *large green pepper, cut into ½-inch pieces*
> 1 *large sweet red pepper, cut into thin 2-inch-long strips*
> 4 *carrots, sliced on the diagonal into ¼-inch pieces*
> 4 *stalks celery, sliced into thin 1-inch-long pieces*
>
> ½ *pound fresh mushrooms, sliced lengthwise (or left whole if very small)*
> ½ *small red onion, finely chopped or 3–4 shallots, finely chopped*
> ½ *cup Low-Cal Vinaigrette Dressing (see Index)*

Mix all ingredients together well; cover and chill for 1–2 hours before serving.

Size of Serving: 1 cup   *Number of Servings:* 8
Per Serving: Calories: 35; Protein: 2 g; Total Fat: —; Sodium: 25 mg
Excellent Source of: Vitamin A, Riboflavin, and Vitamin C

Marinated Dilled Green Bean Salad

1 pound fresh green
beans, trimmed but
left whole

2–3 tablespoons vegetable
oil

2–3 tablespoons lemon
juice

2 large shallots, finely
chopped

2 tablespoons fresh dill
weed or 2 teaspoons
dried dill

¼ teaspoon dry mustard
Garlic salt to taste
Freshly ground pepper
to taste

Cook green beans in a small amount of water briefly—just until they turn bright green (they should be slightly softened but still crisp); drain and run under cold water for several minutes, or until well cooled. Drain well and place in bowl.

Combine oil, lemon juice, shallots, dill weed, dry mustard, garlic salt, and pepper. Mix well; pour over green beans and toss lightly. Cover and refrigerate for 1–2 hours to allow flavors to blend.

Size of Serving: 1 cup   *Number of Servings:* 4
Per Serving: Calories: 110; Protein: 3 g; Total Fat: 10 g; Sodium: 10 mg (unsalted)
Excellent Source of: Vitamin C

Zucchini Salad with Basil

3 small zucchini, thinly
sliced

2 large ripe tomatoes,
sliced in thin wedges

1 small red onion, finely
chopped

¼ cup Low-Cal
Vinaigrette (see Index)

2 tablespoons chopped
fresh basil or 2
teaspoons dried basil

Combine zucchini, tomatoes, and red onion in a bowl. Blend vinaigrette dressing well; add to vegetables. Sprinkle with basil and stir gently.

Cover and chill 1–2 hours before serving to allow flavors to blend.

Size of Serving: 1 cup   *Number of Servings:* 4
Per Serving: Calories: 70; Protein: 2 g; Total Fat: 3 g; Sodium: 15 mg (unsalted)
Excellent Source of: Vitamin C

Marinated Vegetable Salad

1 medium carrot, sliced
  into rounds
1 clove garlic, crushed
1 tablespoon vegetable
  oil
1 medium onion, cut into
  eighths
¼ teaspoon dried basil

1 medium red or green
  pepper, cored, seeded,
  and cut into strips
1 medium zucchini, sliced
10 small mushrooms
¼ cup water
½ cup wine vinegar

In a medium saucepan, sauté carrot rounds and garlic in oil for 4–5 minutes over medium heat—do not brown. Add onion and basil and cook, stirring occasionally, about 3 more minutes. Add pepper, zucchini, mushrooms, and ¼ cup water.

Lower heat, cover pan, and let vegetables steam for about 5 minutes, or until crisp-tender. Remove from heat and add vinegar. Let mixture stand, covered, until cool, then refrigerate. Flavor is best when it is allowed to stand 12 hours or more. This keeps well for several days in the refrigerator. Store in a jar with tight cover.

VARIATIONS: Many other types of vegetables may be substituted or added, such as cauliflowerets, diced eggplant, chopped cabbage, asparagus spears, whole green beans, or turnip strips.

Size of Serving: ¾–1 cup   Number of Servings: 4
Per Serving: Calories: 135; Protein: 2 g; Total Fat: 4 g; Sodium: 20 mg
Excellent Source of: Vitamin A and Vitamin C

Dilled Pickled Carrots

1 pound miniature
  carrots, well scrubbed
  (scraped if necessary to
  remove dark spots),
  with ends trimmed, and
  left whole
1 large green pepper,
  seeded and cut into
  ¾-inch strips
2 bay leaves

½ cup white vinegar
¼ cup water
1–2 tablespoons sugar to
  taste
½ teaspoon mustard seed
½ teaspoon dill weed
¼ teaspoon crushed red
  pepper
¼ teaspoon dill seed
1 garlic clove, crushed

Cook carrots and green pepper until tender but slightly crunchy. Plunge them into cold water to cool quickly; drain.

Pack carrots and pepper strips into clean pint jar with tightly fitting cover. Combine the other ingredients and mix well; pour over the carrots and green pepper. Cover the jar and refrigerate for at least 24 hours before serving to allow contents to marinate. It will keep for several weeks if refrigerated.

Yield: 2 cups
Per ¼ Cup: Calories: 35; Protein: 1 g; Total Fat: —; Sodium: 30 mg
Excellent Source of: Vitamin A and Vitamin C

Tomato Relish

This is particularly delicious with fish.

3 large ripe fresh tomatoes, finely chopped
1 small green pepper, finely chopped
½ sweet red pepper, finely chopped
2 stalks celery, finely chopped
⅓ cup chopped fresh parsley

¼ cup finely chopped onion
2 tablespoons minced fresh basil (or 1 teaspoon dried basil)
1 teaspoon whole mustard seed
Dash hot pepper sauce
⅓ cup wine vinegar
1–2 teaspoons honey to taste
Salt to taste

Combine all ingredients; mix thoroughly.
Cover and chill 1–2 hours before serving to blend flavors.

Yield: 4 cups
Per Tablespoon: Calories: 5; Protein: Trace; Total Fat: —; Sodium: Trace
Excellent Source of: (min. 2½ tbsp.) Vitamin C

Salsa (Mexican Relish)

Particularly good with beef or pork.

1 large tomato, finely diced
½ cup diced green chilies
1 small onion, finely diced
¼ green pepper, finely diced

1 tablespoon minced fresh coriander (or 1 teaspoon dried coriander)
1 teaspoon cider vinegar

Combine ingredients; mix well and chill at least 2 hours before serving.
Yield: about 2 cups
Per ¼ Cup: Calories: 10; Protein: —; Total Fat; —; Sodium: Trace
Excellent Source of: Vitamin C

Fresh Cranberry Orange Relish

Particularly good with poultry or pork.

1 pound fresh cranberries (about 4 cups)
2 oranges, quartered and seeded

⅔ cup honey (or to taste)
1 stalk celery, finely diced
¼ cup chopped walnuts

Grind cranberries and oranges finely in a food chopper or processor. Mix in honey, dissolving well. Add celery and nuts; mix well. Cover and refrigerate for several hours before serving to allow flavors to blend.

Yield: about 6 cups
Per ½ Cup: Calories: 110; Protein: 1 g; Total Fat: 2 g; Sodium: 5 mg
Excellent Source of: Vitamin C

Major White's Chutney

Particularly good with chicken dishes.

1 cup finely chopped dried dates
1 cup finely chopped dried apricots
1½ cups cider vinegar
½ cup finely diced turnip
½ cup finely diced carrot
½ cup tomato purée
1 medium unpeeled apple, cored and finely chopped
1 large onion, peeled and finely chopped

1½ teaspoons minced fresh ginger (or ¾ teaspoon dried ginger)
2–3 tablespoons honey to taste
½ teaspoon ground cinnamon (or to taste)
½ teaspoon ground cloves (or to taste)
½ cup chopped unsalted raw cashew nuts (optional)
⅛ teaspoon cayenne (optional)

Soak chopped dates and apricots in ¾ cup cider cinegar for 4–5 hours.

Meanwhile, combine the turnip, carrot, tomato purée, and remaining ¾ cup cider vinegar in a saucepan. Cook over moderate heat until the vegetables are *just barely* soft—but still crisp. Remove from heat and cool; add to date/apricot mixture and mix well. Cover and refrigerate for remainder of marinating time.

Stir in remaining ingredients; mix well and cover. Allow flavors to blend 1–2 hours before serving. Store in tightly covered jar in refrigerator.

Yield: about 5 cups
Per ½ Cup: Calories: 125; Protein: 2 g; Total Fat: —; Sodium: 65 mg
Excellent Source of: Iron, Vitamin A, and Vitamin C

Salad Dressings

Homemade salad dressings increase the nutritional value of a salad if the ingredients are thoughtfully selected. For example, polyunsaturated oils—such as corn and safflower oil—supply a valuable source of vitamin E and the essential fatty acids. However, despite these benefits, use oils sparingly because of their high caloric value (each tablespoon of oil contains about 120 calories). Vitamin C-rich lemon, orange, grapefruit, or tomato juice can be used in place of, or in addition to, vinegar—vinegar has practically no caloric value, as well as no nutritional value. Plain lowfat yogurt is a good substitute for sour cream in salad dressings because of its lower caloric, saturated fat, and cholesterol content, plus its higher overall nutritional value. (It can also be used to dilute mayonnaise for the same reasons.) And some herbs and spices can substantially increase the vitamin A content of salad dressings: ground basil, cayenne, ground oregano, paprika, and fresh parsley are particularly good sources of vitamin A.

Keep a variety of homemade salad dressings on hand in the refrigerator. Many are useful as complements to cooked vegetables and grain dishes, as well as salads. Try serving salad dressing separately, in a small pitcher or cruet, so people can help themselves and be in control (hopefully) of their caloric intake—and their waistlines. (This also solves the problem of soggy leftover salad.)

Low-Cal Vinaigrette Dressing

3 tablespoons vegetable oil
5 tablespoons wine vinegar
2 tablespoons fresh lemon juice
6 tablespoons water
1 teaspoon Dijon-style mustard
1 large garlic clove, crushed

2 tablespoons finely minced shallots
1 tablespoon honey
1 teaspoon crushed tarragon
¼ teaspoon paprika
⅛ teaspoon freshly ground pepper
Salt to taste (optional)

Mix well in a tightly covered jar; store in refrigerator.

Yield: 1 cup
Per Tablespoon: Calories: 30; Protein: —; Total Fat: 3 g; Sodium: 5 mg (unsalted)

Horseradish Yogurt Dressing

Try this also as a sandwich spread or sauce with cold sliced meats or
as a dip with vegetables.

    1 cup plain lowfat yogurt   2 tablespoons lemon juice
    ¼ cup horseradish   Salt to taste
    ½ cup chili sauce   Pepper to taste
    2 tablespoons vegetable
       oil

Put all ingredients in blender and whirl 10–15 seconds.

Yield: 2 cups
Per Tablespoon: Calories: 15; Protein: —; Total Fat: 1 g; Sodium: 5 mg

Creamy Lime Dressing

    ⅓ cup plain lowfat yogurt   2 teaspoons grated lime
    2 tablespoons lime juice   rind
    1 tablespoon honey

Mix all ingredients together well with a wire whisk.
   Store in tightly covered jar in refrigerator. It's delicious on fruits and
salads.
VARIATION: Lemon (or orange) juice and rind can be used in place of
lime.

Yield: ½ cup
Per Tablespoon: Calories: 15; Protein: —; Total Fat: —; Sodium: 5 mg

Diet Dill Dressing

This is great with broiled salmon steaks.

    ⅔ cup lowfat cottage   2 teaspoons snipped fresh
       cheese   dill weed
    3 tablespoons skim milk   ¼ teaspoon freshly ground
    1 scallion, chopped   pepper (or to taste)
    1 teaspoon lemon juice   1 teaspoon onion powder
                                       (or to taste)

Combine ingredients in blender and purée well. Chill.

Yield: 1 cup
Per Tablespoon: Calories: 10; Protein: 1 g; Total Fat: —; Sodium: 10 mg

Sesame Tahini Dressing

This is delicious with hot vegetables or on salads.

1 cup sesame tahini	Sea salt to taste (or 1
½ cup cold water	tablespoon tamari)
½ cup lemon juice	½ teaspoon garlic powder

In blender, or with egg beater, whip tahini with water and lemon juice until the mixture is smooth. Stir in garlic and sea salt (or tamari). Refrigerate.

If a thinner texture is desired, additional lemon juice or water can be added before serving.
VARIATION: Try adding ⅛–¼ cup sunflower seeds.

Yield: 2 cups
Per Tablespoon: Calories: 60; Protein: —; Total Fat: 7 g; Sodium: —(unsalted)

Creamy-Style Cottage Cheese Dressing

Creamy-style salad dressing becomes lower in fat and calories and higher in protein when cottage cheese is used in place of mayonnaise.

½ cup creamed cottage cheese	1 tablespoon lemon juice
	1 tablespoon vegetable oil
2 tablespoons skim milk	1 tablespoon honey

Combine all ingredients in an electric blender and blend until smooth.

Yield: ¾ cup
Per Tablespoon: Calories: 30; Protein: 2 g; Total Fat: 2 g; Sodium: 30 mg

Avocado Salad Dressing

Good with any green salad, this dressing is spectacular on romaine leaves tossed with marinated artichoke hearts. sliced radishes, and cucumbers.

2 medium fully ripe avocados, peeled, pitted, and cut up	½ cup orange juice
	½ cup mayonnaise (or low-calorie mayonnaise)
½ cup lemon juice	
2 6-ounce jars marinated artichoke hearts, undrained	2 tablespoons finely chopped scallions

(continued)

Mash avocados and lemon juice until smooth. Drain artichoke hearts (save for salad) and pour marinade into avocado mixture. Add orange juice, mayonnaise, and scallions. Beat to blend thoroughly.

Cover and store overnight in refrigerator.

Yield: 3 cups
Per Tablespoon: Calories: 20; Protein: Trace; Total Fat: 2 g; Sodium: 5 mg
Excellent Source of: (min. 2½ tbsp) Vitamin C

Lemon Salad Dressing

¾ cup vegetable oil   ½ teaspoon oregano
½ cup lemon juice   ¼ teaspoon pepper
1½ tablespoons honey   1 garlic clove, crushed
½ teaspoon tarragon   Salt to taste
½ teaspoon thyme

Combine all ingredients and shake well. Chill overnight, then remove garlic.

Yield: 1⅓ cups
Per Tablespoon: Calories: 75; Protein: —; Total Fat: 8 g; Sodium: — (unsalted)

EGG AND
CHEESE DISHES

Soufflés, quiches, fondues, frittatas, and French omelets . . . eggs and cheese are two ingredients that most good cooks would find difficult to live without. And as more people are beginning to live with less meat in their diets, they're also learning to appreciate the merits of eggs and cheese at breakfast, lunch, or dinner.

The egg is at the top of the list for high-quality protein (second only to mother's milk) and it is an excellent source of the B vitamin riboflavin. It also supplies good amounts of folacin, pantothenic acid, and vitamin D. The egg yolk contains respectable amounts of biotin, calcium, iron, phosphorus, and vitamins A, B-12, and K. All neatly packaged, the egg provides about 75 calories. Unfortunately, the yolk also contains all of the egg's fat and cholesterol; so if your doctor has recommended that you eat less cholesterol, keep count of the number of egg yolks that appear in your diet—3 or 4 per week at the most—but go ahead and use the egg whites freely in cooking.

Cheeses are good sources of calcium, phosphorus, protein, riboflavin, and vitamin B-12. Like eggs, however, they also supply substantial amounts of fat and cholesterol. Whenever possible, use cheeses made from partially skimmed milk and save the whole milk varieties for less frequent use in favorite recipes.

BUYING AND STORING EGGS

When buying eggs, choose either brown or white ones (there's no difference nutritionally), and ones that have been *refrigerated*. Eggs deteriorate rapidly at room temperature but can be kept relatively fresh for 1–2 weeks if refrigerated. Fresh, Grade A eggs have thick whites and firm, well-rounded yolks. At home, eggs should be refrigerated in their carton. This will help keep them from absorbing odors from other foods. If an egg is cracked, be sure that it is thoroughly cooked before eating it so that any contaminants will be destroyed.

Cover leftover egg yolks with cold water and store in a covered container in the refrigerator; use in 2–3 days. Egg whites can be covered (without water) and stored in the refrigerator for about 10 days. The whites also freeze well, but egg yolks need a few pinches of salt mixed in before they will freeze successfully. Try using ice cube containers to freeze whites and yolks (or whole eggs—but don't forget the salt); when frozen, transfer them to a plastic bag and seal tightly. This way you'll have individual eggs, whites, or yolks to use in cooking.

Crustless Cheese Vegetable Pie

2–3 tablespoons margarine
¼ pound fresh mushrooms, cut into ½-inch dice
1 small zucchini, cut into ½-inch dice
1 small green pepper, finely diced
1 pound partially skimmed ricotta cheese, well-drained
1 cup partially skimmed mozzarella cheese, coarsely shredded

3 eggs, slightly beaten
½ pound fresh spinach, cooked, squeezed, and finely chopped (will measure about ½ cup)
2 tablespoons vegetable oil (+ oil for pie plate)
1 tablespoon dill weed
Garlic salt to taste
Freshly ground pepper to taste

Preheat oven to 350°F.

Melt 2 tablespoons margarine in a large skillet. Add mushrooms, zucchini, and green pepper and sauté until soft; cool to lukewarm.

Combine cheeses, eggs, spinach, oil, dill, and mushroom mixture. Season to taste with garlic salt and pepper, mixing well. Place mixture in an oiled 9½-inch pie plate; dot with 1 tablespoon margarine (this is not necessary if extra calories are unwanted).

Bake about 45 minutes, or until knife comes out clean when inserted into the middle of the pie. Serve hot or cold.

VARIATION: This can be baked in a rye or whole wheat pie shell or Low-Cal Crust for Quiche (see Index) if desired.

Size of Serving: one-sixth of a 9½-inch pie   *Number of Servings:* 6
Per Serving: Calories: 310; Protein: 21 g; Total Fat: 17 g; Sodium: 405 mg
Excellent Source of: Protein, Calcium, Iron, Vitamin A, Riboflavin, and
Vitamin C

Swiss Potato Pie

2 tablespoons margarine
2 medium raw potatoes,
 peeled
¼ teaspoon salt
1 cup shredded Swiss
 cheese (4 ounces)
½ cup chopped scallions

2 eggs
1 cup skim milk
⅛ teaspoon pepper
2 tablespoons chopped
 parsley
½ teaspoon paprika
½ teaspoon dry mustard

Preheat oven to 375°F.

Spread 1 tablespoon margarine over the bottom of a 9-inch pie plate.

Grate the potatoes in a food processor, blender, or by hand on a coarse grater; drain well. Sprinkle ¼ teaspoon salt on the potatoes and press them into the pie plate, covering the bottom and sides and forming a "crust." Sprinkle shredded cheese over the potato crust.

Melt remaining tablespoon of margarine in a small frying pan; add scallions and sauté until translucent; spread over cheese. Combine the eggs, milk, pepper, parsley, paprika, and mustard. Beat well and pour over the scallions and cheese.

Bake 40–45 minutes, or until pie is golden and a knife inserted into the center comes out clean.

NOTE: This needs a chance to cool slightly (about 10 minutes) before serving since the flavor is masked when hot. Leftover pie can be reheated in foil at 350°F. for 10–15 minutes.

VARIATIONS: Rutabagas may be substituted for the potatoes. Sliced fresh mushrooms can be added on top of the cheese.

Size of Serving: one-sixth of a 9-inch pie   *Number of Servings:* 6
Per Serving: Calories: 185; Protein: 9 g; Total Fat: 13 g; Sodium: 310 mg
Excellent Source of: Calcium and Riboflavin

Spinach Cheese Pie

CRUST:

⅓ cup cold margarine
¾ cup enriched
 all-purpose flour

¼ cup whole wheat flour
3 tablespoons cold water

(continued)

FILLING:

2 tablespoons margarine
1 small onion, diced
½ pound fresh spinach,
    finely chopped
Dash pepper
3 eggs, slightly beaten

1 pound lowfat cottage
    cheese
3 tablespoons enriched
    all-purpose flour
½ cup shredded cheddar
    cheese

To prepare crust, cut margarine into flours and add water. Stir only as much as necessary to blend. Chill 1 hour.

Meanwhile, melt 2 tablespoons margarine in a large skillet; add onion and sauté for 1 minute; add spinach and pepper and sauté 2 minutes. Remove from heat and add eggs, cottage cheese, flour, and cheddar cheese; mix well.

Preheat oven to 375°F.

Roll pie crust dough between two sheets of waxed paper to about a 10-inch diameter and ease into a 9-inch pie pan; flute edges. Add filling to pie crust and bake 45 minutes, or until firm.

Size of Serving: one-sixth of a 9-inch pie   *Number of Servings:* 6
Per Serving: Calories: 390; Protein: 23 g; Total Fat: 28 g; Sodium: 530 mg
Excellent Source of: Protein, Calcium, Iron, Vitamin A, Thiamin, Riboflavin, and Vitamin C

Chilies Rellenos con Queso

8 whole green chilies,
    canned (or fresh if you
    know how to roast,
    sweat, and peel them)
½ pound (approx.) Jack
    cheese, cut into
    ½ x ½-inch pieces

¼ cup enriched
    all-purpose flour plus
    enough to roll chilies in
4 eggs
1 tablespoon water
¼ teaspoon salt
2–3 tablespoons margarine
    or vegetable oil

Remove seeds from chilies and stuff each with 1 piece of cheese. Roll filled chilies in flour.

Separate egg whites from yolks. Beat the whites until they form soft peaks.

Combine ¼ cup flour with water and salt. Add egg yolks and beat well. Fold egg yolk mixture into beaten egg whites.

Heat fat in a large skillet. Place an oval mound of about ½ cup of the egg batter in the pan and quickly lay a stuffed chili in the center; then spoon on enough batter to cover the chili. Cook 2–3 minutes over medium heat; turn and cook 2–3 minutes longer (3–4 chilies can be cooked at once).

Serve immediately with a light tomato sauce or use canned salsa cruda (enchilada sauce is too heavy).

NOTE: Canned green chilies are usually found in the "gourmet" or ethnic foods section of the supermarket.

VARIATIONS: Substitute whole tomatoes with seeds removed, avocados with pits removed, or large whole mushrooms for the chilies if a milder dish is desired.

Size of Serving: 2 chilies   *Number of Servings:* 4
Per Serving: Calories: 490; Protein: 25 g; Total Fat: 33 g; Sodium: 660 mg
Excellent Source of: Protein, Calcium, Iron, Vitamin A, Riboflavin, and Vitamin C

Chile Relleno Soufflé

6 *large eggs*
1 *tablespoon enriched*
  all-purpose flour
¼ *teaspoon salt*
1 *4-ounce can green*
  chilies, seeded and cut
  into small pieces

6 *ounces Jack cheese,*
  sliced
1 *cup hot taco or enchilada*
  sauce (optional)

Preheat oven to 325°F.

Grease a 2 x 7 x 13-inch baking dish.

Separate the eggs; beat the egg whites until stiff. Combine the flour, salt, and egg yolks. Fold into beaten egg whites quickly—only until mixed.

Pour half of this mixture into the baking dish. Spread chilies over the egg batter; then cover chilies with cheese slices. Pour remaining egg mixture on top, distributing it evenly.

Place in oven and bake 28 minutes. Serve immediately with or without sauce.

Size of Serving: ½ cup   *Number of Servings:* 4
Per Serving (without sauce): Calories: 305; Protein: 21 g; Total Fat: 23 g; Sodium: 520 mg
Excellent Source of: Protein, Calcium, Iron, Vitamin A, Riboflavin, and Vitamin C

Frittata (Parslied Spinach Omelet)

1 pound fresh spinach,
washed and coarsely
chopped
1 bunch fresh parsley,
washed and coarsely
chopped
2 medium leeks or 4
scallions, chopped
coarsely (if using leeks,
chop the white bulb end
plus part of the green
stalk if it's tender; if
using scallions, chop all
of it)

6 eggs, slightly beaten
½ teaspoon crumbled
rosemary (or more to
taste)
Salt and pepper to
taste
3–4 tablespoons vegetable
oil

Combine spinach, parsley, and leeks or scallions in a saucepan *without* added water. Cook 2–3 minutes, stirring often to prevent burning. (There is plenty of water in the spinach to cook the vegetables in.)

Remove vegetables from heat; drain and cool. Add eggs, rosemary, salt, and pepper; mix well.

Heat oil in a 12-inch skillet (with tightly fitting cover). Add egg/spinach mixture and cook over *low* heat, covered, about 15 minutes, or until well set. Slide onto a plate, add more oil to the skillet, and slide omelet back into pan with the cooked side up; cook about 1–2 minutes.

Turn onto platter and cut into wedges. Serve hot or cold.

Size of Serving: one-sixth of 12-inch omelet   *Number of Servings:* 6
Per Serving: Calories: 165; Protein: 9 g; Total Fat: 13 g; Sodium: 120 mg
Excellent Source of: Iron, Vitamin A, Riboflavin, and Vitamin C

Spinach Soufflé Crepe

THE SOUFFLÉ:

1 cup cooked, drained,
chopped fresh or frozen
spinach (about 1 pound
uncooked)
2 tablespoons margarine
1 cup skim milk

¼ cup enriched
all-purpose flour
4 large eggs, separated
2 teaspoons finely
chopped onion
¼ teaspoon salt

THE SAUCE:

1½ teaspoons margarine
½ cup skim milk
2¼ teaspoons enriched
all-purpose flour

⅛ teaspoon dry mustard
1 ounce shredded Swiss
cheese

PLUS:

> *8 crepes (see recipe page*   ¼ *cup thinly sliced*
> *215), or any other recipe*   *scallions*
> *for entrée crepes*

Preheat oven to 350°F.

Soufflé:

Grease a 1-quart soufflé dish very well.

Cook spinach, covered, in small amount of water. Drain thoroughly, squeeze out excess water, and chop.

Melt margarine in medium-size saucepan. Mix milk and flour until flour dissolves; add to margarine and cook 3–4 minutes, stirring constantly.

Beat egg yolks 1–2 minutes; add onion, spinach, salt, and milk/flour mixture; beat 1 more minute.

Whip egg white until stiff; gently fold in egg yolk/spinach mixture.

Pour into soufflé dish; place in a larger, shallow pan containing water. Place both pans in oven and bake 40 minutes, or until knife comes out clean.

Sauce:

Melt margarine in saucepan. Mix milk and flour until flour dissolves; add to margarine along with dry mustard. When sauce begins to thicken, add the cheese; stir constantly until cheese melts. Keep warm over low heat, stirring often.

To assemble, place ⅓ cup of soufflé on one side of each crepe, rolling crepes closed. Spoon 1–1½ tablespoons of sauce over each serving. Serve garnished with chopped scallions.

Size of Serving: 2 crepes with ⅓ cup soufflé in each and 1 tablespoon sauce over each   *Number of Servings:* 4

Per Serving: Calories: 295; Protein: 19 g; Total Fat: 19 g; Sodium: 475 mg

Excellent Source of: Protein, Calcium, Iron, Vitamin A, Thiamin, Riboflavin, and Vitamin C

Cottage Cheese Pancakes

> *4 large eggs, beaten*   ⅓ *cup whole wheat flour*
> ¼ *cup melted margarine*   ⅓ *cup enriched*
> *1 cup lowfat small-curd*   *all-purpose flour*
> *cottage cheese*   ¼ *teaspoon salt*

Heat griddle or frying pan; oil lightly.

Combine all ingredients; mix well. Using measuring cup with a lip, pour ¼ cup batter onto griddle for each pancake. When bubbles appear, turn pancakes and brown other side.

Serve with unsweetened applesauce or Fresh Fruit Sauce (see Index).

(continued)

Size of Serving: 2 pancakes   *Number of Servings:* 4
Per Serving: Calories: 300; Protein: 18 g; Total Fat: 18 g; Sodium: 480 mg
Excellent Source of: Protein, Iron, and Riboflavin

Low-Cal Crust for Quiche

1½ tablespoons margarine
⅓ cup wheat germ,
  unprocessed bran,
  cornmeal, or fine
  whole wheat or rye
  bread crumbs

2 tablespoons grated
  Parmesan cheese

Grease an 8-inch pie plate well with the margarine.

Combine the dry ingredients and mix well; sprinkle mixture over the buttered pie plate, covering it well. Using your fingers, pat down in the bottom and around the sides, making sure that the mixture adheres well to the pie plate.

Add your favorite quiche filling and bake according to quiche directions.

Yield: crust for 8-inch pie
Per one-sixth of the Crust: Calories: 45; Protein: 1 g; Total Fat: 4 g; Sodium: 70 mg

Spanakopeta (Greek Spinach Pie)

¾ pound margarine (3
  sticks)
1½ bunches scallions
½ cup chopped onion
1 bunch minced parsley
3 10-ounce packages
  frozen chopped
  spinach, thawed
¾ teaspoon salt

½ teaspoon pepper
2 teaspoons dill weed
½ pound feta cheese,
  crumbled
1 pound lowfat cottage
  cheese
3 large eggs, slightly
  beaten
1 pound filo leaves

Preheat oven to 350°F.

Melt ¼ pound margarine (1 stick) in a large skillet; add scallions, onion, and parsley; sauté for 2–3 minutes. Add spinach, salt, pepper, dill weed, feta cheese, and cottage cheese. Stir and remove from heat. Beat in eggs until frothy. (Use this mixture for the filling.)

Butter 10 filo leaves *very lightly* with margarine (these will be used for the bottom crust and the filling will help to keep them moist). Place leaves in a 9 x 13-inch pan and spread filling on top of them evenly.

Butter 12 filo leaves more generously with remaining margarine and place on top of the filling. Score the top layers with a knife, outlining the shape of the servings. Bake for 50 minutes, or until crust is golden brown.

Size of Serving: about 2½-inch square   *Number of Servings:* 15
Per Serving: Calories: 330; Protein: 15 g; Total Fat: 22 g; Sodium: 570 mg
Excellent Source of: Calcium, Iron, Vitamin A, Riboflavin, and Vitamin C

Lokshen Kugel (Noodle Pudding)

Noodle pudding, or kugel, can be served as a high-protein side dish, light meal, or even dessert—and the leftovers are delicious the next day for breakfast.

2 egg yolks, beaten
2 tablespoons melted margarine
1½ tablespoons honey
1½ cups lowfat cottage cheese (about ¾ pound)
⅔ cup plain lowfat yogurt
¼ teaspoon cinnamon
½ teaspoon vanilla extract

6 ounces medium noodles, cooked and drained (whole wheat noodles are more nutritious)
⅓ cup dark raisins
2 egg whites, stiffly beaten
¼ cup finely crushed whole wheat bread crumbs or wheat germ

Preheat oven to 350°F.

In large bowl, mix together egg yolks, margarine, honey, cottage cheese, yogurt, cinnamon, and vanilla. Add drained, cooked noodles and raisins. Fold in egg whites.

Pour into greased 1½-quart casserole. Top with bread crumbs or wheat germ. Bake for 50 minutes. Serve immediately.

Size of Serving: ¾ cup   *Number of Servings:* 8
Per Serving: Calories: 255; Protein: 13 g; Total Fat: 8 g; Sodium: 310 mg
Excellent Source of: Calcium, Iron, Thiamin, and Riboflavin

Double Swiss Chard

2 pounds Swiss chard, well washed
4 tablespoons margarine
3 tablespoons enriched all-purpose flour
1¼ cups skim milk
1½ cups shredded Swiss cheese

½ teaspoon dry mustard
2 tablespoons minced fresh chives
Salt to taste
¼ teaspoon pepper
¼ teaspoon ground nutmeg

(continued)

Preheat oven to 350°F.

Steam the chard in a steamer or in a small amount of water (just enough to cover the bottom of the pan) about 5 minutes. Stack the chard and slice into ½-inch strips.

Prepare sauce by melting the margarine in a small saucepan; stir in the flour, mixing well, and cook 1 minute over moderate heat. Gradually stir in the milk and cook, stirring constantly, until mixture thickens, about 8–10 minutes. Remove from heat and stir in ¾ cup cheese, dry mustard, chives, salt, and pepper.

Line the bottom of an ungreased 2-quart baking dish with some of the chard; spoon about one-third of the sauce on top. Repeat two more times, alternating chard with sauce. Sprinkle remaining ¾ cup cheese on top and sprinkle with nutmeg. (Cover and refrigerate at this point if being prepared several hours in advance.)

Bake, uncovered, for 20 minutes (25–30 if chilled), or until chard is heated through. Place under broiler 2–3 minutes, or until cheese is lightly browned.

Size of Serving: 1 cup   *Number of Servings:* 8
Per Serving: Calories: 175; Protein: 10 g; Total Fat: 12 g; Sodium: 340 mg
Excellent Source of: Calcium, Iron, Vitamin A, Riboflavin, Vitamin C; (min. 2 cups) Protein

BREADS

One of the oldest known foods, bread has long ranked high on our list of eating basics, both for its nutritional merits and aesthetic qualities. What could be a greater gastronomic pleasure than homemade bread straight from the oven with its freshly baked aroma and flavor? And whole-grain breads provide a large share of our nutritional needs—carbohydrate, B vitamins, iron, zinc, magnesium, fiber, some protein, plus other vitamins and minerals.

Because of the contemporary madness for things that are instant, frozen and, one-step, most people are intimidated by the thought of making bread at home out of a few earthy ingredients. Mistakenly viewed as tedious by the uninitiated, breadmaking can actually be relaxing with its typically short list of ingredients to gather, rhythmic physical action during kneading, and time to do other things while the bread is rising.

Bread hasn't always risen, though. The very early "flat" breads were made with flour and water without a leavening agent and then baked in the sun. Gradually, methods of leavening breads became known. The first ones involved the use of soured grains and sourdough starters, still popular today for preparing delicious sourdough breads. Modern leavening techniques make the art of breadmaking far more reliable in producing perfect results.

Yeast: The principal leavening agent used today is yeast. It comes in two forms: dry, granular yeast in ¼-ounce packets (1 tablespoon), which must be stored in a cool place, and compressed yeast, which comes in cakes (4 teaspoons each) and needs refrigeration. Either type is guaranteed to be active only until the expiration date printed on the package. Yeast needs to be dissolved in *warm* liquid in order to work. The temperature is very important because yeast will not become activated under either extreme in temperature—overheated conditions will kill yeast and a liquid too cool will inhibit its growth. Granular yeast dissolves and activates best at 105°F. to 110°F.; compressed cake yeast works best at a slightly cooler temperature of 95°F. to 105°F. Either way, the yeast will take about 5 minutes to dissolve. And be sure that all the other ingredients used are at room temperature so that the yeast will stay warm throughout the preparation and will continue to do its job.

Sugars: Although breads can be made successfully without sugar, the yeast feed on sugar and will multiply faster when even a very small amount is added. Ideally, a little molasses or honey dissolved with the yeast in the warm liquid works the best. This also helps to brown the crust nicely.

Flours: Wheat flour has traditionally been the main flour used in bread-making because of its high gluten content. Gluten is a protein substance in wheat which has great elasticity and the ability to capture air bubbles formed by the yeast, helping the bread to rise. Flours made from other grains, such as buckwheat, brown rice, corn, and rye, have a very low gluten content; and flours made from soybeans or potatoes have none. When these flours are used to make bread, some wheat flour or gluten flour (a mixture of wheat flour and gluten which has been extracted from selected wheat flours) is usually added to aid in rising.

Since our modern processing methods for turning whole grains into refined flours reduce them to less valuable foods than they are in their natural state, the bread recipes we have included emphasize the use of whole-grain flours as much as possible. Most whole-grain berries from which these flours are made have a structure similar to the following:

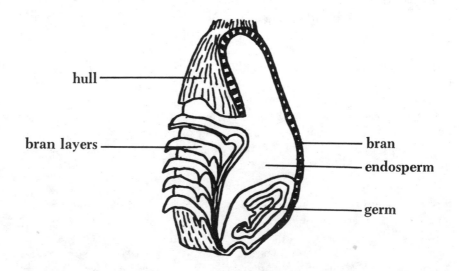

The outer bran layers and the germ contain protein, most of the vitamins (mainly B vitamins) and important minerals, such as iron, zinc, and magnesium. Also, the germ contains the polyunsaturated fatty acids and fat-soluble vitamin E, while the bran is high in fiber.

During the milling process, which "refines" grains, the outer coats and the germ of the whole-grain berry are removed. The endosperm, which contains mainly starch and some protein, is processed into refined flours which may or may not be enriched with some of the lost B vitamins (thiamin, riboflavin, and niacin) and iron. All of the other important nutrients found in the bran and germ are lost. This is a great tragedy, for what could be better than the chewy, nutty-tasting goodness of a slice of whole-grain bread? However, if you do need to use white flour—to prepare a specialty bread that won't be the same with whole-grain flour or perhaps to thicken something elsewhere in your cooking—*be sure* to use flour that has been enriched with at least some of the B vitamins and iron.

Since whole wheat flour is bulkier than white flour, the following formula is helpful in converting favorite bread recipes to whole wheat products: (This is not necessary if a finely ground whole wheat flour is used.)

1 cup white flour = 1 cup whole wheat flour minus 2 tablespoons

> *also,*
>
> decrease the amount of oil called for in the recipe by 1 tablespoon
>
> *and*
>
> increase the liquid called for by 1–2 tablespoons

The result will be a coarser, more compact product—but also one that is much more nutritious and satisfying.

THE TECHNIQUES OF BREADMAKING

Kneading: Almost all bread recipes require that the dough be kneaded in order to develop the gluten and texture. Kneading is a great way to vent your excess energy or frustrations—here's how:

1. Pat the dough into a round mound and place it on a lightly floured surface.
2. Curve your fingers over the dough and press down with the heels of your hands; then push away lightly at the dough.
3. Give the dough a quarter turn; fold it over; press down and push again. Repeat this in a rhythmic pattern for 8–10 minutes, or until the dough feels springy, elastic, and smooth. Be careful not to knead in too much extra flour. The dough should be slightly sticky.

Rising: After kneading, the dough must rise until it doubles in size. To do this, place the dough in a greased or oiled bowl, turning it once to grease the surface on all sides. Cover the bowl to prevent a crust from forming. Place the bowl in a draftfree, warm, humid location, such as:
- the oven if the stove has a gas pilot
- an upper rack in an unheated oven—place a large pan of hot water at the bottom of the oven and replenish the hot water as it cools
- near a hot stove or radiator
- a warm place at room temperature if the weather is warm

Punching Dough Down: After the dough has risen, it needs to be punched down. Punch the dough with your fist; then fold the edges toward the center and turn the dough over. Most recipes require that this process of rising and punching down be repeated twice, and sometimes three times.

Baking Bread: Be sure to preheat the oven so that the yeast will not be subjected to the process of the oven heating up; otherwise, the yeast will begin to act too quickly—this can end in disaster, or heavy bread at least. Also, be sure to grease or oil the baking pans generously, especially for whole-grain breads, since they are more likely to stick. Bake breads on the center rack of the oven with at least 2 inches between the pans so the heat can circulate.

Tests for Doneness
- Bread will pull away slightly from the sides of the pan.
- It will be firm and hollow-sounding when tapped.
- A toothpick inserted into the center will come out clean.
- The loaf should slip out of the pan easily—with or without a whack on the bottom.

If the bread is not done, just put it back in the oven and continue baking.

Cool the bread on a wire rack. If you want a soft crust, brush the top of the bread with melted margarine while it is hot. However, this adds extra calories and most people prefer chewy bread anyway. When the bread is completely cooled, cover it tightly with plastic wrap or aluminum foil to prevent the air from drying it out. Breads can be stored in the refrigerator or freezer if they are to be kept for longer than a few days.

100 % Whole-Grain Bread

1½ cups uncooked
    quick-cooking rolled
    oats
½ cup bran or wheat
    germ
3 cups hot water
2 tablespoons molasses
2 teaspoons salt
½ cup nonfat dry milk

2 tablespoons vegetable
    oil plus enough to
    brush on tops of
    loaves
2 packages active dry
    yeast (2 tablespoons)
1 cup warm water
    (110°F)
9–10 cups whole wheat
    flour

Combine oats, bran, and hot water in a large bowl. Add molasses, salt, dry milk, and 2 tablespoons oil. Stir well and let cool to about 110°F. Dissolve the yeast in 1 cup warm water and add to the oatmeal mixture. Add whole wheat flour gradually, stirring well after each addition, until the dough stiffens and pulls away from the sides of the bowl.

Use some of the whole wheat flour to coat a flat surface and turn dough onto it; cover the dough and let it rest 10 minutes.

Knead 10 minutes, or until smooth and elastic, adding more flour as needed; cover again and let it rest 10 minutes.

Divide dough into 2 greased 9 x 5 x 3-inch loaf pans; brush the tops with oil and cover them with a cloth. Place loaves in a warm place (80°–85°F.) until double in size.

Meanwhile, preheat the oven to 350°F. Bake loaves about 50 minutes, or until they sound hollow when tapped. Remove from oven; remove bread from pans and cool on a rack.

Yield: 2 9 x 5-inch loaves (16 slices per loaf)
Per Slice: Calories: 160; Protein: 7 g; Total Fat: 2 g; Sodium: 140 mg
Excellent Source of: Iron, Thiamin, and Riboflavin; (min. 2½ slices) Protein

Whole Wheat Oatmeal Bread

⅓ cup warm water
    (110°F.)
1 package active dry
    yeast
2 teaspoons salt
2 tablespoons vegetable
    oil
¼ cup molasses

2 cups cooked oatmeal
    plus ⅔ cup warm
    water
3 cups enriched
    all-purpose flour
2½–3 cups whole wheat
    flour

Pour ⅓ cup warm water into bowl. Sprinkle yeast onto water and allow it to dissolve gradually.   *(continued)*

Stir in salt, oil, molasses, and oatmeal mixed with ⅔ cup warm water. Stir in 2 cups all-purpose flour; beat in well. Add whole wheat flour; beat in well. Cover with a towel and let it rest 15 minutes.

Sprinkle remaining 1 cup all-purpose flour onto clean surface. Knead dough, working in all of the flour, for about 10 minutes.

Place dough in greased bowl; turn dough to grease top; cover and let rise in a warm place until it doubles.

Punch down and knead again; divide dough in half and pat into the greased loaf pans; cover and put in warm place to rise. Bake at 375°F. for 35–45 minutes.

Yield: 2 loaves (16 slices per loaf)
Per Slice: Calories: 100; Protein: 4 g; Total Fat: 2 g; Sodium: 140 mg
Excellent Source of: Thiamin and Riboflavin; (min 1½ slices) Iron and Niacin

Oatmeal Bread

1 cup warm skim milk
1 cup old-fashioned rolled oats
1 tablespoon margarine
¼ cup molasses
¼ cup honey
1 package active dry yeast

¼ cup warm water
3 cups unbleached, enriched all-purpose flour
1 teaspoon salt
½ cup raisins or currants

Pour milk over rolled oats and add margarine. Add molasses and honey; mix well.

Dissolve yeast in warm water and add to oatmeal mixture. Add the flour and salt; mix well. Stir in the raisins.

Knead the dough, adding flour as needed, until it is shiny and elastic, then pat into round ball. Grease the dough and let it rise in a warm place (covered) until double in size.

Grease a 9 x 5-inch loaf pan. Punch the dough down with your fists and shape into a loaf; place in pan and allow to rise until double.

Preheat oven to 350°F.

Bake bread for 45 minutes; then reduce oven temperature to 325°F. and bake 10 more minutes, or until bread sounds hollow when tapped. (Bread may need to be covered with aluminum foil toward the end of the baking time since it browns quickly.)

Yield: 1 9 x 5-inch loaf (16 slices)
Per Slice: Calories: 120; Protein: 5 g; Total Fat: 1 g; Sodium: 155 mg
Excellent Source of: Iron, Thiamin, and Riboflavin

Russian Rye Bread

2 tablespoons honey
¼ cup warm water
1 package active dry
   yeast
¼ cup nonfat dry milk
1 cup warm liquid skim
   milk
2 cups rye flour
1 cup raisins (presoaked
   in warm water and
   drained)

2 tablespoons melted
   margarine
1 orange rind, grated
1½ teaspoons salt
¾ tablespoon anise seed
1½ cups unbleached,
   enriched all-purpose
   flour
2 tablespoons boiling
   water
1 teaspoon instant
   decaffeinated coffee

Dissolve honey in the warm water; add the yeast and dissolve.

Combine the dry and liquid milk; add to the yeast mixture. Beat in 1 cup of the rye flour, the raisins, margarine, orange rind, salt, and anise seed. Beat in the remaining rye flour and the white flour.

Knead the dough until smooth and elastic. Cover and allow to rise in a warm spot until it has doubled, then punch down and knead a few times.

Shape into a round loaf and place on a greased baking sheet that has been dusted with cornmeal; cut a cross in the top of the loaf. Cover and allow to rise again until the cross opens.

Preheat oven to 375°F.

Brush the loaf with 2 tablespoons boiling water mixed with the instant coffee. (This helps to brown the bread nicely.) Bake for 35–40 minutes, or until done.

Yield: 1 round loaf (16 slices)
Per Slice: Calories: 150; Protein: 4 g; Total Fat: 2 g; Sodium: 240 mg
Excellent Source of: (min. 2 slices) Calcium and Riboflavin

Bohemian Rye Bread

¼ cup honey
2 cups warm water
3 packages active dry
   yeast (3 tablespoons)
2 tablespoons melted
   margarine plus some for
   top when baked

3 teaspoons salt
1 tablespoon caraway
   seeds
3 cups rye flour
3½ cups unbleached,
   enriched all-purpose
   flour

(continued)

Dissolve the honey in ¾ cup of the water. Add the yeast and dissolve. Combine yeast mixture with the rest of the ingredients. Mix well to make a stiff dough.

Knead dough until smooth and elastic. (This may take 20–30 minutes, as described in basic directions, page 199.)

Pat the dough into a large ball, and put it in a bowl. Cover and let it rise in a warm place until double in size. (This may take 3 hours.)

Punch down and knead a few times, then shape it into 2 loaves or 1 large loaf. Cover loaf and allow to double in size.

Remove the towel and place a greased baking sheet over the bowl(s). Turn upside down to remove the dough.

Preheat oven to 450°F.

Slash the top of the bread decoratively (with an X, for example). Bake at 450°F. for 10 minutes, then at 350°F. for 45 minutes, or until done. If a softer crust is desired brush the loaf with melted margarine when it comes out of the oven.

Yield: 2 medium-size round loaves (16 slices per loaf)
Per Slice: Calories: 100; Protein: 3 g; Total Fat: 1 g; Sodium: 210 mg
Excellent Source of: Riboflavin

Cottage Cheese-Dill Bread

¼ cup warm water (110°F.)	1 tablespoon vegetable oil
1 package active dry yeast	1 tablespoon dill seed
2 tablespoons sugar	1 teaspoon salt
1 cup lowfat cottage cheese at room temperature	¼ teaspoon baking soda
	1 egg, beaten
½ small onion, finely minced	1 cup sifted enriched all-purpose flour
	1½ cups whole wheat flour

Pour warm water in bowl and sprinkle yeast over surface; let it dissolve completely.

Add the sugar, *room temperature* cottage cheese, onion, oil, dill seed, salt, baking soda, and egg. Mix well. Gradually add flours, beating to form a stiff batter.

Cover and put in a warm place until it doubles in size (about 1½–2 hours).

Beat well to stir down dough and put in a well-greased 1½-quart casserole dish, turning once to grease top. Cover and put in a warm place until it has almost doubled (about 30–40 minutes).

Preheat oven to 350°F.

Bake bread for 40–50 minutes, or until browned and hollow sounding when tapped. If necessary, cover with foil during the last 10–15 minutes to prevent excessive browning. Remove from pan and cool on a wire rack. NOTE: Do not cover during the last 10–15 minutes if a thick, dark crust is desired.

Yield: 1 7-inch round loaf (16 slices)
Per Slice: Calories: 90; Protein: 4 g; Total Fat: 2 g; Sodium: 170 mg

Whole Wheat Hamburger Buns

2½ cups warm water   ¾ cup vegetable oil
½ cup honey   3 cups whole wheat flour
¼ cup active dry yeast   4–5 cups enriched
2 eggs   all-purpose flour
1½ teaspoons salt

Combine water and honey; sprinkle yeast into liquid gradually; let mixture rest 15 minutes.

Add eggs, salt, and oil; beat to mix well. Stir in whole wheat flour and let water soak up flour for 20–25 minutes. Add all-purpose flour gradually to make a stiff dough. Knead well (see directions, page 199).

Flatten dough to 1 inch thickness. Cut into 2½-inch rounds and place on cookie sheets. Cover and place in a warm place; let them rest 10 minutes and rise. Flatten tops and allow to rise again. Meanwhile, preheat oven to 400°F.

Bake for about 15 minutes.

NOTE: These rise quickly because the yeast is doubled.

Yield: 2 dozen buns
Per Bun: Calories: 230; Protein: 6 g; Total Fat: 2 g; Sodium: 160 mg
Excellent Source of: Iron, Thiamin, and Riboflavin

Whole Wheat Pita Loaves

Pita, or Syrian bread, is a traditional flat bread from the Middle East. It is split and stuffed with sandwich fillings or cut into triangular pieces to serve with dips, such as Garbanzo Bean Dip (see Index). Try making this gratifying bread—it only takes about 25 minutes from start to finish— and the pockets are fun.

1 package active dry yeast   1½ cups enriched
1 cup lukewarm water   all-purpose flour
1 tablespoon sugar   1½ cups whole wheat flour
                               ½ teaspoon salt

(continued)

Dissolve yeast in warm water. Add sugar and the all-purpose flour; mix well. Gradually add whole wheat flour and salt. Mix flour in well until the dough pulls away from the bowl.

Place dough on lightly floured surface and knead about 2–3 minutes. Divide dough into 8 balls; cover and let rest for 10 minutes.

Preheat oven to 450°F.

Flatten each ball and roll into a 5-inch round circle. (Be careful to avoid creases in dough or it will not separate after baking. Also, the rounds should not rise before baking—if they do, flatten them again.) Arrange on lightly greased baking sheets and place on top oven shelf. Bake 8–10 minutes.

To serve, split one side open to form a pocket and fill with all types of salad *or* cut each in two and stuff each half with filling.

Yield: 8 pitas
Per Pita: Calories: 180; Protein: 7 g; Total Fat: 1 g; Sodium: 135 mg
Excellent Source of: Thiamin

Pumpkin Rolls

¼ cup honey
¼ cup warm water
1 package active dry yeast
2½ cups unbleached enriched all-purpose flour
½ teaspoon salt

¼ cup pumpkin purée
½ cup warm skim milk
¼ cup melted margarine (cooled to 110°F.)— reserve 1½ teaspoons to grease the dough before baking

Dissolve the honey in warm water; add the yeast and dissolve. Combine with the rest of the ingredients, making sure that the warmed ingredients are no warmer than 110°F. or the yeast will be killed.

Knead the dough, adding flour as needed, until it is shiny and elastic (see kneading directions at the beginning of this chapter). Grease the dough with margarine; put in a bowl; cover and allow to rise in a warm place until double in size.

Grease the muffin tins. Punch down the dough and roll it into 1-inch balls; place 3 balls in each muffin tin. Cover and allow to rise until double.

Preheat oven to 450°F.

Brush rolls with reserved melted margarine and bake for 8–10 minutes, watching them closely to prevent burning.

Yield: 1 dozen rolls (large)
Per Roll: Calories: 160; Protein: 3 g; Total Fat: 4 g; Sodium: 140 mg
Excellent Source of: (min. 2 rolls) Iron, Thiamin, and Riboflavin

QUICK BREADS

Muffins, biscuits, loaf breads, popovers, coffee cakes, waffles, pancakes, and crepes are called "quick" breads because they can be quickly mixed and appear hot out of the oven or pan just in time for a meal. This speed is made possible by the use of quick-acting leavening agents—mainly baking powder and baking soda. *Baking soda* reacts with acidic ingredients, such as buttermilk, vinegar, fruit juices, or molasses, and releases carbon dioxide bubbles, which make the bread rise. *Baking powder* contains both baking soda and an acidic ingredient such as tartaric acid or an acid phosphate which, when the batter is mixed, release carbon dioxide. Some baking powders are "double acting" and react while the batter is being mixed and again in the oven. Air and water vapor also act as leavening agents (in popovers, for example).

Since baking powder and baking soda react when the ingredients are being combined, it is most important not to overmix the batter. Quick breads should be prepared just as the name suggests—*quickly*. Stir the ingredients just until mixed and dampened—don't worry if the batter is a bit lumpy; the lumps will work themselves out as the bread bakes.

Be sure to use *finely ground* whole wheat flour (or use whole wheat pastry flour) to avoid a heavy product. Or use part whole wheat flour and part enriched all-purpose flour.

Quick breads are meant to be eaten soon after they are baked. They usually keep only a few days, so wrap them tightly in plastic wrap or foil and store in the refrigerator—or freeze them for later use and reheat in foil. The following quick bread recipes can be used at any meal or for snacks, and they are particularly good as desserts.

Walnut Rhubarb Bread

¾ cup honey
⅓ cup melted margarine
plus 1 teaspoon for top
2 large eggs, beaten
½ cup skim milk
1 teaspoon vanilla extract
2 cups finely ground
whole wheat flour or
whole wheat pastry
flour

1½ teaspoons baking
powder
½ teaspoon baking soda
1½ cups diced fresh
rhubarb
½ cup chopped walnuts

Preheat oven to 350°F. Grease a 9 x 5 x 3-inch loaf pan very well.

Mix together the honey, ⅓ cup margarine, eggs, milk, and vanilla. Mix together the flour, baking powder, and baking soda, then combine with

(continued)

the liquid ingredients, mixing just until moistened. Add rhubarb and walnuts.

Pour into pan and drizzle 1 teaspoon melted margarine over the top. Bake for 1 hour; allow bread to cool 10 minutes before removing from pan.

Yield: 1 9 x 3-inch loaf (16 slices)
Per Slice: Calories: 180; Protein: 4 g; Total Fat: 7 g; Sodium: 130 mg
Excellent Source of: (min. 2 slices) Iron, Thiamin, and Riboflavin

Grandma's Brown Bread

This bread contains about twice the protein available in regular whole wheat bread. When served with a legume soup or main dish, a valuable complementary protein relationship is established.

⅓ cup molasses	¾ cup whole wheat or
2 cups plus 1 tablespoon	graham flour
buttermilk	¼ cup soy flour
1¼ teaspoons baking soda	1 cup yellow cornmeal
1 teaspoon baking	¼ cup wheat germ
powder	1 teaspoon salt
1 cup enriched	
all-purpose flour	

Preheat oven to 350°F.

Grease a 9 x 5 x 3-inch loaf pan.

Mix the molasses, buttermilk, baking soda, and baking powder together. Add the flours, cornmeal, wheat germ, and salt; mix well until smooth. Pour batter into pan and bake for 1 hour. (If the bread becomes nicely browned on top after 30–45 minutes, reduce the oven temperature to 325°F.)

NOTE: Soy flour is seldom available in the supermarket but can be purchased in a health food store.

VARIATIONS:

- ¼ cup whole wheat or graham flour may be substituted for the ¼ cup soy flour. However, this will reduce the protein content of the loaf.
- If necessary, 1 cup whole wheat flour may be substituted for the graham and soy flour.
- ½ cup dark raisins or nuts can be added to the batter to vary the texture.

Yield: 1 9 x 5 x 3-inch loaf (16 slices)
Per Slice: Calories: 115; Protein: 4 g; Total Fat: 2 g; Sodium: 215 mg
Excellent Source of: Iron and Thiamin

Better Banana Bread

½ cup margarine
½ cup brown sugar
3 tablespoons plain lowfat yogurt
2 medium eggs, well beaten
1 cup whole wheat flour
1 cup unbleached enriched all-purpose flour

¾ teaspoon baking powder
½ teaspoon (rounded) baking soda
½ teaspoon ground mace
1 cup mashed ripe bananas
1 whole orange rind, grated
½ cup chopped raw sunflower seeds

Preheat oven to 350°F. Grease a 9 x 5 x 3-inch loaf pan.

Cream the margarine and sugar in a large bowl. Stir in yogurt and eggs.

Sift the flours together on a sheet of waxed paper or in a separate bowl, then sift flours again with the baking powder, baking soda, and mace.

Add sifted dry ingredients to the creamed mixture alternately with the mashed banana. Stir in the grated orange rind and seeds.

Pour mixture into greased loaf pan and bake 50–60 minutes, or until it tests done.

VARIATION: ½ cup of chopped unsalted peanuts may be used in place of sunflower seeds.

Yield: 1 9 x 5 x 3-inch loaf (16 slices)
Per Slice: Calories: 175; Protein: 4 g; Total Fat: 9 g; Sodium: 100 mg
Excellent Source of: Thiamin; (min. 1½ slices) Iron

Pumpkin Nut Bread

This is a delicious way to get vitamin A—and to use leftover pumpkin or sweet potatoes.

½ cup plus 2 tablespoons sugar
1½ cups finely ground whole wheat flour°
¾ teaspoon cinnamon
½ teaspoon ginger
1 teaspoon baking soda
½ teaspoon nutmeg
1 teaspoon salt

Dash ground cloves
½ cup vegetable oil
2 eggs, beaten
⅓ cup water
1 cup cooked pumpkin (freshly cooked or canned)
½ cup chopped pecans

° Whole wheat pastry flour or 1 cup whole wheat flour plus ½ cup enriched all-purpose flour may be substituted.

(continued)

Preheat oven to 350°F. Grease a 9 x 5 x 3-inch loaf pan.

Place all dry ingredients in a large bowl and mix well. Add oil and beaten eggs; blend in well. (This recipe is easy to mix by hand.) Add water, pumpkin and pecans; stir until batter is well blended.

Place in greased loaf pan and bake in top half of oven for 1 to 1¼ hours, or until it tests done. Remove from oven and allow to cool in the pan; then place pan on its side and gently ease the loaf out.

NOTE: This bread is excellent for freezer storage and can be frozen up to three months. It also keeps well for about a week tightly wrapped in foil in the bread box.

VARIATIONS:
- Other nuts, such as walnuts, can be used in place of pecans.
- Experiment with other spices, such as allspice or mace, to vary the flavor.
- Substitute mashed sweet potato for the pumpkin.
- Add ½ cup raisins.

Yield: 1 9 x 5 x 3-inch loaf (16 slices)
Per Slice: Calories: 170; Protein: 3 g; Total Fat: 10 g; Sodium: 140 mg
Excellent Source of: Vitamin A

Apricot-Oat-Nut Bread

2 cups finely ground whole wheat flour (or use whole wheat pastry flour)
½ teaspoon baking soda
½ cup sugar
1 teaspoon salt
¾ cup quick-cooking oats
2 tablespoons wheat germ
1 cup chopped dried apricots
1 cup skim milk
⅓ cup vegetable oil
2 eggs, slightly beaten
⅔ cup chopped walnuts (or pecans)

Preheat oven to 350°F. Grease a 9 x 5 x 3-inch loaf pan.

Mix together the flour, soda, sugar, salt, oats, wheat germ, and apricots. Add the milk, oil, and eggs; mix well. Stir in the nuts.

Pour into pan and bake 55–60 minutes; allow to cool for 5 minutes, then remove from pan and cool on rack before slicing.

Yield: 1 9 x 5 x 3-inch loaf (16 slices)
Per Slice: Calories: 180; Protein: 5 g; Total Fat: 9 g; Sodium: 150 mg
Excellent Source of: Thiamin; (min. 1½ slices) Iron, Vitamin A, and Riboflavin

Plum Oatmeal Bread

1 cup chopped pitted
    purple plums
2 cups sifted unbleached
    enriched all-purpose
    flour
3 teaspoons baking
    powder

1 teaspoon salt
½ teaspoon baking soda
1 cup rolled oats
¾ cup honey
2 large eggs, beaten
¼ cup melted margarine
½ cup skim milk

Preheat oven to 350°F. Grease a 9 x 5 x 3-inch loaf pan very well.
Prepare plums and set aside.

Sift flour, baking powder, salt, and baking soda together; stir in rolled
oats. Combine honey, eggs, margarine and milk; add to dry ingredients
and stir just enough to moisten completely. Add the plums and pour batter
into pan.

Bake for 45 minutes, or until it tests done.

VARIATION: Use 1 cup chopped fresh peaches in place of plums.

Yield: 1 9 x 5 x 3-inch loaf (16 slices)
Per Slice: Calories: 155; Protein: 3 g; Total Fat: 4 g; Sodium: 265 mg

Zucchini Walnut Bread

4 large eggs
¾ cup granulated brown
    sugar
¾ cup vegetable oil
3 cups finely ground
    whole wheat flour (or
    whole wheat pastry
    flour)
1½ teaspoons baking soda

¾ teaspoon baking powder
¾ teaspoon salt
2 teaspoons ground
    cinnamon
2 cups grated, unpeeled,
    uncooked zucchini
1 cup coarsely chopped
    walnuts
1 teaspoon vanilla extract

Preheat oven to 350°F. Grease and flour a 9 x 5 x 3-inch pan.

Beat eggs with a wire whisk or fork. Gradually beat in sugar and then
the oil. Combine all dry ingredients in a separate bowl; add dry ingredients, alternately with the zucchini, to the egg mixture. Stir in the walnuts
and vanilla.

Pour into pan and bake for 50 minutes; allow bread to cool 10 minutes
before removing from the pan.

Yield: 1 9 x 5 x 3-inch loaf (16 slices)
Per Slice: Calories: 260; Protein: 6 g; Total Fat: 17 g; Sodium: 225 mg
Excellent Source of: Iron and Thiamin

Chili and Cheese Cornbread

2 eggs, beaten
2 cups buttermilk
1 teaspoon baking soda
2 cups enriched cornmeal
1 teaspoon salt

½ cup shredded cheddar
   cheese
2 tablespoons chopped
   canned green chilies
2 tablespoons chopped
   canned pimiento

Preheat oven to 450°F. Grease an 8 x 8 x 2-inch baking pan.

Stir together eggs, buttermilk, and soda; set aside.

Combine the cornmeal, salt, and cheese. Blend liquid mixture into dry ingredients; stir just until blended. Add green chilies and pimiento to batter; blend well.

Pour batter into greased baking pan and bake for 20–25 minutes.

Yield: 16 squares
Per Square: Calories: 105; Protein: 4 g; Total Fat: 2 g; Sodium: 210 mg
Excellent Source of: (min. 1½ squares) Calcium, Niacin, Riboflavin, and Vitamin C

Ready Bake Bran Muffins

This recipe may be completely mixed and stored in a tightly covered container in the refrigerator for up to two weeks—make the whole recipe and bake the muffins fresh as needed.

3 cups unprocessed bran
1 cup boiling water
2 eggs, slightly beaten
2 cups buttermilk, lowfat
   yogurt, or soured skim
   milk
½ cup vegetable oil
1 cup raisins, currants, or
   chopped pitted dried
   dates, prunes, or apricots

2½ teaspoons baking soda
½ teaspoon salt
⅓ cup sugar
1 cup unsifted enriched
   all-purpose flour
1½ cups whole wheat flour

Preheat oven to 425°F.

Mix bran and boiling water together in a large bowl; stir to moisten evenly and set aside to cool.

In another bowl, mix together the eggs, buttermilk, oil, and raisins; stir into the bran mixture.

In a third bowl, stir together the baking soda, salt, sugar, all-purpose flour and whole wheat flour; stir into the bran mixture.

Put in greased muffin pans and bake about 20 minutes.

Yield: about 2 dozen muffins
Per Muffin: Calories: 120; Protein: 4 g; Total Fat: 3 g; Sodium: 160 mg
Excellent Source of: (min. 1½ muffins) Iron

Whole Wheat Banana Nut Muffins

1 medium very ripe banana
1 egg, beaten
½ cup skim milk
3 tablespoons melted margarine
1 cup finely ground whole wheat flour or whole wheat pastry flour

2 tablespoons sugar
1½ teaspoons baking powder
¼ teaspoon salt
¼ cup coarsely chopped walnuts

Preheat oven to 425°F. Grease 8 muffin tins.

Mash the banana with a fork until smooth. Combine banana with the egg, milk, and margarine in a large bowl. Combine the dry ingredients in a sieve or sifter and sift all together into the banana mixture. Add walnuts and stir briefly—only until the dry ingredients are just moistened.

Fill greased muffin tins about two-thirds full and bake 25 minutes, or until muffins are nicely browned.

Yield: 8 muffins
Per Muffin: Calories: 155; Protein: 4 g; Total Fat: 7 g; Sodium: 135 mg

Corn Muffins

⅓ cup vegetable oil
⅓ cup sugar
1¼ cups skim milk
1 egg
1 cup whole wheat flour

½ teaspoon salt
4 teaspoons baking powder
1 cup whole-grain cornmeal

Preheat oven to 425°F. Grease muffin tins.

Combine oil and sugar in a large bowl. Add milk and egg; stir to mix thoroughly.

In a separate bowl, combine the flour, salt, and baking powder; add to liquid mixture and mix thoroughly. Add cornmeal and stir *only to mix.*

Put into greased muffin pans and bake 20–25 minutes.

Yield: about 12 muffins
Per Muffin: Calories: 160; Protein: 4 g; Total Fat: 7 g; Sodium: 115 mg

Whole Wheat Popovers

1 cup whole wheat pastry
    flour
½ teaspoon salt
2 large eggs, beaten

1 cup skim milk
1 teaspoon sugar (or brown
    sugar or honey)

Preheat oven to 450°F. Oil 6 popover or muffin tins and place in preheated oven.

Sift together the flour and salt. Add eggs and milk to flour mixture; beat thoroughly for 4–5 minutes with a rotary beater or put in blender and blend for 2 minutes (these are minimum times needed to develop the gluten in the flour). Add the sugar and beat another ½ minute to mix in completely.

Remove the tins from the oven and quickly fill them half full with batter. Return filled tins to oven for 15 minutes; reduce heat to 350°F. and bake for 15 minutes more, then turn off heat.

Slit tops of popovers and leave them in oven for 5–10 minutes to allow them to dry out slightly. Serve hot.

Yield: 6 popovers
Per Popover: Calories: 110; Protein: 5 g; Total Fat: 2 g; Sodium: 220 mg

Sweet Potato Biscuits

½ cup cooked sweet
    potato (baked in the
    skin; then skin removed)
¼ cup melted margarine
½ cup skim milk
¾ cup (rounded) finely
    ground whole wheat
    flour or whole wheat
    pastry flour, stirred

1½ teaspoons sugar
1½ teaspoons baking
    powder
¼ teaspoon salt

Preheat oven to 450°F. Lightly grease medium-size baking sheet.

Mash the sweet potato until light and fluffy. Stir in the margarine and milk.

Combine the stirred flour, sugar, baking powder, and salt; stir well into a large bowl. Blend in the sweet potato mixture and stir until the dough comes away from the sides of the bowl.

Form into a ball and knead lightly on a floured surface for about 1 minute. Roll out to a ½-inch thickness, then dip the edge of a 2-inch biscuit cutter or glass in flour and cut rounds from the dough.

Place on the lightly greased baking sheet. Bake 15 minutes, or until lightly browned.

NOTE: Boiled or canned sweet potatoes are too moist and make the mixture too wet to roll and cut. Sweet potatoes for this recipe should be baked in their skins with dry heat.

Yield: 8 biscuits
Per Biscuit: Calories: 120; Protein: 2 g; Total Fat: 6 g; Sodium: 210 mg
Excellent Source of: Vitamin A

Wheat Germ Waffles

3 eggs
1 cup skim milk
⅓ cup wheat germ
¼ cup chopped walnuts
6 tablespoons melted margarine

1¼ cups finely ground whole wheat flour or whole wheat pastry flour
3 teaspoons baking powder
¼ teaspoon salt

Preheat waffle iron.

Beat eggs in a medium-size bowl. Stir in milk, wheat germ, walnuts, and margine.

Combine flour, baking powder, and salt and sift into liquid ingredients; *mix just until smooth* (but no more). Add more milk if mixture seems too stiff—batter should be thin.

Pour ¼ cup batter into the center of the hot waffle iron, covering to about 1 inch from the outside edge. Close lid quickly and bake until all steaming stops and waffle is brown and crisp (about 4–6 minutes). Unplug iron, lift waffle off with a fork, and keep warm until ready to serve.

NOTE: Leftover batter can be covered and stored in the refrigerator for a few days. Leftover baked waffles can be cooled, tightly wrapped in plastic wrap, and frozen. To reheat, unwrap and place, frozen, directly in pre-heated 350°F. oven.

Size of Serving: 2 4½-inch waffles   *Number of Servings:* 8
Per Waffle: Calories: 240; Protein: 8 g; Total Fat: 14 g; Sodium: 365 mg
Excellent Source of: Iron, Thiamin, and Riboflavin; (min. 2 waffles) Protein, Calcium, and Vitamin A

Cornmeal Crepes

1 cup whole-grain cornmeal
1 teaspoon salt
1 tablespoon sugar
1 cup boiling water
1 egg
½ cup skim milk

2 tablespoons vegetable oil
½ cup finely ground whole wheat flour or whole wheat pastry flour
2 teaspoons baking powder

(continued)

Combine cornmeal, salt, and sugar in a large bowl. Pour 1 cup boiling water over the mixture; cover and let soak 10 minutes.

Meanwhile, beat together the egg, milk, and oil; add to the cooled cornmeal mixture.

In a separate bowl, mix flour and baking powder together thoroughly; stir it into the batter with a few swift strokes.

To cook, oil a 6–7-inch crepe pan or frying pan and heat until it just begins to smoke. Pour ¼ cup of batter into pan and quickly tilt pan in all directions to allow batter to spread and form a thin coating over the bottom. Cook about 1 minute, or until edges begin to brown and crepe can be shaken loose from the bottom of the pan. Turn crepe and cook about ½ minute on other side. (Crepes should be light and lacy looking.)

Serve hot with Fresh Fruit Sauce (see Index) or use as wrappers for sandwich fillings.

Size of Serving: 3 crepes   *Number of Servings:* 4
Per Serving: Calories: 265; Protein: 15 g; Total Fat: 3 g; Sodium: 460
Excellent Source of: Thiamin; (min. 4 crepes) Protein, Calcium, Iron, and Riboflavin

French Toast

4 *eggs (or 1 cup liquid*
   cholesterol-free egg
   substitute)
½ *cup skim milk*
2 *teaspoons vanilla*
   extract
⅛ *teaspoon freshly grated*
   nutmeg (or ground
   nutmeg)

½ *teaspoon cinnamon*
2 *tablespoons margarine*
8 *slices whole wheat*
   bread
   Cinnamon and honey
   (optional)

Beat the eggs well and mix with the milk, vanilla, nutmeg, and cinnamon in a shallow dish.

Melt some of the margarine in a large frying pan.

Dip 2–3 slices of bread in the egg mixture, coating both sides of the bread; drain off any excess egg. Put the bread in the frying pan and cook over medium heat, turning once, until both sides are golden brown. Repeat until all the bread has been dipped and cooked; keep cooked slices warm in oven.

Serve hot with cinnamon sprinkled on top and/or a drizzle of honey; or use for French toast sandwiches.

Size of Serving: 2 slices   *Number of Servings:* 4
Per Serving: Calories: 265; Protein: 14 g; Total Fat: 14 g; Sodium: 450 mg
Excellent Source of: Calcium, Iron, Thiamin, and Riboflavin; (min. 3 slices) Protein and Vitamin A

Caraway Rye Croutons

Croutons are a good way to use leftover bread as well to as create a variety of garnishes for soups and salads.

4 slices slightly stale caraway rye bread	1 large garlic clove, sliced, or 1 teaspoon garlic powder
3 tablespoons margarine	

Preheat oven to 325°F.

Cut bread into ½-inch cubes.

Melt margarine in a skillet over moderate heat. Add garlic and sauté until golden brown, then remove garlic and discard. Add bread to margarine; toss lightly and remove from heat. Spread bread cubes on a cookie sheet and toast in the oven until lightly browned (watch them carefully, as they burn easily!).

VARIATIONS: Substitute whole wheat, corn, pumpernickel, bran, or any other whole-grain bread in place of the rye bread. *Cheese Croutons:* Add ¼ cup grated Parmesan cheese and a few dashes of paprika to the melted margarine. *Herbed Onion Croutons:* Substitute 1 teaspoon of onion juice (or ½ teaspoon onion powder) and 2 teaspoons dried herbs (such as basil, dill weed, or oregano) in place of the garlic.

Yield: about 2 cups

Per ⅛ cup: Calories: 35 (45 with cheese); Protein: 1 g; Total Fat: 2 g; Sodium: 70 mg (80 with cheese)

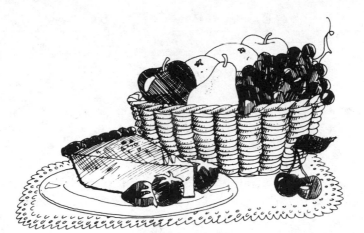

DESSERTS

Nutritionists are often thought of as the people who tell you to "cut out desserts." But most nutritionists would agree that desserts have their place in the diet if they are prepared with a minimum of sugar and fat, and if they take advantage of the more nutritionally dense ingredients (such as skim milk, lowfat yogurt, partially skimmed ricotta cheese, eggs, nuts, whole wheat flour, wheat germ, oatmeal, fruits, and even some vegetables—for example pumpkin, squash, and sweet potato). With these ingredients involved, desserts become as nutritionally valuable as any other part of a meal.

By far, fresh fruits are the simplest and most delicious items on the approved dessert list. These neat packages of good nutrition provide fiber; vitamin C (particularly high are grapefruit, mangoes, melons, oranges, papayas, tangerines, and strawberries); vitamin A (apricots, cantaloupe, mangoes, papayas, and watermelon); potassium (apricots, bananas, cantaloupe, dried fruits, and oranges); and iron (dried fruits). In addition fruits are naturally low in sodium and most contain no fat—which helps to keep the calories low also. Depending on the size, a serving of fruit is generally in the neighborhood of only 50–100 calories.

Fruits can be served in combination with each other; accompanied by cheese, yogurt, or a light sauce; baked with nuts; blended into fruit frappés and mousses; or, for fancier occasions, turned into a fresh fruit pie with a whole-grain/crushed nut shell. But the simplest and perhaps best dessert of all is a bowl of fresh fruit passed around the table after dinner.

Fresh Fruits

Try these favorite fruit combinations with Creamy Lime Dressing (see Index) or plain, garnished with wedges of fresh lemon or lime and fresh mint. For each serving (1 tbsp.) of the dressing add 15 calories and 5 mg sodium to the nutrient breakdowns below.

Size of Serving: 1 cup fruit   *Number of Servings:* 4

CANTALOUPE AND KIWI:

1 large ripe cantaloupe, seeded, peeled, and diced

2 ripe kiwifruit, seeded, peeled, and sliced or 4 unpeeled Italian prune plums, pitted and sliced

Per Serving: Calories: 70; Protein: 1 g; Total Fat —; Sodium; 20 mg
Excellent Source of: Vitamin A and Vitamin C

PAPAYA WITH FRESH BERRIES:

2 large chilled ripe papayas, halved and seeded,
filled with

1 cup small whole fresh raspberries or sliced strawberries or blueberries

Per Serving: Calories: 80; Protein: 1 g; Total Fat: Trace; Sodium: 5 mg
Excellent Source of: Vitamin A and Vitamin C

PINEAPPLE WITH POMEGRANATE SEEDS:

½ fresh, ripe pineapple, peeled and diced
2 medium bananas, peeled and sliced

½ cup pomegranate seeds or ½ cup pitted and sliced fresh cherries

Per Serving: Calories: 100; Protein: 1 g; Total Fat: Trace; Sodium: Trace
Excellent Source of: Vitamin C

NECTARINES WITH GREEN AND PURPLE GRAPES:

4 medium unpeeled ripe nectarines, pitted and sliced

½ cup whole seedless green grapes
½ cup halved and seeded purple grapes

Per Serving: Calories: 105; Protein: 1 g; Total Fat: Trace; Sodium: 10 mg
Excellent Source of: Vitamin A and Vitamin C

MELON AND BERRIES:

1 small ripe honeydew melon, seeded, peeled, and diced

½ cup fresh blueberries
½ cup halved fresh strawberries

Per Serving: Calories: 95; Protein: 2 g; Total Fat: 1 g; Sodium: 30 mg
Excellent Source of: Riboflavin and Vitamin C

SPLENDID WINTER FRUIT CUP:

1 large ripe avocado, pitted, peeled, and sliced (and sprinkled with lemon juice to prevent discoloration)
1 large ripe papaya, seeded, peeled, and diced

2 large tangerines (or 1 large orange or ½ large grapefruit), peeled, seeded, and sectioned
1 cup halved and seeded purple grapes

Per Serving: Calories: 170; Protein: 3 g; Total Fat: 10 g; Sodium: 10 mg
Excellent Source of: Vitamin A, Thiamin, Riboflavin, and Vitamin C

Cantaloupe Ice

2 cups seeded, cubed cantaloupe (approximately ½ medium-size melon)

1½ tablespoons lime or lemon juice
1–2 tablespoons honey or sugar (or less to taste)

Put all ingredients in a blender or food processor and blend thoroughly. Pour into a shallow metal pan. Cover and freeze until solid.

Remove from freezer, break into chunks, and blend again until there is a velvety slush. (This can also be done by smashing the ice into small pieces and beating it with an electric mixer.)

Pour into a bowl, cover, and freeze. Allow ice to soften slightly before serving.

VARIATIONS:

· *Watermelon Ice:* Same as above recipe using 2 cups ripe cubed watermelon in place of cantaloupe.
· *Papaya Ice:* Substitute 2 medium-size ripe papayas for cantaloupe; double the lime or lemon juice (use 3 tablespoons); prepare as for above recipe.
· *Strawberry Ice:* Substitute 4 cups fresh hulled strawberries in place of cantaloupe.

Size of Serving: ½ cup   *Number of Servings:* 4
Per Serving: Calories: 40; Protein: 1 g; Total Fat: Trace; Sodium: 10 mg
Excellent Source of: Vitamin A and Vitamin C

Peach Zabaglione

3 large egg yolks
1 large whole egg
2 tablespoons sugar
¼ cup white wine

½ teaspoon fresh lemon
juice
¼ teaspoon ground ginger
4 unpeeled fresh peaches,
sliced

In a large mixing bowl, beat the egg yolks and whole egg until thick. Gradually beat in the sugar; continue to beat until the mixture is light and tripled in bulk. Slowly beat in the wine, lemon juice, and ginger.

Pour mixture into top of a double boiler; place over simmering water and beat with rotary beater or electric mixer until it is light and frothy or the consistency of whipped cream (about 8 minutes.)

Spoon sauce over sliced peaches.

VARIATION: Use fresh orange sections or freshly sliced pears in place of peaches.

Size of Serving: 1 peach plus 2 tablespoons of sauce   *Number of Servings:* 4
Per Serving: Calories: 140; Protein: 4 g; Total Fat: 6 g; Sodium: 25 mg
Excellent Source of: Iron and Vitamin A

Flan

It's no wonder that this simple, elegant custard has been a longtime favorite of the Spanish and is the national dessert of Mexico.

4 tablespoons brown
sugar
2 eggs, beaten
⅓ cup sugar

¼ teaspoon salt
2 cups skim milk
½ teaspoon vanilla extract

Preheat oven to 350°F.

Press 1 tablespoon of brown sugar into the bottoms of each of 4 custard cups.

In a large mixing bowl, beat together the eggs, sugar, and salt. Stir in milk and vanilla. Slowly pour mixture into custard cups.

Place custard cups in a baking pan that contains about 1 inch of hot water. Bake for 50–60 minutes, or until a knife inserted 1 inch from edge comes out clean.

Size of Serving: about ⅔ cup   *Number of Servings:* 4
Per Serving: Calories: 180; Protein: 7 g; Total Fat: 3 g; Sodium: 95 mg
Excellent Source of: Calcium and Riboflavin

Upside-Down Yogurt Sundae

1 cup plain lowfat yogurt
1 tablespoon honey
4 raw, unpeeled apples
¼ cup fresh or reconstituted frozen unsweetened orange juice

2 tablespoons raisins
1 tablespoon raw shelled sunflower seeds
¼ teaspoon cinnamon (plus a dash)
Dash nutmeg

In a small bowl combine the yogurt and honey.

Wash the apples and slice them into bite-size pieces; place in a medium mixing bowl and cover with orange juice. Add the raisins, sunflower seeds, and ¼ teaspoon cinnamon to the apples and orange juice; mix well.

Divide the fruit mixture into 4 equal portions and place in serving bowls. Pour ¼ cup of the yogurt mixture over each portion of fruit mixture. Sprinkle a dash of cinnamon and nutmeg over the top of each serving and enjoy!

VARIATIONS: Toasted almonds can be used in place of the sunflower seeds. Pineapple juice can be used in place of the orange juice.

Size of Serving: ¼ cup yogurt topping and ¼ cup fruit mixture *Number of Servings:* 4
Per Serving: Calories: 150; Protein: 1 g; Total Fat: 3 g; Sodium: 35 mg

Pumpkin Pudding

1 cup cooked mashed pumpkin
2 eggs, slightly beaten
¼ cup honey
1 cup skim milk

½ teaspoon grated orange peel
Dash powdered ginger
Dash powdered cinnamon
Dash powdered cloves

Mix all ingredients together (this is most easily done in a blender). Pour into 4 small custard cups. Set custard cups in large skillet. Fill skillet with water to within ½ inch of top of custard cups. With moderate heat, heat water just to simmer; cover skillet and gently simmer 15 minutes, or until pudding is just set. Remove cups immediately and refrigerate at least 1 hour, or until well chilled.

VARIATIONS: Substitute mashed squash or sweet potato for the pumpkin. Add ½ cup chopped pecans or walnuts (only if you can afford the extra calories).

Size of Serving: ⅔ cup *Number of Servings:* 4
Per Serving: Calories: 140; Protein: 6 g; Total Fat: 3 g; Sodium: 60 mg
Excellent Source of: Calcium, Vitamin A, and Riboflavin

Cranberry Nut Pie

Buy cranberries at the height of the season, since they can be kept in the freezer for months.

2 cups fresh cranberries
⅔ cup honey or sugar
½ cup chopped walnuts
1 egg, well beaten
½ cup whole wheat flour

1 teaspoon grated orange rind
3 tablespoons melted margarine
2 tablespoons melted shortening

Preheat oven to 325°F.

Spread the cranberries in the bottom of a well-greased 9-inch pie pan. Sprinkle with ⅓ cup honey and walnuts.

In a small bowl, add ⅓ cup honey to the egg, beating well. Beat in the flour, orange rind, margarine, and shortening. Pour over the cranberries. Bake about 1 hour, or until crust is golden brown.

Size of Serving: one-eighth of 9-inch pie *Number of Servings:* 8
Per Serving: Calories: 220; Protein: 4 g; Total Fat: 13 g; Sodium: 60 mg

Fruit Custard Pie

2 eggs
1–1½ cups sugar
1 cup skim milk
Dash salt
½ teaspoon vanilla extract
1 9-inch Whole Wheat Pie Crust (see Index)

¼ cup uncooked tapioca
3 cups sliced fresh peaches, rhubarb, papaya, cherries, blackberries, strawberries, or raspberries.

Preheat oven to 375°F.

Beat eggs slightly. Add ¼ cup sugar, milk, salt, and vanilla and mix well.

Sprinkle the bottom of the pie crust with tapioca, just to lightly cover it. Add the fruit. Sprinkle 1–1¼ cups sugar over the fruit. (The amount of sugar will need adjustment, depending on how sweet or sour the fruit is—use as *little* as possible to keep the calories to a minimum.) Pour egg mixture over the fruit to within ½ inch of the top of the pie plate.

Place pie plate on a cookie sheet to catch any spills. Bake for 30–40 minutes, or until a knife comes out clean when inserted into the pie.

VARIATIONS: This pie may also be prepared with Low-Cal Pie Crust (see Index). Canned fruit may be substituted for fresh fruit; if canned fruit is used, do not include the sugar called for in the recipe.

Size of Serving: one-eighth of 9-inch pie   *Number of Servings:* 8
Per Serving (with Whole Wheat Pie Crust): Calories: 245 (165 without crust); Protein: 4 g (3 g without crust); Total Fat: 7 g (1 g without crust); Sodium: 200 mg (95 mg without crust)
Excellent Source of: Vitamin C

Impossible Coconut Custard Pie

The pie and crust are all in one in this delicious easy-to-to-make dessert.

1⅓ *cups skim milk*	¾ *teaspoon baking powder*
3 *eggs*	⅓ *cup enriched*
2 *tablespoons margarine*	*all-purpose flour*
½ *cup sugar*	⅔ *cup shredded coconut*
1 *teaspoon vanilla*	
extract	

Preheat oven to 350°F.
  Grease and flour a 6-inch pie plate (using fat and flour over and above amounts called for in recipe).
  Put *all* ingredients into an electric blender and blend for 1 minute. Pour into pie plate. Bake for 45 minutes and turn off oven heat. Let pie set in oven for 10 minutes before removing.

Size of Serving: one-quarter of 6-inch pie   *Number of Servings:* 4
Per Serving: Calories: 330; Protein: 10 g; Total Fat: 15 g; Sodium: 160 mg
Excellent Source of: Calcium, Thiamin, and Riboflavin

Almond Wheat Pie Shell

Perfect for pie fillings that do not require baking, such as chiffon, frozen yogurt, or fruit whips.

1 *cup whole wheat pastry*	½ *cup ground almonds*
flour	⅓ *cup vegetable oil*
1 *cup wheat germ*	3 *tablespoons honey*

Preheat oven to 350°F.
  Mix flour, wheat germ, and almonds.
  Combine oil and honey; add to dry ingredients, mixing well with a fork. Press into a pie pan and flute the edges. Prick surface with a fork. Bake 8–10 minutes, or until golden.

(continued)

Yield: 2 9-inch pie shells
Per one-eighth of Pie Shell: Calories: 110; Protein: 3 g; Total Fat: 7 g;
Sodium: Trace
Excellent Source of: Thiamin

Whole Wheat Pie Crust

1 cup whole wheat pastry
  flour
¼ cup wheat germ
¼ teaspoon salt

½ cup margarine, cut into
  pieces
¼ cup cold water

Preheat oven to 450°F.

Combine flour, wheat germ, and salt in a bowl. Add margarine and cut into the dry ingredients using a pastry cutter or 2 knives until the fat particles are about ⅛ inch. Sprinkle with the cold water and toss lightly with a fork to form a ball.

Roll dough between 2 sheets of floured waxed paper to about 1½ inches larger than the inverted pie pan. Ease dough into the pan; trim crust to ½ inch beyond the rim of the pan. Fold edge under and seal by fluting edge with your fingers or pressing closed with the tines of a fork. Prick bottom and sides of crust; bake 8–10 minutes. (If crust is to be baked with a filling, do not prick the bottom and sides.)

Yield: 2 9-inch pie crusts
Per one-eighth of Pie Crust: Calories: 80; Protein: 1 g; Total Fat: 6 g;
Sodium: 105 mg

Low-Cal Pie Crust

2 tablespoons margarine
⅓ cup fine whole wheat
  bread crumbs

½ teaspoon ground
  cinnamon
1 teaspoon brown sugar

Grease an 8-inch pie plate well with margarine. Combine dry ingredients. Mix thoroughly and sprinkle over the surface of the pie plate, covering it well. Add pie filling and bake according to directions for baking filling.

Yield: 1 8-inch pie crust
Per one-eighth of Pie Crust: Calories: 40; Protein: 1 g; Total Fat: 3 g;
Sodium: 70 mg

The Ultimate Oatmeal Cookie

2 cups old-fashioned rolled oats	1 teaspoon cinnamon
½ cup whole wheat flour	¼ teaspoon nutmeg
½ cup wheat germ	½ teaspoon salt
½ cup unprocessed bran	¼ cup water
½ cup nonfat dry milk powder	¼ cup vegetable oil
½ cup chopped dates or raisins (or some of each)	1 cup brown sugar (not packed)
½ cup unsalted roasted peanuts	2 large eggs, slightly beaten
	2 teaspoons vanilla extract

Preheat oven to 325°F. Grease 2 cookie sheets well.

Combine all ingredients in a large bowl; mix thoroughly. Drop heaping teaspoonfuls of the mixture onto the greased cookie sheets. Bake for 20 minutes, or until lightly browned; cookies should spring back when pressed lightly. Cool for a few minutes and remove to a wire rack.

Yield: about 3 dozen cookies
Per Cookie: Calories: 90; Protein: 3 g; Total Fat: 4 g; Sodium: 40 mg
Excellent Source of: (min. 2 cookies) Iron and Thiamin

Almond Frozen Yogurt Sticks

¼ cup wheat germ	1 pint frozen vanilla lowfat yogurt
2 tablespoons crushed almonds	

Combine wheat germ and crushed almonds.

Using hands, shape yogurt into 4 balls. Roll yogurt in wheat germ/almond mixture until completely coated. Insert 3-inch popsicle stick in each ball. Cover loosely and freeze until ready to serve.

Size of Serving: ½-cup ball   *Number of Servings:* 4
Per Serving: Calories: 100; Protein: 6 g; Total Fat: 5 g; Sodium: 60 mg
Excellent Source of: Calcium, Thiamin, and Riboflavin

Spiced Wheat Germ Bars

1 cup raisins
1½ cups water
½ cup margarine (1 stick)
1 cup finely ground
   whole wheat flour (or
   whole wheat pastry
   flour)
1 cup wheat germ
½ cup nonfat dry milk
1 teaspoon baking soda

½ teaspoon salt
2 teaspoons ground
   cinnamon
½ teaspoon ground
   nutmeg
½ teaspoon ground cloves
1 cup brown sugar (firmly
   packed)
2 eggs, slightly beaten

Preheat oven to 325°F. Grease and flour 15 x 10-inch jelly roll pan.

In 2½-quart saucepan, simmer raisins in water with margarine, uncovered, 15 minutes; cool 10 minutes.

Measure flour, wheat germ, dry milk, soda, salt, and spices onto piece of waxed paper and stir with fork to partially mix.

Add sugar and eggs to cooled raisins and water and beat well. Add dry ingredients and mix with wooden spoon for about 1 minute. Spread batter evenly in prepared pan. Bake until top springs back when touched lightly (about 20 minutes).

These are quite moist and keep well in a tightly covered place for about a week. They also freeze well.

Yield: 24 2 x 3-inch bars
Per Bar: Calories: 135; Protein: 3 g; Total Fat: 5 g; Sodium: 120 mg
Excellent Source of: (min. 2 bars) Iron

APPETIZERS, SNACKS, AND SANDWICHES

These recipes can often be called upon to stand in for each other. To demonstrate their versatility, we have grouped them together here. But first, a few words about each . . .

APPETIZERS (hors d'oeuvres) are meant to do just what the name suggests: to tease the appetite, and to appease it until the next meal. Since most of us do not need to have our appetites teased, our goal here is to make them as nutritionally valuable and low in calories as possible. They can be used as snacks, small meals, or as part of a larger meal.

SNACKS, like appetizers, are generally intended to satisfy us until the next meal. But for many people snacks often function as small meals. So to satisfy these varied needs, the snacks suggested here range from crunchy, nutritious, low-calorie nibbles to meal-in-one sandwiches.

SANDWICHES were first designed by the Fourth Earl of Sandwich (1718–92), so he could stay at the gambling table without being interrupted for meals. Despite some not-so-nutritious permutations on the original sandwich, the Earl's idea was a good one. The sandwich can be a nutritious, easy-to-prepare small meal that can be called into service anytime, even at breakfast, or cut into smaller shapes for snacks. Of course, how nutritious a sandwich is depends very much on what we put in, on, and around it. Here are some favorite sandwich ingredients with high nutritional value:

High-Protein Sandwich Fillings

> peanut butter or cashew butter with sunflower or sesame seeds
> cheeses, all types
> spreads made with garbanzo, pinto, soy, or kidney beans
> spreads made with split peas
> mashed tofu (soybean curd) with fruit and nuts
> hard-cooked egg
> tuna, crab meat, or other flaked fish
> any leftover meat or poultry

Sandwich Sources of Crunch, Vitamins, and Minerals

These are also good to use with dips and spreads for appetizers and light snacks.

> chopped raw broccoli
> thinly-sliced raw cauliflower
> alfalfa sprouts
> sliced raw mushrooms
> thin strips of raw carrot
> fresh tomatoes, sliced or chopped
> green pepper strips or circles
> sliced cucumber
> finely chopped celery
> all types of onion, thinly sliced or chopped
> romaine lettuce—or any other type
> spinach
> mustard greens
> chopped fresh parsley
> sweet red pepper strips
> thin slices of apple
> thin strips of raw turnip
> whole, lightly cooked green beans
> thin strips of raw zucchini or summer squash
> crispy Chinese pea pods

And to contain them try:

> any whole-grain bread or roll—rye, whole wheat, oatmeal, corn and
>   molasses, cracked wheat, pumpernickel
> Syrian bread, preferably whole wheat
> large romaine lettuce leaves, secured with a toothpick
> taco shells
> whole-grain pancakes or crepes

Garbanzo Bean Dip

Good with raw vegetables, such as broccoli, cauliflower, mushrooms, celery, carrots, and cherry tomatoes, or wedges of pita bread.

1 1-pound-4-ounce can garbanzo beans (chick-peas), drained

3 tablespoons sesame seed paste (tahini)

¼ cup unsweetened lemon juice (fresh or bottled)

1 tablespoon vegetable oil

3 garlic cloves, peeled and crushed

1 small red onion, thinly sliced

Mash the chickpeas, tahini, lemon juice, olive oil, and garlic very well to make a thick paste. Serve with red onion slices.

Yield: 2½ cups
Per Tablespoon: Calories: 20; Protein: 1 g; Total Fat: 1 g; Sodium: Trace

Guacamole

Guacamole was popular in Mexico even before the Spanish *conquistadores* arrived in the early 1500s. Originally made with avocados, onions, and salt, the following recipes are two variations of the classic guacamole. Delicious as a dip for raw vegetables or corn chips; use guacamole also as a stuffing for cherry tomatoes or as a garnish for tacos.

2–4 tablespoons chopped green chilies

½ small onion, finely chopped

2½ teaspoons lemon or lime juice

1 garlic clove, crushed

¼ teaspoon salt

¼ teaspoon freshly ground pepper

2 medium ripe avocados, cut up

Place all ingredients, except for the avocados, in an electric blender or food processor and blend thoroughly (or mash with a fork). Add avocados and blend very lightly.

Put mixture in bowl (placing avocado pit in center, if desired); cover and refrigerate until serving time.

VARIATION: Include 1 tablespoon minced fresh coriander (or ¼ teaspoon dry ground coriander); omit the garlic and pepper.

Yield: 1 cup
Per Tablespoon: Calories: 50; Protein: 1 g; Total Fat: 5 g; Sodium: 35 mg
Excellent Source of: (min. 1½ tbsp.) Vitamin C

Chicken Liver Pâté

Serve this high-protein, high-iron pâté in celery or cherry tomatoes, spread on cucumber slices or crackers, or as an appetizer on lettuce with Bermuda onion rings.

2 tablespoons margarine
½ pound chicken livers
¼ cup chopped onion (or more to taste)
2 hard-cooked eggs (optional)

1½–3 tablespoons mayonnaise (or low-calorie mayonnaise)
Salt and pepper to taste

Melt margarine in frying pan. Add livers and onion and sauté until pinkish color is gone from livers and onions are translucent.

Place in electric blender or food processor. Add eggs and 1½ tablespoons mayonnaise; process until finely chopped. If desired, add more mayonnaise to achieve smoother consistency.

Season to taste with salt and pepper. Pack into a mold or bowl and chill before serving.

NOTE: This recipe is high in cholesterol and is not recommended for anyone on a cholesterol-restricted diet.

Yield: 2 cups
Per Tablespoon: Calories: 30; Protein: 2 g; Total Fat: 2 g; Sodium: 20 mg
Excellent Source of: (min. 1½ tbsp.) Vitamin A; (min. 2½ tbsp.) Iron

Bean Salad Spread

Try bean spreads served on crackers, as a filling for sandwiches and pita bread, or as a stuffing for vegetables, such as celery or whole tomatoes.

⅔ cup dried beans (pinto, kidney, lima, garbanzo, or Great Northern) or use 1½ cups cooked, canned beans and omit salt from the recipe
⅓ cup lowfat cottage cheese
1½ tablespoons lemon juice (or juice from ½ fresh lemon)
3 tablespoons vegetable oil
¼ teaspoon salt

⅛ teaspoon dry mustard
⅛ teaspoon ground cumin
Dash cayenne
1 tablespoon fresh parsley, minced
¼ teaspoon dried basil
1 small onion, minced (or 3 whole scallions minced)
½ cup minced green pepper (or ½ cup minced celery or a combination of both)

Wash beans and soak them overnight, or about 6 hours.

Cook in soaking water until beans are tender (see Cooking Timetable, page 96.) Drain (save cooking water for soup stock) and cool. Mash the beans until about half of them are a paste (use a fork, a masher, or a food mill—all work well). Add the cottage cheese and mash any large pieces. Add the lemon juice, oil, salt, spices, and herbs; mix together well. Then add the minced vegetables and mix again.

Refrigerate to allow flavors to blend; taste and correct seasonings, if necessary.

VARIATIONS:

- The cottage cheese may be omitted by adding another ⅓ cup of beans.
- Other herbs, such as savory, thyme, dill, or crushed celery seed, may be used in place of or in addition to the basil.
- Use ¼ cup low-calorie mayonnaise instead of the oil and lemon juice.
- To decrease calories, increase the lemon juice to 3 tablespoons and bind the mixture with 1½ tablespoons tahini (sesame paste).

Size of Serving: ⅓ cup   *Number of Servings:* 8
Per one-third Cup: Calories: 115; Protein: 5 g; Total Fat: 5 g; Sodium: 95 mg
Excellent Source of: Iron, Thiamin, and Vitamin C

HOMEMADE YOGURT

Often touted as a "health" food, yogurt supplies the same nutrients found in the milk from which it is made—plenty of protein, calcium, vitamins A and D, riboflavin, and other B vitamins. It also provides bacteria that help to maintain the normal balance of the microorganisms needed in a healthy intestinal tract. Once you've tried honest-to-goodness yogurt, you'll wonder how those commercial concoctions made with artificial flavors, stabilizers, and sugary preserves have become such a big craze. These commercial varieties often contain 250–300 calories per 8-ounce container—or as many calories from the sweet ingredients added to flavor them as from the yogurt itself. A cupful of pure homemade yogurt contains only about 90–160 calories, depending on how much fat was in the milk from which it was made.

For the very best taste and lowest calories, flavor your own plain lowfat yogurt for desserts and snacks. Fresh fruits are particularly good with yogurt—berries, sliced banana, chopped orange sections, diced melon, papaya, pineapple, nectarine, peaches, chopped apple or applesauce—or add a dash of vanilla extract and a little honey if the yogurt is too tart for your taste buds.

Yogurt has many other uses—most notably in recipes calling for cream and sour cream where yogurt can reduce the fat and caloric value of the recipe substantially—for example, in cold soups, salad dressings, sauces, baked goods, and classics such as stroganoff and paprikash (see Index).

Homemade Lowfat Yogurt

1 quart fresh skim milk

3 tablespoons fresh plain lowfat yogurt at room temperature (either homemade or commercial yogurt without stabilizers added because they do not allow the bacteria to multiply)

Sterilize all utensils thoroughly with soap and hot water. This is very important to prevent unwanted microorganisms from contaminating the yogurt and adversely affecting the flavor and texture. You will need to sterilize:

1 1½-quart heavy saucepan or a 1½-quart double boiler
1 measuring tablespoon
1 large glass or ceramic bowl or a 1-quart jar or several small jars to equal 1 quart

Pour the milk into the sterilized heavy saucepan or the top of the double boiler (over boiling water). Scald the milk by heating until it almost reaches the boiling point.

Cool the milk until it feels warm when tested on your wrist—it should be about 110°F. (bacteria multiply between 95° and 120°F.—below this range they will be inactive; above this they will die).

Stir in the room-temperature yogurt and mix well. Pour into the sterilized bowl, quart jar, or smaller jars (depending upon how you are planning to use the yogurt—the bowl is fine if you will be using it right away; jars with tight covers are better for storage).

Cover with plastic and wrap the bowl or jar(s) completely in a thick towel or blanket (or use an electric yogurt maker).

Place the yogurt in a warm place (on a heating pad, near a heating unit, or in a gas stove with a pilot light). Let the yogurt stand for about 4–5 hours (or overnight) until it has set.

Cover well and store in the refrigerator.

Size of Serving: 1 cup   *Number of Servings:* 4 (or 1 quart)
Per Serving: Calories: 95; Protein: 9 g; Total Fat: Trace; Sodium: 135 mg
Excellent Source of: Calcium and Riboflavin

Dutch Yogurt Cheese

This tastes like a cross between a very smooth cottage cheese, ricotta cheese, and cream cheese.

1 *quart fresh Homemade*   *2-foot length clean*
  Lowfat Yogurt (see   *cheesecloth*
  above)

Rinse the cheesecloth, squeeze well, and line a colander with it, double thickness, so that it hangs over the edges. Pour in the fresh yogurt.

Cover the colander with a plate or plastic wrap, or gather the edges of the cheesecloth together, tie it tightly at the top, and hang the bag from the faucet or a cabinet handle. Place a container under the colander or cheesecloth bag to catch the whey (the liquid that will separate from the curd, or solid part, of the yogurt). Save the whey for use in baking. Let the yogurt stand at room temperature for about 12 hours (or longer if it is still dripping).

Remove the cheesecloth and use the yogurt as you would any soft cheese.

Yield: about 2 cups
Per Tablespoon: Calories: 15; Protein: 1 g; Total Fat: Trace; Sodium: 20 mg
Excellent Source of: (min. 3 tbsp.) Calcium and Riboflavin

Curried Yogurt Dip

1 *cup plain lowfat*   1 *tablespoon onion juice*
  yogurt   1 *teaspoon garlic powder*
2–3 *teaspoons curry*
  powder to taste

Mix ingredients together well and chill.
VARIATION: *Herbed Yogurt Dip:* Combine yogurt with 2 teaspoons each of dried onion and dried parsley flakes, ¼ teaspoon each of dried dill weed and dried chervil, and ⅛ teaspoon celery salt. Mix well and chill.

Yield: 1 cup
Per Tablespoon: Calories: 8; Protein: 1 g; Total Fat: Trace; Sodium: 25 mg

Cheddar Cheese Ball

½ pound shredded
cheddar cheese

3 ounces Neufchâtel
cheese made with skim
milk

¼ cup dry sherry

½ teaspoon
Worcestershire sauce

2 dashes garlic powder

2 dashes onion powder

2 dashes celery salt

½ cup chopped walnuts

Blend everything together except for the walnuts. Form into a ball and chill for 1–2 hours. Roll in nuts. Cover tightly with plastic wrap and store in refrigerator.

Yield: about 2½ cups
Per Tablespoon: Calories: 40; Protein: 2 g; Total Fat: 3 g; Sodium: 50 mg
Excellent Source of: (min. 3 tbsp.) Calcium

French Herbed Cheese

1 tablespoon water
1½ teaspoons lemon juice
8 ounces partially
skimmed ricotta cheese

3 ounces Neufchâtel
cheese made with skim
milk

½ teaspoon crushed dried
basil

½ teaspoon crushed dried
tarragon

2 teaspoons minced fresh
parsley

2 teaspoons minced fresh
dill weed or ½ teaspoon
dried dill weed

1 large garlic clove,
crushed

Combine water, lemon juice, and cheeses in blender; purée for 30 seconds. Add remaining ingredients and blend for 10 seconds. Cover and chill.

Yield: 1½ cups
Per Tablespoon: Calories: 10; Protein: 1 g; Total Fat: Trace; Sodium: 25 mg

Curried Egg Salad Spread

Try creating your own egg salad specialties by using any available raw vegetables, such as radishes, broccoli buds, sweet red pepper, or chopped escarole in place of, or in addition to, the vegetables suggested in the recipe. This egg salad is particularly delicious served on caraway rye bread.

4 hard-cooked eggs
1 cup finely shredded cabbage
1 carrot, finely shredded
1 small sour pickle, finely diced
½ cup finely diced celery
2 scallions, finely sliced
2 tablespoons mayonnaise (or low-calorie mayonnaise)
1 teaspoon Dijon-style mustard
½ teaspoon paprika
¼ teaspoon garlic powder
1 teaspoon dill weed
¼ teaspoon ground tarragon
½ teaspoon finely chopped parsley
½ teaspoon caraway seed (optional)
½ teaspoon curry powder (or more to taste)
1 teaspoon lemon juice
Salt and pepper to taste

Mash eggs and add other ingredients; mix all well. Chill before serving.

Size of Serving: ½ cup   *Number of Servings:* 6
Per Serving: Calories: 110; Protein: 5 g; Total Fat: 8 g; Sodium: 185 mg
Excellent Source of: Vitamin A and Vitamin C

Mushroom Caps with Crab Meat Stuffing

1½ cups lump crab meat (fresh, frozen, or canned)
2 tablespoons margarine
4 tablespoons finely chopped shallots or scallions
1 cup Medium White "Cream" Sauce (see Index)
¼–½ teaspoon lemon juice
Salt to taste
White pepper to taste
2 dozen 2-inch mushroom caps

Preheat oven to 350°F.

Carefully inspect the crab meat and remove any bits of cartilage, then shred with a fork.

(continued)

In a heavy 8–10-inch skillet, melt 2 tablespoons margarine over moderate heat. Add the shallots and cook for 2 minutes, stirring constantly, until they are soft. Stir in the crab meat and toss it with the shallots for about 10 seconds.

Transfer the mixture to a large bowl. Stir in the white sauce. Season to taste with lemon juice, salt, and white pepper.

Lightly grease a shallow baking dish large enough to hold the mushroom caps in one layer. Sprinkle the inside of the caps lightly with salt. Spoon in the crab filling and arrange the caps in the pan. Bake in the upper third of the oven for 10–15 minutes, or until the mushrooms are tender when pierced with the tip of a sharp knife and the filling is bubbly.

Yield: 2 dozen mushroom caps
Per Mushroom: Calories: 35; Protein: 2 g; Total Fat: 2 g; Sodium: 140 mg

Nut Butter

3 *cups raw peanuts (or cashew nuts or almonds, shelled and skinless)*	1–2 *tablespoons vegetable oil* *salt to taste (optional)*

Preheat oven to 300°F.

Spread nuts in a shallow pan and roast, stirring often, about 15–20 minutes, or until lightly browned. Remove from oven and cool.

Put nuts in blender (or put through meat grinder) and grind about 2 minutes, gradually adding the oil to make a spreadable paste. Spoon peanut butter into jar; cover and store in refrigerator.

NOTE: Nuts may be purchased freshly roasted if you want to skip the roasting step.

Yield: 2 cups
Per Tablespoon: Calories: 80; Protein: 2 g; Total Fat: 6 g; Sodium: Trace
Excellent Source of: (min. 3½ tbsp.) Iron

Plum "Butter"

This delicious spread contains about half, or less, the calories found in most commercially prepared jams and jellies.

1½ *pounds unpeeled Italian prune plums, pitted and sliced* ⅓ *cup sugar (or to taste)*	½ *teaspoon cinnamon* *Dash ground nutmeg* *Dash ground cloves* *Dash ground allspice*

Combine plums and sugar in a heavy pot over low heat; when the juices begin to flow, bring to a boil. Cook 5 minutes, or until the fruit is tender.

Cool slightly and put into blender; chop on low speed 2 seconds (mixture should not be smooth).

Return mixture to pot; add spices and bring to a boil. Reduce heat but keep it bubbling; cook 5–8 minutes.

Ladle into hot sterilized screw-top jars; store in refrigerator.

NOTE: If storing longer than 1 week, seal jars by pouring melted paraffin on top of contents.

VARIATIONS: Try substituting other fruits for the plums, such as apricots, berries, nectarines, and peaches.

Yield: about 2–2½ cups
Per Tablespoon: Calories: 20; Protein: Trace; Total Fat: Trace: Sodium: Trace

Spicy Peach Jam

5 cups peeled, thinly sliced fresh peaches	1 envelope unflavored gelatin
1 tablespoon lemon juice	¼ cup cold water
¼ teaspoon ground cinnamon	2½ tablespoons honey (or less, to taste)
Dash ground nutmeg	3 tablespoons sugar (or less, to taste)
⅛ teaspoon ground cloves	

In a medium saucepan combine the peaches, lemon juice, cinnamon, nutmeg, and cloves. Simmer over low heat 5 minutes, crushing peaches with a spoon.

Meanwhile, sprinkle gelatin over cold water in a small bowl and allow to dissolve for about 1 minute. Add honey and sugar to taste to peach mixture, using as little as possible; bring to a boil and boil rapidly for 1 minute, stirring constantly; lower the heat. Add dissolved gelatin and stir over low heat about 3 minutes, or until gelatin is thoroughly dissolved.

Let stand about 5 minutes, skimming off any foam.

Ladle into 3 sterilized ½-pint jars; cover and allow to cool slightly before storing in the refrigerator.

Yield: 3 cups (3 ½-pint jars)
Per Tablespoon: Calories: 15; Protein: Trace; Total Fat: —; Sodium: Trace

Crabby English

¼ cup margarine
1 6½-ounce can crab
   meat
6 ounces finely shredded
   cheese (any mild
   cheese)

1 tablespoon Worcester-
   shire sauce
1 teaspoon garlic salt
6 English muffins, split
   (preferably whole wheat
   muffins)

Mix all ingredients together except muffins.

Lightly toast English muffins. Spread with crab-cheese mixture and cut each muffin half into 4 wedges.

Place wedges on cookie sheet and freeze individually. When frozen, place in plastic bag in freezer until ready to use.

To serve, remove from freezer and place under broiler until bubbly and light brown.

VARIATION: Use whole wheat pita bread (split) in place of English muffins.

Yield: 4 dozen wedges
Per Wedge: Calories: 45; Protein: 2 g; Total Fat: 2 g; Sodium: 140 mg

Spinach Calzone

These tasty Italian turnovers can be filled with an endless variety of vegetables, cheeses, meat, fish, poultry, and eggs—try creating your own specialities.

½ recipe for Whole Wheat
   Hamburger Buns (see
   Index)
1 pound cooked fresh
   spinach
1 tablespoon margarine
½ pound fresh mushrooms,
   sliced

6 ounces shredded
   partially skimmed
   mozzarella cheese
½ tablespoon dill weed
   Salt to taste
   Freshly ground pepper
   to taste
1 egg white
1–2 tablespoons skim milk

Prepare recipe for Whole Wheat Hamburger Buns up to the point where the dough rises the first time.

Meanwhile, cook the spinach in a small amount of water; drain well, squeeze out all the moisture and chop.

Melt the margarine in a medium-size skillet. Sauté the mushrooms for 3–4 minutes; drain well. Combine the mushrooms, spinach, cheese, dill, salt, and pepper; mix well.

Divide the dough into 8 balls; roll each out on a lightly floured surface to 5-inch-round circles.

Preheat oven to 400°F.

Place mixture on *half* of each dough circle to within ¼ inch of the edge. Brush edges with egg white. Fold the empty half of the dough over and seal. Place on a greased baking sheet; brush each turnover with milk. Bake 15–20 minutes.

Yield: 8 calzone
Per Serving: Calories: 455; Protein: 17 g; Total Fat: 8 g; Sodium: 550 mg
Excellent Source of: Protein, Calcium, Iron, Vitamin A, Thiamin, Riboflavin, Niacin, and Vitamin C

Toasted Mushroom Sandwich Rolls

2 tablespoons margarine
½ pound fresh mushrooms, sliced
4 ounces pimientos, chopped
1 small onion, finely minced

2 tablespoons flour
Salt to taste
Cayenne to taste
8 slices whole-grain bread, crusts removed (use for bread crumbs)

Melt margarine in a skillet; add vegetables and sauté over low heat for 5 minutes. Stir in flour until thick. Season to taste with salt and cayenne. Allow to cool.

Preheat oven to 400°F.

Spread mixture over slices of bread; *roll* each slice into small finger sandwiches (like small jelly rolls). Place on a cookie sheet and bake until toasty.

Size of Serving: 1 roll   *Number of Servings:* 8
Per Roll: Calories: 105; Protein: 4 g; Total Fat: 4 g; Sodium: 160 mg
Excellent Source of: Riboflavin; (min. 1½ rolls) Iron and Thiamin

Cheese-Mushroom-Sprout Sandwich

This is a flavorful, crunchy hot sandwich that is also good at room temperature. So don't hesitate to pack it for lunches that travel.

8 slices whole wheat or rye bread
4 teaspoons margarine
12 large mushrooms, sliced

4 ounces Jack cheese, coarsely shredded
1 cup alfalfa sprouts

(continued)

Toast bread lightly. Spread 1 teaspoon of margarine on 4 slices of toast, then add mushrooms and cheese, divided evenly among the 4 slices. Place under broiler until cheese melts. Add sprouts and top with other slice of toast.

Number of Servings: 4
Per Sandwich: Calories: 290; Protein: 15 g; Total Fat: 15 g; Sodium: 510 mg
Excellent Source of: Calcium, Iron, Thiamin, and Riboflavin

Crispy Crunchy Sandwich

4 ounces Neufchâtel cheese made with skim milk

8 slices whole wheat bread

¼ cup raisins

4 tablespoons slivered almonds

½ lemon

1 medium apple, cored and thinly sliced

Spread Neufchâtel cheese on 4 slices of bread (about 1 ounce each slice). Press about a tablespoonful of raisins onto cheese. Sprinkle 1 tablespoonful of almonds on top of the raisins. Squeeze lemon juice over apples so they won't brown, and place several apple slices on each sandwich half.
    Cover with top slice of bread, wrap, and chill until ready to serve.

Number of Servings: 4
Per Sandwich: Calories: 345; Protein: 17 g; Total Fat: 6 g; Sodium: 340 mg
Excellent Source of: Protein, Calcium, Iron, Thiamin, and Riboflavin

Classic Italian Pizza

THE DOUGH:

1 package active dry yeast

⅔ cup warm water

½ teaspoon brown sugar

½ teaspoon salt

2 tablespoons vegetable oil

1 cup whole wheat flour

¾ cup sifted unbleached enriched all-purpose flour

THE TOPPING:

2 tablespoons vegetable oil

8 ounces fresh Italian sausage, sliced

¼ pound fresh mushrooms, sliced, or use 1 4-ounce can mushrooms, drained

1 cup Basic Italian Tomato Sauce (see Index)

¼ cup grated Parmesan cheese

2 ounces imported provolone cheese, shredded

8 ounces partially skimmed mozzarella cheese, shredded

1 green pepper, thinly sliced

Mix yeast with warm water and brown sugar; let stand 15–20 minutes, or until a good head of foam is developed.

Combine yeast with salt, oil, and flours in large bowl; stir well.

Lightly flour a flat surface and knead dough 8–10 minutes (see Index for directions for kneading).

Put dough in lightly oiled bowl; turn it once and cover with a damp cloth. Allow to double in size in a warm place (about 1½ hours).

Meanwhile, heat the oil in a frying pan and lightly brown the sliced sausage. Remove sausage and drain well, then lightly sauté the mushrooms and drain well.

Preheat oven to 425°F.

Roll the dough out on a floured surface to a circle about 14 inches in diameter, then ease the dough into a 12-inch pizza pan, pressing it into the bottom and sides of the pan. (An 11 x 13¼-inch cookie sheet can also be used.)

Spread the tomato sauce on top of the dough; sprinkle on the three cheeses, in the order given; top with sausage, mushrooms, and green pepper.

If you are using a *gas* oven, place the pizza directly on the hot surface of the bottom of the oven, rather than on one of the racks, so that the bottom crust will not become soggy. Bake 25 minutes, or until the edges of the crust are browned. If the oven is *electric*, bake the pizza 15 minutes on oven rack, then remove it from the pan and bake another 5 minutes directly on rack to get a crispy bottom crust.

NOTE: Imported provolone and Parmesan cheeses have a more distinctive flavor than most domestic varieties, but they are also more expensive. They can be found in cheese shops and Italian speciality markets.

VARIATION: Use chopped fresh broccoli in place of green pepper.

Size of Serving: one-eighth of 12-inch pie or 15 3 x 2½-inch pieces   *Number of Servings:* 8

Per Serving: Calories: 410; Protein: 19 g; Total Fat: 20 g; Sodium: 580 mg

Excellent Source of: Protein, Calcium, Iron, Thiamin, Riboflavin, and Vitamin C

Hearty Whole Wheat Pizza

THE DOUGH:

1 cup lukewarm water
1 tablespoon active dry
  yeast
1 teaspoon honey

1 tablespoon
  vegetable oil
½ teaspoon salt
2–2½ cups whole wheat
  flour

THE TOPPING:

1 tablespoon olive oil
1 medium onion, chopped
1 15-ounce can tomato
  purée
1 green pepper, diced
¼ pound fresh mushrooms,
  thinly sliced
½ teaspoon basil

½ teaspoon oregano
½ teaspoon pepper
1 teaspoon brown sugar
  Dash cayenne
6 ounces shredded cheese
  (half sharp cheddar,
  half partially skimmed
  mozzarella)

Preheat oven to 425°F.

Combine water, yeast, honey, oil, and salt in a medium mixing bowl; let stand 5 minutes. Add 2 cups whole wheat flour and mix until a stiff dough is formed. (Additional flour, up to ½ cup, may need to be added to form a stiff dough.)

Turn dough onto a floured work surface and knead 15 strokes; roll dough into circle about 14 inches in diameter (see Index for kneading instructions).

Press dough into bottoms and sides of a 12-inch pizza pan; set aside.

Pour olive oil into a medium saucepan; add chopped onion and sauté over medium heat until translucent. Add tomato purée, green pepper, mushrooms, basil, oregano, pepper, brown sugar, and cayenne. Simmer, uncovered, 10 minutes. Spread tomato mixture over pizza crust.

If you are using a *gas* oven place the pizza directly on the hot surface of the bottom of the oven, rather than on one of the racks, so that the bottom crust will not become soggy. Bake 15–20 minutes, or until the edge of the crust is lightly browned. Sprinkle cheese evenly on top of the pizza and bake 5 more minutes, or until cheese has melted. If the oven is *electric*, bake the pizza on oven rack for 15–20 minutes; then remove pizza from the pan, sprinkle on cheese, and bake 5 minutes directly on oven rack to melt cheese and to crisp the bottom.

Let pizza cool a bit before slicing. (This makes the pizza easier to slice and prevents the flavor from being masked by the heat.)

NOTE: Any leftover pizza can be covered with aluminum foil and refrigerated. It can then be reheated at 350°F. for 15 minutes.
VARIATION: Sliced sausage may be added to the pizza just before the cheese is added.

Size of Serving: one-eighth of 12-inch pie   *Number of Servings:* 8
Per Serving: Calories: 280; Protein: 12 g; Total Fat: 12 g; Sodium: 495 mg
Excellent Source of: Calcium, Iron, Vitamin A, Riboflavin, and Vitamin C

Navajo Taco

1 cup dried pinto beans	4 tacos
12 ounces lean ground beef	2 cups shredded lettuce
¼ cup chopped onion	1 cup shredded cheddar
¼ teaspoon salt	cheese
¼ teaspoon pepper	2 fresh tomatoes, chopped
½ teaspoon chili powder	1 green chili, chopped
1 16-ounce can tomatoes	

Wash beans; place in a large, heavy pan and cover with water. Heat to boiling and boil 2 minutes, then remove from heat and let stand 1 hour.

Add water, if necessary, cover beans; simmer, partially covered, for 50 minutes, or until tender.

Brown beef and onion in a large skillet. Add salt, pepper, chili powder, canned tomatoes, and drained pinto beans. Cook for 1 hour, stirring occasionally.

To serve, place tacos on plate. Pour chili mixture over tacos and top with shredded lettuce, chopped tomatoes, shredded cheese, and chopped green chili.

Size of Serving: 1 taco and 1 cup sauce   *Number of Servings:* 4
Per Serving: Calories: 530; Protein: 39 g; Total Fat: 19 g; Sodium: 560 mg
Excellent Source of: Protein, Calcium, Iron, Vitamin A, Thiamin, Riboflavin, Niacin, and Vitamin C

Whole Wheat Pretzels

THE DOUGH:

1 package active dry yeast	4 cups whole wheat flour
1½ cups warm water (about 110°F.)	1 teaspoon salt

THE COATING:

1–2 egg whites, beaten (begin with 1)	1 cup sesame seeds

(continued)

Sprinkle yeast over warm water; let it rest for 5 minutes.

Measure 3½ cups of flour into a large bowl; stir in the salt. Gradually pour yeast mixture into flour and mix well.

Sprinkle remaining flour on board and place dough *on* it. Knead 3–5 minutes to form a soft dough.

Place in a lightly greased bowl, turning once to grease entirely. Cover and put in a warm place for about 2 hours, or until it doubles in size. Punch dough down. (If preparing it for the next day, cover and place in refrigerator at this point. Bring back to room temperature the next day before proceeding.)

Place on *unfloured* board and knead lightly. Divide into 12 equal parts and form each into a ball; place balls on a plate and lightly cover with plastic wrap. Let them rest 15 minutes.

Preheat oven to 425°F.

Grease 2 baking sheets very well.

Stretch each ball into a 2-foot rope and shape into pretzels. Place on greased baking sheets; then brush each pretzel with beaten egg white and sprinkle with sesame seeds. Bake about 10 minutes, or until bread springs back when touched; it should not brown very much.

VARIATIONS: Try sprinkling with poppy seeds or caraway seeds in place of the sesame seed.

Yield: 12 pretzels
Per Pretzel: Calories: 210; Protein: 8 g; Total Fat: 7 g; Sodium: 180 mg
Excellent Source of: Iron and Thiamin; (min. 2 pretzels) Protein, Riboflavin, and Niacin

Frisbees

Chewy and nutritious, these whole wheat bread discs are good for snacks and to accompany soups or salads. For breakfast, they replace Danish pastry, and are better for you.

1 dough recipe from Whole Wheat Pretzels (see above)	*4 tablespoons melted margarine*

Follow dough preparation for Whole Wheat Pretzels, through "Grease 2 bakings sheets very well."

Stretch and press each ball into a 6-inch circle, depressing each slightly in the center. Place circles on greased baking sheets; brush tops of circles with melted margarine and sprinkle with any of the toppings suggested below. Bake about 8 minutes, or until bread springs back when lightly touched; it should not brown very much.

VARIATIONS: Use any of the following toppings:

- 2 tablespoons tomato sauce
- 1 tablespoon grated cheese
- 1 tablespoon diced green chilies
- 3 tablespoons sautéed, finely diced fresh vegetables, such as 1 tablespoon mushrooms,

2 tablespoons broccoli, and 1 teaspoon onion
- 2 tablespoons chopped fresh cranberries
- 1 tablespoon chopped walnuts
- 1 teaspoon honey

Yield: 12 frisbees
Per Frisbee (without topping): Calories: 170; Protein: 6 g; Total Fat: 5 g; Sodium: 315 mg
Excellent Source of: Thiamin; (min. 1¼ frisbies)Iron
FRISBEE TOPPINGS
Per Frisbee:
Tomato/Cheese/Chilies (4 tbsp): Calories: 60; Protein: 2 g; Total Fat: 4 g; Sodium: 90 mg
Vegetables (3 tbsp): Calories: 25; Protein: 1 g; Total Fat: 2 g; Sodium: 25 mg
Cranberry/Nut (3 tbsp): Calories: 45; Protein: 1 g; Total Fat: 2 g; Sodium: —
Excellent Source of: Vitamin C (except Cranberry/Nut)

Syrian Cheese Toasts

These toasts can be eaten hot or at room temperature. Try them with soups, salads, or for snacks.

- 3 medium-size whole wheat Syrian breads
- 6 tablespoons margarine
- ¾ cup grated Parmesan cheese

1–2 teaspoons paprika
½ teaspoon garlic powder

Split the Syrian bread through the middle to make 6 rounds. Spread each half with 1 tablespoon of margarine. Sprinkle with Parmesan cheese, paprika, and lightly with garlic powder. Cut each round into 6 wedges. Place on sheet of aluminum foil and broil 3–4 minutes, or until lightly browned (they burn easily so watch them closely).

Yield: 3 dozen cheese triangles
Per Wedge: Calories: 30; Protein: 1 g; Total Fat: 3 g; Sodium: 40 mg

Whole Wheat Sesame Wafers

2 cups whole wheat pastry flour	¼ teaspoon salt
⅓ cup wheat germ	2 tablespoons grated dry Jack or
¼ cup soya flour	Parmesan cheese
¼ cup sesame seeds	(optional)
2 tablespoons nonfat dry milk	½ cup vegetable oil
	½–⅔ cup water

Preheat oven to 375°F.

Combine the first 7 ingredients and stir to mix. Add oil and ½ cup water and mix gently with fork or hands as you would for pie dough. Add more water as needed to form a stiff dough that holds its shape and is not sticky. (Don't overmix as it will cause the product to be tough.)

Roll out on floured board to ¼-inch thickness (less if you prefer thinner wafers). Cut in diamond shapes about 2 x 1-inch size. Place on ungreased cookie sheet and bake for 10–15 minutes, or until lightly browned.

These are excellent with yogurt dip or cheese.

Yield: about 2 dozen wafers
Per Wafer: Calories: 95; Protein: 3 g; Total Fat: 6 g; Sodium: 30 mg
Excellent Source of: (min. 3 wafers) Iron and Thiamin

Crunchy Garbanzos

This makes a tasty snack that can also be used as a topping for soups, salads, or casseroles.

2 teaspoons vegetable oil	¼ teaspoon onion powder
1¼ cups cooked garbanzo beans (chickpeas)	⅛ teaspoon dry mustard
	½ teaspoon chili powder
¼ cup pumpkin seeds	¼ teaspoon dry crushed parsley
¼ cup sunflower seeds	¼ teaspoon paprika
¼ cup raw peanuts	¼ cup raisins (optional)
¼ teaspoon garlic powder	

Preheat oven to 375°F.

Heat oil in skillet. Add garbanzos, seeds, and peanuts. Sauté over medium heat, stirring often; the beans will turn golden brown. Add spices and stir.

Transfer to a cookie sheet and bake until the beans are crunchy. If desired, add raisins after baking the mixture.

VARIATIONS: After beans have browned, add ¼ cup soy sauce with the spices. Stir until it is absorbed. Continue with recipe preparation as given. Any other nuts may be added or substituted (such as almonds, cashews, walnuts, or Brazil nuts). Substitute 2 teaspoons curry powder in place of the chili powder.

Size of Serving: ¼ cup   *Number of Servings:* 8
Per Serving: Calories: 210; Protein: 10 g; Total Fat: 9 g; Sodium: 10 mg
Excellent Source of: Iron and Thiamin

Granola

1 cup buckwheat groats
½ cup vegetable oil
⅓ cup honey
1 cup rolled oats
1 cup whole wheat flakes
(or macro wheat flakes)
½ cup sesame seeds
½ cup hulled sunflower
seeds

1 cup broken-up walnuts
1 cup sliced almonds
½ cup wheat germ
1 cup chopped dried
apricots
1 cup currants
3 teaspoons vanilla
extract

Heat oven to 300°F.

Oil a very large roasting pan (large enough to hold all the ingredients, spread out in a thin layer) or 2 2 x 9 x 13-inch baking pans. (Pans with sides are good so that the granola can be stirred without spilling.) Place buckwheat groats in baking pan; place in oven and toast about 10 minutes, stirring once or twice.

Measure oil and honey into a small saucepan; heat until warm.

Add oats and wheat flakes to groats; add oil/honey mixture, stirring well. Toast in oven 15 minutes, stirring 2–3 times. Add seeds and nuts; stir well and return to oven and toast 10 minutes, stirring once or twice.

Remove from oven; add wheat germ, apricots, currants, and vanilla extract; stir well. Continue to stir every 5–10 minutes until cereal is cool (otherwise it will stick). Store in mason jars or tightly sealed plastic bags.

Serve with milk or yogurt or eat plain as a snack.

NOTE: Macro wheat flakes are available at most health food stores.

Size of Serving: ½ cup   *Number of Servings:* 18 (recipe makes approximately 9 cups)
Per Serving: Calories: 265; Protein: 6 g; Total Fat: 15 g; Sodium: 10 mg
Excellent Source of: Iron and Thiamin

Peanut Butter Balls

¾ cup peanut butter
(plain ground
unsalted peanuts
with a small amount
of oil)

2 tablespoons molasses

2 tablespoons honey
(or to taste)

1–1½ teaspoons vanilla
extract

⅔ cup nonfat dry milk

½ cup rolled oats

½ cup toasted wheat
germ

¼ cup toasted sesame
seeds

1–2 tablespoons boiling
water

⅓–½ cup finely chopped
unsalted peanuts or
sesame seeds

Combine the peanut butter, molasses, honey, and vanilla extract; mix well.

Mix together the powdered milk, rolled oats, wheat germ, and sesame seeds; gradually add to the peanut butter mixture, blending well. As mixture begins to stiffen, add boiling water, blending well.

Using the palms of your hands, shape mixture into 1-inch balls. The balls will be dry, so dip them in hot water before rolling them in the chopped nuts or seeds. Chill well before serving to allow flavors to blend.

Yield: about 2½ dozen balls
Per Ball: Calories: 80; Protein: 4 g; Total Fat: 5 g; Sodium: 10 mg
Excellent Source of: (min. 3 balls) Calcium, Thiamin, and Riboflavin

SAUCES

Sauces have long been notorious for their *la grande cuisine*-style salt, fat, and calorie content. The following recipes have been designed so that even weight-conscious people can enjoy the luxury of sauces without the traditionally high levels of fat—particularly saturated fat—calories, and salt.

Basic White "Cream" Sauces (Béchamel Sauces)

Basic white sauce, a universal recipe of varying consistency, is called upon to "cream" soups, sauces, vegetables, meats, fish, poultry, and eggs or to bind spreads, casseroles, croquettes, and soufflés. These recipes are much lower in fat and calories than the traditional white sauces.

It's easy to adjust the thickness of white sauces by simply increasing or decreasing the amounts of margarine and flour—just remember to keep the proportions of these two ingredients *equal to each other,* no matter what the desired consistency.

	Margarine	Enriched All-Purpose Flour	White Pepper	Salt (optional)	Hot Skim Milk
VERY THIN (for thin soups)	1 tablespoon	1 tablespoon	dash	¼ teaspoon	1 cup
THIN (for thick "cream" soups)	1½ tablespoons	1½ tablespoons	dash	¼ teaspoon	1 cup
MEDIUM (all-purpose sauce for creamed or scalloped foods)	2 tablespoons	2 tablespoons	dash	¼ teaspoon	1 cup
HEAVY (for binding recipes)	4 tablespoons	4 tablespoons	dash	¼ teaspoon	1 cup

Melt margarine in a heavy saucepan over low heat. Stir in flour, salt, and pepper gradually; cook, stirring constantly (a wide whisk is good for this), *over low heat for* about 3 minutes, or until the mixture is smooth—*do not brown.*

Remove from heat and gradually stir in hot milk.

Return to heat and bring sauce to slow boil, stirring constantly; reduce heat and cook for 3 minutes, or until the mixture is smooth and has thickened.

NOTE: White sauces may be tightly covered and refrigerated for a few days or frozen.

VARIATION:

- *Gruyère Sauce:* (Yield: 1½ cups)
  Combine 1 cup hot Medium White Sauce with 1 cup shredded Gruyère cheese and a pinch of cayenne. Stir until mixture is smooth.

Yield: 1 cup

VERY THIN "CREAM" SAUCE
Per Tablespoon: Calories: 15; Protein: 1 g; Total Fat: 1 g; Sodium: 45 mg

THIN "CREAM" SAUCE
Per Tablespoon: Calories: 20; Protein: 1 g; Total Fat: 1 g; Sodium: 45 mg

MEDIUM "CREAM" SAUCE
Per Tablespoon: Calories: 25; Protein: 1 g; Total Fat: 2 g; Sodium: 50 mg

HEAVY "CREAM" SAUCE
Per Tablespoon: Calories: 40; Protein: 1 g; Total Fat: 3 g; Sodium: 55 mg

GRUYÈRE SAUCE
Per Tablespoon: Calories: 30; Protein: 2 g; Total Fat: 2 g; Sodium: 60 mg
Excellent Source of: (min. 2 tbsp.) Calcium

BBQ Sauce

This is good for basting chicken or meats.

¼ *cup molasses*
½ *cup tomato purée*
½ *cup minced fresh onion*
2 *teaspoons finely shredded orange peel*
⅓ *cup orange juice*
2 *tablespoons vinegar*
1 *teaspoon Dijon-style mustard*

1 *tablespoon Worcestershire sauce*
¼ *teaspoon garlic powder*
¼ *teaspoon pepper*
¼ *teaspoon hot pepper sauce (optional)*
3 *cloves*

In small saucepan, combine all ingredients and bring to a boil. Reduce heat and simmer, uncovered, for 10 minutes; remove cloves.

Yield: 2 cups
Per Tablespoon: Calories: 15; Protein: —; Total Fat: —; Sodium: 5 mg
Per ¼ Cup: Calories: 50; Protein: 1 g; Total Fat: —; Sodium: 20 mg

Cucumber Sauce

This is good on broiled fish or vegetables.

1 cup plain lowfat
yogurt
1 large cucumber, peeled
and grated (and seeded
if desired)

½ teaspoon prepared hot
mustard or ¼ teaspoon
hot pepper sauce
2 tablespoons minced
fresh chives

Mix together and chill before serving.

Yield: 2 cups
Per Tablespoon: Calories: 5; Protein: —; Total Fat: —; Sodium: 5 mg
Per ¼ Cup: Calories: 20; Protein: 1 g; Total Fat: Trace; Sodium: 22 mg

Classic Green Sauce

A piquant embellishment for hot or cold meats, fish, shellfish, hard-cooked
eggs, and vegetables—particularly artichokes, broccoli, and cauliflower.

2 tablespoons drained
capers
1 tablespoon minced
onion
1 garlic clove, crushed
1 anchovy fillet, chopped

2 cups chopped fresh
parsley
1 teaspoon dried basil
½ cup vegetable oil
Juice of 2 lemons
Salt to taste
¼ teaspoon pepper

Place all ingredients in blender and purée thoroughly. May be heated
before serving if desired.

Yield: 1 cup
Per Tablespoon: Calories: 50; Protein: —; Total Fat: 5 g; Sodium: 5 mg
Excellent Source of: Vitamin C; (min. 2½ tbsp.) Vitamin A

Spanish Sauce

This is a particularly good way to perk up scrambled eggs and omelets.

2 tablespoons margarine
½ cup sliced onion
½ green pepper, cut into strips
½ sweet red pepper, cut into strips

2 8-ounce cans tomato sauce
2 teaspoons sugar
1 teaspoon Worcestershire sauce
1 garlic clove crushed

Melt margarine in a 10-inch frying pan. Sauté onion and green and red pepper in margarine until tender but not browned. Stir in tomato sauce, sugar, Worcestershire, and garlic. Cook over low heat for 10–15 minutes.

Yield: 3½ cups
Per Tablespoon: Calories: 10; Protein: —; Total Fat: —; Sodium: 35 mg
Per ¼ Cup: Calories: 35; Protein: 1 g; Total Fat: 2 g; Sodium: 140 mg

Taco Sauce

2 medium ripe tomatoes, peeled and finely chopped
1 small onion, finely chopped
3 mild chili peppers, fresh or canned, finely chopped

1 teaspoon cider vinegar (or to taste)
Salt to taste
½ teaspoon ground coriander
¼ teaspoon ground cumin

Place half of the tomatoes, onion, and chili peppers in a blender with the vinegar, salt, coriander, and cumin; purée. Combine this mixture with remaining finely chopped vegetables.

Chill about 1–2 hours before serving to allow flavors to blend.

Yield: about 1 cup
Per Tablespoon: Calories: 10; Protein: —; Total Fat: —; Sodium: Trace (unsalted)
Per ¼ Cup: Calories: 30; Protein: 1 g; Total Fat: —; Sodium: 3 mg (unsalted)
Excellent Source of: (min. 1 tbsp.) Vitamin C; (min. ¼ cup) Vitamin A

Basic Italian Tomato Sauce

This classic Italian tomato "gravy" can be served with meatballs, Italian sausages, or vegetables and is also great on pizza.

3 tablespoons vegetable oil
1 cup chopped onion
2 tablespoons minced fresh garlic (about 3 cloves)
4 cups canned Italian tomatoes with liquid (or fresh peeled Italian plum tomatoes)
1 6-ounce can tomato paste

2 tablespoons crushed oregano
1 tablespoon crushed basil
2 bay leaves
1 tablespoon fennel seeds (a must)
1 tablespoon crushed thyme
2 teaspoons sugar
Salt to taste
½ teaspoon freshly ground pepper

Heat oil in a large heavy pot; add onion and sauté until translucent (do not brown them). Add garlic and cook 1–2 minutes, stirring constantly. Add remaining ingredients; stir well. Simmer, uncovered, for 1 hour; stirring occasionally.

Remove bay leaves and, if desired, cool sauce slightly and purée in blender.

NOTE: It is important to use Italian tomatoes. Other types of tomatoes have a sharper taste, and the sauce seems to lack body.

Yield: 4 cups
Per Tablespoon: Calories: 15; Protein: —; Total Fat: 1 g; Sodium: 20 mg
Per ½ Cup: Calories: 100; Protein: 2 g; Total Fat: 5 g; Sodium: 170 mg
Excellent Source of: (min. ½ cup) Vitamin A and Vitamin C; (min. ¾ cup) Iron

Fresh Fruit Sauce

This is a delicious way to add vitamin C, folacin, and potassium to pancakes, waffles, crepes, and blintzes—or use it to flavor plain yogurt.

¼ cup boiling water
¼ cup raisins
3 ripe bananas
2 oranges, peeled

Juice of 1 lemon
Dash ground mace or nutmeg

Pour water over raisins and let stand until plump.

Combine raisins with bananas, oranges, lemon juice, and ground mace or nutmeg in a blender; purée until smooth.

(continued)

Yield: 2 cups
Per Tablespoon: Calories: 20; Protein: —; Total Fat: —; Sodium: —
Per ¼ Cup: Calories: 70; Protein: 1 g; Total Fat: —; Sodium: 2 mg
Excellent Source of: (min. ¼ cup) Vitamin C

Leafy Green "Butter"

This "butter," or any of its varations, can be dabbed on fish, vegetables, grains, and pasta as the finishing touch.

¼ **pound fresh spinach, stems removed and washed, or ½ 10-ounce package frozen spinach**	¼ **pound margarine, softened at room temperature (or use tub margarine)**
2 **tablespoons minced fresh parsley**	1 **small garlic clove, crushed, or ½ teaspoon garlic powder (or to taste)**

Combine spinach and parsley in saucepan with a small amount of water; cook 3 minutes. Drain in a strainer; rinse with cold water and squeeze out excess water. Chop finely; then mash into a paste. Beat in margarine and garlic; mash and mix together well.

NOTE: To serve "butters" at the table, pack mixture into a small soufflé cup and chill.

VARIATIONS:

· *Herb "Butter"*
Combine ¼ pound margarine with 1 teaspoon minced fresh parsley, 1–2 tablespoons minced fresh tarragon (or dill weed), and a dash of lemon juice.

· *Mustard "Butter"* (Great on green beans)
Combine the margarine with 2–3 teaspoons Dijon-style mustard, 1 tablespoon minced fresh parsley, and a dash of lemon juice.

· *Lemon "Butter"* (Good with fish and shellfish)
Combine the margarine with the juice of 1 lemon and 1–2 tablespoons minced fresh parsley.

· *Garlic "Butter"* (Good with pasta)
Combine the margarine with 2 large crushed garlic cloves and 1–2 tablespoons minced fresh parsley.

Yield: about ⅔ cup
Per Tablespoon: Calories: 80; Protein: Trace; Total Fat: 10 g; Sodium: 115 mg
Excellent Source of: Vitamin A

BEVERAGES

Beverages have become an integral part of our modern customs and social occasions—from coffee breaks to the "pause that refreshes." However, many of our most popular drinks have come under scrutiny in recent years—some because of their caffeine, others because of their high sugar content, as well as the artificial colorings, flavorings, and other chemical additives found in many of these commercially prepared beverages.

Delightfully refreshing, nutritious substitutes can be quickly prepared from combinations of vegetables, fruits, lowfat milk and yogurt, vanilla, and other extracts. Plain club soda mixed with unsweetened fruit juice used in place of sweetened carbonated sodas offers the same sparkle without added sugar. Beverages provide a natural place to boost the nutrient content of the diet by introducing extras such as instant nonfat dry milk, nutritional yeast, and juices high in vitamins A and C. And this can often be done without their presence being noticed.

So stir up your imagination with these recipes and have fun creating your own specialties. And keep in mind that many of these beverages not only serve as great pick-me-up snacks and accompaniments to meals but can even stand alone as desserts.

"Make Me A Malted!"

4 cups skim milk (or skim buttermilk)

4 teaspoons sugar

4 teaspoons any extract, such as vanilla, almond, maple, or chocolate

(continued)

Blend on low speed, gradually adding 4 ice cubes per cup of milk. Serve chilled and frothy.

VARIATIONS:
- Flavor with 4 teaspoons powdered coffee or decaffeinated coffee.
- Add fruits such as bananas or strawberries or blueberries or melon to blender.
- Add sesame seeds or nuts such as almonds or cashews.

Size of Serving: 1 cup   *Number of Servings:* 4
Per Serving: Calories: 100; Protein: 9 g; Total Fat: —; Sodium: 130 mg
Excellent Source of: Calcium and Riboflavin

Eggnog

1 cup skim milk	*1 tablespoon wheat germ*
1 large egg	*Few dashes freshly*
1–2 teaspoons honey	*grated nutmeg (or use*
½ teaspoon vanilla	*ground nutmeg)*
extract	

Measure all ingredients into a blender or beat by hand until forthy.
NOTE: ¼ cup of cholesterol-free liquid egg substitute may be used in place of the egg.

VARIATION:
- *Banana Nog:* Add 1 small ripe banana to the basic recipe and blend.

Yield: about 1 cup
Per Cup: Calories: 225 (310 with banana); Protein: 17 g; Total Fat: 7 g; Sodium: 190 mg
Excellent Source of: Protein, Calcium, Iron, Thiamin, and Riboflavin

Fruit Milk Shake

This is a delicious, nutritious snack which can also double as a dessert.

3 bananas	*1 teaspoon sugar*
2 cups cold skim milk	*1 teaspoon vanilla extract*
1 apple, chilled	

Peel bananas and freeze at least 8 hours in plastic bag (a good way to save excess bananas before they become overripe).

Measure milk and pour into blender. Peel, quarter, and seed apple and add to blender. Add sugar and vanilla extract, then bananas, cut into thirds. Blend at slow speed, then medium speed, about ½ minute, or until smooth and thick.

VARIATIONS:

- Many different flavors are possible by omitting the apple and vanilla and using instead about 1 cup of other chilled, fresh fruit, such as strawberries, berries, peach, pineapple, cantaloupe, or 1 cup orange juice.
- Add 1 teaspoon finely grated or minced ginger.
- Turn this into a malted milk shake by adding 2 tablespoons of instant malted milk to any variation.
- Substitute buttermilk for the skim milk.

Size of Serving: 1 cup   *Number of Servings:* 4
Per Serving: Calories: 130; Protein: 5 g; Total Fat: Trace; Sodium: 65 mg
Excellent Source of: Calcium and Riboflavin

Iced Melon Frappé

3 cups seeded and diced   *Juice of 1 lime*
fresh cantaloupe or other   4 ice cubes
melon (½ small   *Fresh mint (optional)*
cantaloupe, cut up, = 1
cup)

Blend all ingredients together in blender.
VARIATION: Use ripe papaya or peaches in place of melon.

Size of Serving: 1 cup   *Number of Servings:* 4
Per Serving: Calories: 40; Protein: Trace; Total Fat: —; Sodium: 15 mg
Excellent Source of: Vitamin A and Vitamin C

Fresh Fruit Sparkle

1 quart fresh orange juice   1 lemon, sliced and cut in
1 quart pineapple juice   half
1 pint cranberry juice   1 lime, sliced
2 oranges, sliced and cut   2 cups crushed ice
   in fourths   Sugar to taste (optional)
                                 1 pint club soda

Combine juices. Prepare fruit and add to juices. Add sugar to taste if necessary. Add ice and chill. Just before serving, mix in the club soda.

Size of Serving: 1 cup   *Number of Servings:* 12–14
Per Serving: Calories: 120; Protein: 2 g; Total Fat: —; Sodium: Trace
Excellent Source of: Vitamin C

Hot Spiced Cranberry Juice

4 cups cranberry juice   4 thin lemon or lime slices
2–3 whole cloves   2 cinnamon sticks
    Pinch nutmeg

Mix together the juice, cloves, and nutmeg. Heat without boiling.
    Serve each with a slice of lemon or lime and ½ cinnamon stick.

VARIATION:

 · *Mulled Apple Cider:* Substitute unsweetened apple cider or apple
    juice for the cranberry juice.

Size of Serving: 1 cup   *Number of Servings:* 4
Per Serving: Calories: 165 (95 with apple); Protein: —; Total Fat: —;
Sodium: Trace
Excellent Source of: Vitamin C

Super Sangria

1 quart dry red wine   1 teaspoon cinnamon
2–3 ounces brandy   3 lemons
    (depending on desired   4 oranges
    strength)   Club soda
¼ cup sugar (or to taste)

In a large pitcher with cover, combine the wine, brandy, sugar, and cinnamon. Squeeze 2 lemons and 3 oranges; add juices to the wine mixture
and blend well. Slice remaining lemon and orange thinly, remove seeds,
and add to mixture.

    Allow sangria to chill for several hours, if possible, so that flavors can
blend. Serve over ice with club soda to taste (half and half is a good
mix) and the marinated lemon and orange slices.

Yield: about 2 quarts (before diluting with club soda)
Per ½ Cup: Calories: 80; Protein: Trace; Total Fat: —; Sodium: Trace
Excellent Source of: Vitamin C

HERBS AND SPICES

Good cooks often place as much importance on the merits of herbs and spices as they do on the food they are complementing. The need for most people to cut down on salt (see Index), makes a working knowledge of herbs and spices even more essential to successful cooking. A few herbs and spices provide surprising nutritional value: 1 teaspoon of paprika, for example, supplies nearly 1300 I.U.s of vitamin A (which makes it an excellent source of this nutrient), and 1 tablespoon of chili powder supplies about 2600 I.U.s of vitamin A and over 1 milligram of iron. But overall, herbs and spices do not provide appreciable amounts of nutrients or calories—their main value is in the flavor they add.

The Herb and Spice Chart in this chapter provides a cross reference of various foods with the herbs and spices recommended for use with them. This makes it easy for the uninitiated cook to quickly locate the herbs and spices to enhance the food at hand. But don't hesitate to experiment. There's no absolute rule that one herb or spice has to go with a particular food.

The following are some tips on buying and using herbs and spices:

- To get the maximum flavor from dried herbs and spices, be sure that they are not stale when you buy or use them. You can quickly find this out by giving them the sniff test—fresh dried herbs and spices have a strong aroma.
- It's best not to buy large quantities of herbs and spices (unless you plan to use them quickly)because they tend to lose their flavor if stored for a long time.

- Store herbs and spices in tightly closed containers in a cool, dry place. Avoid exposing them to sunlight or heat from the stove to prevent rapid aging.
- Fresh herbs can be frozen. For best results, do not defrost them before adding them to the food—this way, more of their natural flavor is retained.
- Chop or crush fresh herbs before using to bring out their aromatic oils.
- Pulverize dried herbs just before adding them to food; you can also soak dried herbs in a small amount of the liquid called for in the recipe for 15–20 minutes before adding them to the other ingredients.
- Whole spices can be put in a cheesecloth bag or tea ball before adding to the other ingredients so they can be removed easily before serving.
- It's best to add herbs to long-cooking dishes (such as some soups, sauces, and stews) during the last hour of cooking; dishes that cook in a shorter time (such as broiled meats or vegetables) should have the herbs added at the beginning of the cooking time.
- For most recipes, you will need about three times as much fresh herbs as dried. For example:

1 tablespoon fresh herbs = 1 teaspoon dried herbs

or

⅓ teaspoon ground
dried herbs

Bouquet Garni

Good for flavoring stocks, sauces, soups, stews, and other liquid dishes, Bouquet Garni usually includes the following herbs.

1 *bay leaf*	4–5 *sprigs fresh parsley,*
1 *tablespoon fresh thyme*	*including the stems or*
or ½ teaspoon dried	1 *tablespoon dried*
thyme	*parsley*

Place bay leaf and thyme on the parsley sprigs; roll parsley lengthwise into a tight bundle. Tie bundle together with a clean string, leaving a 5–6-inch tail. If using dried parsley, proceed directly as follows:

Place herbs in the center of a 2½-inch square of cheesecloth and tie closed tightly with a clean string, leaving a 5–6-inch tail.

or

Place herbs in a perforated metal tea ball.

To use, place Bouquet Garni in pot as directed in recipe, allowing the string or metal chain to dangle 1–2 inches over the side so that it can be removed easily after the food has cooked.

NOTE: Other herbs may be added to Bouquet Garni, such as basil, chervil, chives, marjoram, mint, savory, or thyme, depending on the recipe.

Cambridge Curry

Although people in the Western world frequently classify curry powder as a spice unto itself, it contains several spices in a wide variety of blends. Here is a favorite mixture, but don't hesitate to blend your own to taste, as the cooks in India do.

2 tablespoons ground fenugreek + 1 teaspoon
1 tablespoon ground cumin
1 tablespoon ground turmeric
1 teaspoon dry mustard
2 teaspoons Spanish paprika
1½ teaspoons dried dill weed
1½ teaspoons ground mace
1 teaspoon ground coriander

1 teaspoon garlic powder
½ teaspoon ground ginger
½ teaspoon ground cardamom
½ teaspoon celery seed
½ teaspoon ground allspice
½ teaspoon ground cloves
½ teaspoon cayenne (grown in Zanzibar, if possible)
½ teaspoon ground black pepper

Combine all ingredients very well. Store in jar with tightly fitted cover.

Yield: about ½ cup

HERB AND SPICE CHART

BREADS anise, caraway seed, cardamom, cinnamon, coriander, dill, fennel, nutmeg, parsley, poppy seed

CHEESES basil, caraway, cayenne, celery seed, chervil, chives, coriander, cumin, dill, marjoram, oregano, parsley, pepper, sage, thyme

DIPS cayenne, chili powder, chives, curry powder, dill, oregano, parsley, pepper, sage

EGGS basil, cayenne, celery seed, chervil, chili powder, chives, cumin, curry powder, dill, marjoram, mustard seed, oregano, paprika, parsley, pepper, rosemary, saffron, sage, savory, tarragon, thyme, turmeric

FISH basil, bay leaf, cayenne, celery seed, chervil, cumin, curry powder, dill, ginger, marjoram, mustard seed, oregano, paprika, parsley, pepper, saffron, sage, savory, tarragon, thyme, turmeric

FRUIT   allspice, anise, basil, cardamom, cinnamon, cloves, curry powder, fennel, ginger, mace, mint, nutmeg, rosemary

GRAINS   basil, celery seed, chili powder, cumin, curry powder, dill, marjoram, mint, oregano, parsley, pepper, rosemary, saffron, savory, thyme

JAMS & JELLIES   allspice, cardamom, cinnamon, cloves, ginger, mace, mint, nutmeg

MARINADES   allspice, bay leaf, cayenne, celery seed, chili powder, cloves, ginger, mustard seed, oregano, parsley, rosemary, tarragon, turmeric

PASTA   basil, oregano, parsley, pepper, poppy seed

PICKLED VEGETABLES   allspice, bay leaf, cardamon, cinnamon, cloves, coriander, dill, ginger, mint, mustard seed, pepper, tarragon, turmeric

POULTRY   basil, bay leaf, chervil, coriander, curry powder, dill, ginger, marjoram, paprika, parsley, pepper, rosemary, saffron, sage, savory, tarragon, thyme, turmeric

RELISHES   allspice, cayenne, chili powder, cloves, coriander, ginger, mace, tarragon

SALAD DRESSINGS   caraway seed, celery seed, chervil, chili powder, chives, coriander, curry powder, dill, ginger, mint, mustard seed, paprika, parsley, pepper, poppy seed, tarragon, turmeric

SHELLFISH   basil, bay leaf, cayenne, curry powder, marjoram, oregano, paprika, parsley, saffron, sage, savory, tarragon, thyme

SOUPS & STEWS   allspice, basil, bay leaf, caraway seed, cayenne, celery seed, chervil, chili powder, chives, cloves, coriander, curry powder, dill, ginger, marjoram, oregano, paprika, parsley, pepper, rosemary, saffron, tarragon, thyme

STUFFINGS   basil, marjoram, oregano, pepper, rosemary, sage, savory, tarragon, thyme

Meats

BEEF   allspice, basil, bay leaf, caraway seed, chervil, chili powder, cloves, coriander, cumin, curry powder, dill, fennel, ginger, marjoram, oregano, paprika, pepper, savory, tarragon, thyme

KIDNEYS   caraway, dill, oregano, rosemary, thyme

LAMB   basil, bay leaf, chervil, cinnamon, cloves, cumin, curry powder, dill, marjoram, mint, nutmeg, oregano, parsley, pepper, rosemary, saffron, sage, savory, thyme

LIVER   basil, bay leaf, caraway seed, chives, tarragon, thyme, turmeric

Meat loaf chili powder, cumin, curry powder, marjoram, nutmeg, oregano, parsley, pepper, sage, savory, thyme

Pork allspice, basil, bay leaf, caraway seed, chervil, cinnamon, cloves, coriander, fennel, ginger, marjoram, nutmeg, pepper, rosemary, sage, savory, thyme

Tongue allspice, bay leaf, chervil, chives, cloves, dill, parsley, tarragon, thyme

Veal basil, fennel, marjoram, mustard seed, oregano, paprika, parsley, pepper, rosemary, saffron, sage, savory, tarragon, thyme, turmeric

Vegetables

Artichoke bay leaf, coriander, parsley, savory, thyme

Asparagus chives, marjoram, mustard seed, parsley, tarragon, thyme, turmeric

Beans, Lima cumin, dill, marjoram, nutmeg, oregano, sage, savory, tarragon, thyme

Beans, Snap basil, caraway seed, chili powder, dill, marjoram, mustard seed, oregano, sage, savory, tarragon, thyme

Beets allspice, anise, bay leaf, caraway seed, cinnamon, dill, fennel, ginger, mustard seed, savory, tarragon, thyme

Broccoli caraway seed, dill, mustard seed, oregano, tarragon

Brussels Sprouts basil, caraway seed, dill, mustard seed, sage, thyme

Cabbage caraway seed, celery seed, cumin, dill, fennel, mustard seed, nutmeg, oregano, paprika, savory, tarragon, turmeric

Carrots allspice, anise, bay leaf, caraway seed, cinnamon, cloves, dill, fennel, ginger, mace, marjoram, mint, nutmeg, parsley, rosemary, sage, thyme

Cauliflower caraway seed, celery seed, coriander, dill, mace, nutmeg, paprika, parsley

Corn chili powder, chives, oregano, parsley, sage, savory

Cucumber basil, chives, cinnamon, cloves, dill, mint, parsley, pepper, tarragon

Dried Beans allspice, bay leaf, celery seed, chili powder, cloves, cumin, mint, mustard seed, oregano, sage, savory, tarragon, turmeric

Eggplant basil, marjoram, oregano, parsley, sage, thyme

Greens, dark leafy allspice, basil, mace, marjoram, nutmeg, oregano, tarragon

Greens, Salad basil, celery seed, chervil, chives, dill, marjoram, oregano, parsley, pepper, sage, savory, tarragon

LENTILS   cinnamon, curry powder, dill, sage, savory, thyme

MUSHROOMS   chives, dill, marjoram, parsley, tarragon, thyme

ONIONS   caraway seed, curry powder, mustard seed, nutmeg, oregano, parsley, sage, thyme, turmeric

PARSNIPS   chervil, dill, marjoram, parsley, rosemary, sage, thyme

PEAS   allspice, basil, chervil, chives, dill, marjoram, mint, oregano, poppy seed, rosemary, sage, savory, tarragon, thyme

POTATOES, SWEET   allspice, cardamom, cinnamon, cloves, ginger, mace, nutmeg

POTATOES, WHITE   basil, bay leaf, caraway seed, celery seed, chives, dill, mustard seed, oregano, parsley, pepper, poppy seed, rosemary, savory, tarragon, thyme

PUMPKIN   allspice, cardamom, cinnamon, cloves, ginger, mace, nutmeg

SQUASH, SUMMER   chervil, marjoram, parsley, pepper, savory

SQUASH, WINTER   allspice, basil, cardamom, cinnamon, cloves, fennel, ginger, mace, mustard seed, nutmeg, rosemary

SQUASH, ZUCCHINI   marjoram, oregano, parsley

TOMATOES   basil, bay leaf, celery seed, chervil, chili powder, chives, curry powder, dill, oregano, parsley, sage, savory, tarragon, thyme

TURNIPS   allspice, dill, mace, nutmeg, paprika, thyme

VEGETABLE JUICES   basil, bay leaf, oregano, parsley, pepper, tarragon

Index

Lard, 27
"Lasagne," Zucchini, 141
Leafy Green "Butter," 256
Leeks, 75–76
Legumes, 9–10
 cooking, 95–96
 gas from, 95n, 96n
 herbs and spices with, 266
 lack of cholesterol in, 27
 protein and calories in, 15
 recipes with, 103–7
 sodium in, 30
Lemon "Butter," 256
Lemon Salad Dressing, 186
Lentils. *See* Legumes
Lentil Soup with Tomatoes,
 Greek (Fakisoupa), 60
Lentil Surprise Stew, 105
Lettuce, 75
Lima Beans, Cowboy Steak with,
 139
Linoleic acid, 25
Lipids, 23, 25
Lithuanian Cold Beet Soup, 54–55
Liver, 10, 127–28
 cholesterol in, 27
 herbs and spices for, 264
Liver Creole, 148
Lobster, 14, 111
Lobster with Crab Sauce, 116
Lokshen Kugel (Noodle Pudding),
 195
Low-Cal Coquilles, 118–19
Low-Cal Crust for Quiche, 188, 194
Low-Cal Pie Crust, 226
Low-Cal Vinaigrette Dressing, 183
Lysine, 17

M

Machaca, 143
Macrominerals, 4
Magnesium, 4
 in legumes, 95
 in whole grains, 197, 199

Major White's Chutney, 182
"Make Me A Malted!" 257–58
Malted milk shakes, 257–59
Manganese, 4
Margarines, 5, 24–25
 lack of cholesterol in, 27
 sodium in, 31
Marinades, 124, 264
Marinated Barbecued Beef Hearts
 (Anticuchos Teriyaki), 143–44
Marinated Dilled Green Bean
 Salad, 179
Marinated Mussels, 118
Marinated Salmon, 113–14
Marinated Squid Salad, 122
Marinated Vegetable Salad, 180
Marsala Chicken with Herbs, 164
Mayonnaise, 27, 31
Meatballs, Spinach, 134
Meat loaf herbs, 265
Meat Loaf, Kim's Zucchini, 133–34
Meat Loaf Pot Roast, 133
Meats:
 about, 123–24
 cholesterol in, 27
 cooking methods for, 125–31
 cooking times for, 131–32
 cuts of, 125–27
 fat in, 23
 herbs and spices for, 264–65
 nutrient calculations for,
  explained, 48
 protein and calories in, 9–10, 15
 recipes with, 132–53
 sodium in, 29
 stock from, 51–52
 storage of, 124–25
 variety, 15, 26–27, 127–28
Megaloblastic anemia, 35
Melon and Berries, 221
Melon Frappé, Iced, 259
Methionine, 17
Metric units, *xiv*
Mexican Chicken Stew, 166
Microminerals, 4